WHEN YOU'RE GREAT
THEY REMEMBER YOUR NAME

HOW TO CREATE A Personal Brand Image

The
SUPERHERO
Inside You

Paulette Bazerman

D1228002

Dedicated to all those who will read this book
and find their **Personal Brand Image**

Table of Contents

Introduction

There are many stories in books, movies, and blogs about people having a dream who fought their way through adversity, challenged every obstacle, and finally reached their goal. What if you have no passion to fantasize about, nothing to fight for, no career to pursue, but still have the deep desire to be successful at something? Where do you start? How do you have a chance to accomplish a goal if you don't have specialized training or even have a dream?

As a child you are eventually confronted by a well-meaning person who asks, "What do you want to be when you grow up?" The child blurts out a familiar job from his or her reality. Ballet dancer, fireman, doctor, talk show host! Perhaps the job you will become expert in hasn't even been invented. How many children born before the 1960s ever dreamed of becoming an astronaut? At that time, this was still a science fiction story.

The myth continues when you finish high school, complete college, or even reach retirement age: you will always have a clear direction toward your next step in life. Even more frustrating, what if you have no special talent, you don't excel in anything, and have no particular desire to do so? The probability is that you don't know in your early years what steps to take to achieve positive results.

Okay, the comments I just made seem simple, and one might say, "Doesn't everyone know this?" The answer is, I certainly didn't and from my many years of working, trust me—the majority of folks don't know how to manage their careers or their lives. They lack common sense. They assume that somehow it will all magically work out if they put in the time, and eventually their boss, or all of humanity, will recognize them and good things will happen. But soon the wake-up call arrives: success is not guaranteed.

This story shares what I did to find my way from being an impoverished girl in Brooklyn, New York to becoming a Vice President in Asia for the world's largest toy company, without any training or skills in toy manufacturing. This is a business memoir meant to be a career how-to guide, via my own experiences, to help others who, like me, have no clue about their own dreams or potential.

You don't need to have resources, whether financial or academic, to change the world. It all starts with you. If only I'd had someone tell me a fraction of what I will share with you, perhaps I could have been a more exceptional colleague, boss, or mentor. Being great at something takes planning and emphasis on what you excel in to develop a **Personal Brand**. No matter how insignificant you think your skill is, you must be better than anyone else at it, or you will never be noticed.

Personal Brand Image

Right now, you may not know what foundation to build your Brand on, but that's irrelevant. You can identify what small thing you do best and repeat it. The result is a reputation for being excellent at what you do best. It may not necessarily be related to your career, but will affect the way you are perceived. You must be consistent with that image, so it becomes part of who you are—a trusted Brand.

Let's say you are really good at creating attractive gift wrapping. You tie great bows and meticulously fold the carefully selected wrapping paper. This skill doesn't seem like much, but you do it so well that you wrap thank-you notes to give to friends, give your teacher or boss a small gift-wrapped item like it came from a luxury store. Everyone now knows you're good at this, and they ask you to wrap their gift boxes. You gladly do it and do it better than anyone. You are now referred by friends to wrap their friends' gifts. The word gets out about how good you are, and you start to charge for supplies and then up the price for profit, create a website, and offer your services for your entrepreneurial business, "Wrap-it-Up." You now have a small business with a **Personal Brand Image** of being the best gift-wrap service in your town.

Everyone has their own special Brand. You may not know your potential, since it's like a Superhero inside you that needs to be discovered. Similar to valuable jewelry locked in a treasure chest, it needs to be taken out for everyone to see. These jewels are totally wasted inside a locked box, if no one can admire their powerful beauty. These items don't have to be diamonds or gold. It's even better if they're elaborate costume jewelry, since those items can be bigger, shine brighter, and make an impact. Small, twinkling diamonds will never get the attention that a magnificently embellished, rhinestone-encrusted item—worn with attitude—can attract. Your Brand, like the jewelry, should make a recognizable statement about you.

Brands are more commonly associated with products, especially luxury products like **Louis Vuitton** or **Tiffany & Co**. Then there are the easily identifiable mass-produced Brands, like **Coca-Cola**, **Apple**, **Nike**, **McDonald's**, etc.

As for **Personal Brand Images**:

- You can be **Queen Elizabeth**, who was born into a Royal Brand. She lives in the palace and performs the traditional formalities that project her Queen Brand Image.

- If you were born as Miss Norma Jean Mortenson, without a Brand, you could completely invent your image and Brand yourself into the legendary **Marilyn Monroe**, the Brand of vulnerable, blonde sex symbol that becomes a legend.

- You could be an unknown US senator, who worked as a lawyer, college professor, and community organizer. Building a National Brand in spite of the odds and in spite of being African American, **Barack Obama** was elected president of the United States based primarily on emphasizing his **Personal Brand Image** as a passionate orator and man of the people, not his experience. Whether you agree or disagree with his politics isn't the issue—he became a Historic Brand and the most powerful man in the world through a consistent, strong **Personal Brand Image**.

I lived in Hong Kong, China, employed by Mattel, Inc. as Vice President of Soft Goods Design & Development in Asia, leading teams that developed the fabrics and fashions for dolls, mainly Barbie.

Yes, the famous doll, the pink-glittered, blue-eyed, blonde American icon who claimed nearly two hundred careers to inspire girls. My life had a series of events which took me from being shy, introverted, and financially challenged, to becoming an executive creating a design and development organization for a multibillion-dollar toy company.

I never had a dream job or even a dream in my mind. Basically, survival was my only goal. Throughout my life I depended on creating a series of **Personal Brand Images**, being the best at what I was able to do, no matter how trivial, just being great at it. Then I'd expand the scope of that success to lead to the next level of accomplishment. Being great at something small would make up for what I didn't know or the experience I lacked. How I became employed by Mattel and moved to Asia, though totally unqualified for the job, as well as all my other careers, is my story.

Developing my talents was like wearing those jewels that were locked in the treasure chest. Just like taking ordinary costume jewelry, wearing it proudly, and creating a memorable style is an example of how to do a lot with not much. I soon learned the lesson that with each success your Brand is strengthened, and

When You're Great They Remember Your Name

Chapter 1

One Room

I wasn't groomed for success, nor was I a shining star in school. I was considered shy and never displayed any unique characteristics. My childhood story isn't unusual—there are no famous people or alien abductions—but it provides insight to what caused my childhood dysfunction and pushed me to find a way to change or be eternally stuck in a life of feeling hopeless and helpless.

My mom, Gertrude, and my dad, Harry, were born in Montreal, Canada, at the beginning of the twentieth century. They married in 1930 in Montreal. Photos indicate they were quite a stunning couple. Dad was handsome, artistic, athletic, and well groomed. He was extremely handy and earned his electrician license in Montreal. My mother was a fashionista by today's standard and looked fabulous, at ninety-five pounds in her clothes. Her father was a tailor in Montreal, and he made all her clothes. She had the custom-tailored look of a Hollywood glamour girl, although she never thought of herself that way. Mom did some secretarial work but focused on her housewife duties, as was the norm for early twentieth-century women.

The details of their romance and their early life together were never talked about in front of me. Most conversations were spoken in their second language, French, and they never translated what they were discussing. I wouldn't know what they were saying unless mom interjected a few words in English, like "Don't let her hear this—speak French."

The most memorable story that mom shared, in English, was about her wedding dress. She insisted on a purple silk chiffon cocktail dress, not a white formal gown. Quite the trendsetter and eccentric for her time. My dad's family was furious that she wasn't wearing the traditional white gown and they didn't attend the wedding. My mother said they had little money, and she thought a white dress impractical because it would never be worn again. She held her ground and continued with the plan to wear the luscious, rich purple dress she designed. So fierce was the memory of her in-laws' anger that all the wedding day photos were destroyed. I have never seen a picture of my parents' wedding. However, I do have the purple dress. The fabric is a transparent, flowing silk chiffon with an opaque purple slip worn underneath. I also have the remnants of the lovely, dried purple bouquet and the purple boutonniere my father wore. These items were saved and sealed in a box, but anything purple was forbidden in our home. Probably one of the reasons that my *signature* color is purple, and the sight of it makes me smile and feel really happy.

Personal Brand Image:

Find something that you will instantly be recognized for, even if it is as simple as the color Purple.

My parents moved to Brooklyn, New York, from Canada in 1930 and became naturalized US citizens in 1945. I was born in 1948. Yes, I was the only child after an eighteen-year year marriage. My parents' explanation was that they didn't want any children because they couldn't afford to support a family. A similar reason to not wanting a white wedding gown, I suppose. Mom was forty-two years old when she became pregnant, and Dad was forty-three years. In 1948, they were considered ancient to be new parents. My mother even thought about an abortion after learning she was pregnant with me, which at the time was illegal.

Of course, mom always told me how blessed she was that she changed her mind and gave birth to me. She said I was the best thing that ever happened to her. Intellectually, I know this was true and she meant well by explaining my history. I'm sure she was genuinely happy to have me in her life. However, the one thing a child doesn't want to hear from her mother is that she wasn't wanted, and her mom thought about destroying her before she was born. Was I like the unwanted wedding pictures?

That this memory has remained in my mind for over sixty years shows how monumental this incident was, and even today writing down the facts makes me feel ill. The same feeling I had when I suffered from nausea and vomiting every morning. I thought the feeling was normal. I woke up, declined breakfast, and went straight to the bathroom. I tried to cope but was overwhelmed with nausea, and if I didn't throw up immediately I felt as if I would die. So I muffled the noise and made myself heave even though I hadn't eaten any food.

My ritualistic vomiting was kept secret from my parents as I locked myself in the bathroom every morning. Breakfast was hardly ever a formal event, so it wasn't strange at all for me to have no appetite. The ritual of vomiting or just dry heaving made me feel better. This went on daily until I was almost thirty years old.

It was hard to hide anything from my parents, since we lived in a one-room apartment. I truly mean one room, except for the small bathroom. The apartment would be called a studio in today's terms, more suitable for a single person. The neighborhood that we lived in was nice, and I have fond memories of the area known as Sheepshead Bay, Brooklyn, New York, located a few miles from famous Coney Island and within walking distance to the Atlantic Ocean. Our building was opposite Sheepshead Bay, where fishing boats constantly hauled in their daily catch. My mom would cross the street, walk on the promenade, and buy the daily catch for dinner. I loved all the fresh fish, and going to the boats and picking out dinner was entertainment.

When you opened our apartment door, there was a closet on the left and a small bathroom on the right. Taking a couple of steps, you entered the one room. The kitchen wasn't separate; it was in the wall of the room. Small refrigerator, mini stove, and sink, with a few cabinets above the appliances. Forget the luxury of counter space—there was none. In front of this cooking area was a classic mahogany wooden dining table to eat your meal and to function as a counter.

Straight ahead was my dad's desk and two couches in the daytime, which transformed into my parents' beds at night. To the right, two windows facing another apartment overlooked a fire escape and an alley.

Between the windows sat a television that was purchased when we could afford this new invention. In the early 1950s the TV was in a wooden cabinet with doors that closed to hide the screen. The doors were also used to block the glare at night when I was trying to sleep. My bed was against the wall, next to the TV. I used to stand on my bed and pretend that the top of a tall cabinet next to my bed was my secret playhouse for dolls and my private space. My parents created a loving environment, and I don't believe they could have been more caring if we'd had six rooms.

When I was four years old, my mother disappeared. She had taken me to kindergarten as usual, but at the end of the day, when I expected her to take me home, she wasn't there. Instead my mom's sister, Leah, was waiting for me. We walked home together, and I expected to see Mom when we reached home. As we entered the one-room apartment, it wasn't difficult to see that my mother wasn't there.

Aunt Leah told me my mom would be home soon. By this time I was hysterical, thinking that my mother had left me forever—after all, she'd almost aborted me! Days went by, and my Aunt stayed with me until my dad came home from work. "Where's Mommy?" I cried. I was told she was in a secret place. I was so upset I refused to leave the house or go to school.

A few days passed, and my dad took me to a big building. We stood on the street and looked up at one of the open windows. Dad pointed and said, "Look up at the window and you will see mommy." In a few seconds she appeared. With outstretched arms I ran toward Mom, but Dad wouldn't let me go into the building. I was once again hysterically crying. My memory isn't clear about what Dad told me at that point. My mother was in the hospital. It was 1952, and hospital policy didn't allow children into patients' rooms. I was heartbroken and scared.

Mom was released from the hospital a few days later, and we all went to her brother's home, in Rockaway, New York. Mom needed rest and help with me after her surgery. I didn't understand what was happening, and all my dad, aunts, and uncles were speaking French to keep what was going on a secret. Mother was weak, and I wouldn't leave her for fear that she would disappear again or die. I became extremely attached to her, as well as introverted and quiet.

We went home the next week, and Mom told me that she had a lump in her breast that was bad and the doctors needed to remove that cancerous lump and her breast. I didn't understand why this happened. My mother, in her desire to have me know the truth, showed me the scar across her chest and her missing left breast. Horrible and shocking! I was sure my mother was going to die from this mutilation.

My daily routine of vomiting intensified, since I now had more reason to believe I was unworthy. Perhaps if I was a better daughter, or if mom had aborted me, she wouldn't have this horrendous scar. There was no chemotherapy in 1952, and the doctors gave my mother only six months to live. However, my mother lived another twenty-four years, until I was twenty-eight years old. Years later I asked her what kept her alive. She replied, "The day I saw you crying on the street below my hospital window and you were not allowed in my room, I said to myself, 'I will not leave her.'" She kept her promise.

My mother quickly recuperated, and life got back to normal. Okay, she had an artificial silicone breast that she put into her bra. But Mom had courage and never seemed depressed. Quite the opposite—she was filled with energy and caring. She was my role model for courage.

Personal Brand Image:

When faced with disaster, keep your attitude positive to create a better situation.

After Mom's surgery not much changed for our family, including living in one room. The older I got the more embarrassed and humiliated I felt, realizing we were the only family I knew that lived in such a small space. Therefore, I limited my friends to one girl, Judy, who lived in the same building. Her family had a one-bedroom apartment. I thought she was the rich girl in the building, with an extra room.

When I invited Judy to our apartment to play, the bathroom became the art studio. We put shaving cream on the mirrors, then added red lipstick to turn the foam pink. We pretended that the dining room table was a secret room when we covered it with a big tablecloth and hid underneath. Judy preferred to come to my apartment since it was more fun. My mother let us be creative with the small space and do stuff that most parents would think was destructive.

Mom was always in a good mood, and I couldn't understand why she didn't feel trapped in the small space. In fact she acted as if the one room wasn't a problem. I remember her giving parties in that room that were fit for royalty. Mom had great tableware accessories that she'd collected or received as gifts. Nothing matched but they were all beautiful and one of a kind. When she had family or friends over, the eye-catching, delicate porcelain dinnerware would be set on the small table with fine linens. The guests proclaimed her "the hostess with the mostess."

Knowing we had no extra money for entertaining, I was a surprised that the guests were so happy. Mom told me that even if you only serve tuna fish sandwiches, present them in grand style on nice plates and use pretty linens. Presenting food in this manner will make everything taste better and the guests will feel special. Pretty good advice and way before Martha Stewart. To this day I cannot serve even a slice of toast on a paper plate or water in a plastic cup. Served in style, tuna sandwiches become gourmet delicacies when they're placed on bone china plates, and water is tastier than wine when sipped from a crystal glass.

Personal Brand Image:

Be creative and change your weakness into a strength.
Presentation style can change perception.

I was obsessed with the thought that if I could have my own bedroom, then everything would be okay. My schoolwork was difficult to complete at home. I had no place for quiet study or privacy. After work, dad watched TV all night, and my work area was on my bed or on the floor, next to the TV. My survival strategy to complete schoolwork was to memorize details. I read, but the noise, my low self-worth, and my worry that my mother was going to die affected my reading comprehension. I resorted to memorizing to pass tests and write reports. I was like a robot, repeating what I memorized from books or my class notes, not necessarily understanding the meaning.

Creativity and fun came from art. I remember the best gift I ever received as a child was a giant art set with paints, colored pencils, and pastels. Wow—I could do something that didn't require a quiet atmosphere. I could paint or draw on the floor by the TV and let my imagination soar.

My father's after-work routine was to watch TV and smoke lots of cigarettes. However, Dad helped with my art projects, and this was our special time together. I loved it. Dad was a professional window trimmer for pharmacies and liquor stores. He never told me why he was no longer an electrician, and the reason remains a mystery. Most stores displayed products in their windows to attract passersby, a popular trade before TV advertising.

I was nearly eight years old when my mother decided to tell me a secret. According to Mom and Dad, they were thirty years old, similar to other parents of kids my age. Now Mom felt I needed to know the truth: she was fifty years old and Dad was fifty-one. I was devastated. All of a sudden my parents were twenty years older! Now I was sure they would die at any moment. This reality fed into my lack of self-worth and ignited my fear of losing both my parents. Another reason to keep vomiting!

From my perspective, my parents' time on earth would end soon. I had no other family to depend on and we had no savings. What would I do when my parents died? Who would support me? I was just a kid. How could I survive? I needed to find a way to take care of myself. My parents were high-school graduates and they instilled in me that college was important for my future. I must go to college. I saw this as a way to insure my employment and live alone if necessary.

By the time I was eleven years old, living in a one-room apartment was becoming more problematic. We couldn't afford to move and pay more rent. The dream of college seemed as impossible to afford as an apartment with a bedroom.

I have no idea where the extra money came from for my clothing. Mom occasionally took her gold and diamond jewelry to the pawn shop, until enough money was saved to buy the items back. When Mom wasn't wearing her diamond ring, I knew we had trouble. The reappearance of that stunning ring on her finger meant all was well. Mom promised Dad she would cut back expenses and get a part-time job in a factory to help pay for any additional rent if we moved. In 1959 we finally moved into a three-room apartment around the corner from our old apartment. It had a small kitchen, living room, and most important to me, a separate bedroom that my parents gave me while they used the living room.

Now that the worry of one-room humiliation was gone, it was replaced by the fear of not being able to afford the new apartment. I was always thinking about what could happen next, like the day my Mom had disappeared. I learned that anything could happen, and I was constantly worried about when the next bad thing would occur. I was an only child, with a mother who could die at any time from breast cancer. I had a Dad who was diagnosed with emphysema, due to smoking four packs of cigarettes a day. Becoming an orphan could soon be a reality.

Chapter 2

College

In 1961 I was a freshman at Lincoln High School in Brighton Beach, Brooklyn. It was the first day of school, and we all gathered in the assembly hall for an orientation. The principal, Mr. Lass, stood in front of hundreds of freshman students and told us the story of a student who'd left a paper lunch bag on the cafeteria table a few years earlier and received a demerit from the school's security officer. This violation was noted on the student's permanent record. The student's behavior was identified as irresponsible and caused their rejection for employment by a government agency after graduation. This was our "Warning: Welcome to High School." Times have changed in the twenty-first century. However, this statement frightened me, especially since I was focusing on attending college. If I left a paper bag or a tissue on school property, would I be denied entrance to college?

My high desire to attend college was always lowered, because my family had no money to support tuition and my grades weren't good enough for a scholarship. Adding to my layers of worry, I didn't excel in any particular academic area. Even if I were accepted to a college, I had no expertise that could be considered a major and as a result, probably no career opportunities. I felt locked in the one-room again, until a door opened when New York City offered a plan for students to attend any of the New York City Colleges tuition free, as long as students meet each year's academic standard. I was lucky that during the 1960s New York was offering this gift. Now I had to find a way to receive it.

My reading comprehension had never improved. Although I finally had my own quiet bedroom at home, the habits I'd learned in a distracted one-room environment made it difficult for me to focus. I still depended on memorization to pass tests, versus actually understanding what I was reading. My grades were average, not good enough to gain the tuition-free entrance to college.

I did really well in mathematics, my best subject as a result of my memorizing formulas and not needing to read and comprehend information. Art was a close second in my scoring excellence, since memory and concentration weren't factors in being artistic. My mental chaos made me more creative in my art classes. With extreme effort and lots of memorization, I focused on math and art to achieve high grades. It paid off. I successfully pulled up my grade average in junior year, garnering me the opportunity to attend college.

Personal Brand Image:

Use the skills you have to reach another opportunity.

Hunter College was my choice, a two-hour round-trip sub-way ride from Brooklyn to Manhattan. I selected Hunter because of the outstanding art faculty, who taught a vast number of creative disciplines. The majority of the professors were reputable artists who exhibited in the nearby art galleries. Hunter was on the Upper East Side of New York City, at 68th Street and Park Avenue. My campus would be the Madison Avenue art galleries, Museum of Modern Art, The Whitney Museum, The Metropolitan Museum, and the legendary Bloomingdale's department store. To me this was cosmopolitan-campus heaven.

The most common careers for women in the 1960s that I could actually accomplish were limited to teaching or secretarial positions. At the time I felt that the best way to earn a living would be teaching. I declared math as my major and art as my minor and entered Hunter College in 1965. I was still secretly vomiting every morning and hoped that acceptance to college and the positive outlook would finally cure me.

The daily journey to Manhattan was a stressful adventure and caused me to immerse myself in the New York Attitude mode: Do not make eye contact with anyone. I was afraid. The danger on the train, especially for women, was high. Armed Transit Police constantly patrolled each subway car, but pickpocket incidents remained rampant and men exposing themselves on the crowded trains was commonplace. I became vigilant in suspecting the evil men who might prey on the subway ladies.

Identifying math as my major meant I had to enroll in basic classes, and my ambition was to complete all the math requirements in the first year. This was an aggressive decision. I had no advice on what to do, since my parents never went to college and I had no siblings to rely on to advise me on how to work the system. I did what I thought was best and could handle. This was math, I was good at it. Little did I know that this was college math, quite different from high school, and the teaching method was more accelerated and demanding. In addition, the requirements for a math degree included physics, chemistry, and advanced calculus. I hadn't anticipated that my memorization methodology would be a failure in these courses. I was overwhelmed and beyond my area of expertise.

My first year in college was an academic nightmare. I was struggling, barely making the *C* average to stay matriculated at Hunter. I continued to be very introverted and never made any friends. However, the few students I spoke with shared their approach to selecting courses. They made sure to take some easy classes along with the requirements, to lower the emotional pressure and achieve a good grade average. Of course this made complete sense and seemed obvious, but it was too late for me. I took the full load of difficult classes, and I was paying the price for my registration ignorance with low grades and unrelenting morning vomiting.

After two semesters at Hunter my average was below *C* and I was dropped from full-time studies until I could bring up my grade average to at least *B*. This meant I needed to enroll in evening classes to get my matriculated status back. Now I knew how to work the system and rethink my major. Math was definitely the wrong choice. I was embarrassed to be dropped from full-time college yet also relieved that my academic nightmare was over. I changed my major to graphic design, enrolled in the beginning art classes, and took a few low-level requirements that weren't too intense.

Personal Brand Image:

After trial and error, identify what you are good at to accomplish a goal.

After a semester of evening classes my grade average was a *B+* and I was able to get my matriculation status back. Graphic design was officially my major, and what a difference the selection made to my academic success. My graduation target was now January 1970. I felt that I would pursue a career in advertising, something to do with a Madison Avenue company, and become involved with product promotion. I had a really good sense of style and a minimalist approach to convey a message with some humor and deep thought. I felt I had something inside me that could make me successful in the competitive field of advertising. Therefore, my art classes focused on the basics, with an emphasis on graphic design like in stationery, posters, business promos, and interior design. The timing is 1967-1969. There are no personal computers and I am actually drawing, painting, sculpting, and constructing by hand in my bedroom back in Brooklyn.

One of the requirements to complete my BA degree was an introductory drawing class taught by Professor Robert Huot. I didn't realize at the time that this basic drawing class would have a major impact on my life. I always thought of it as a small, meaningless incident. Retracing my steps on how I achieved my career, I thought back to 1967 and Mr. Huot's drawing class. Perhaps the origin of my **Personal Brand Image** began with Mr. Huot, who inspired me to change my outlook on life.

Robert Huot was a professional artist, exhibiting his abstract paintings in the local galleries. I heard from other students that he was somewhat famous and we were all lucky to have him teaching at Hunter. Mr. Huot's drawing class was held at 8:00 a.m. twice a week. To be on time, I left Brooklyn before 6:30 a.m., taking the long walk and subway ride to the Upper East Side. The class was held in a studio environment, with a table in the room's center. Mr. Huot started the class by carefully placing a large gauntlet in the middle of the table. This protective styled glove was grayish in color and looked like something a gladiator would wear. This was the subject for our drawings. White paper and pencils were provided, and the class became intensely quiet with all the students' eyes mesmerized with The Glove.

This exact same object and setting continued for weeks, until Mr. Huot held a private meeting with each student to review our drawings, comment, and advise. He was an overwhelming figure with an intimidating style. I was only nineteen years old with a small frame, short at five foot two. My personality was quiet and I never spoke in class, particularly never uttered a word to Mr. Huot, who was tall, deep voiced, and heavyset. He prominently displayed lots of facial hair, which he stroked while pacing the room and making a brisk sound when his denim overalls rubbed on his boots.

So here I am in the classroom with this intimidating famous art professor. He calls my name and I enter his office with my portfolio of a few dozen black-and-white pencil drawings of The Glove. He shuffles through them in a few seconds and looks at me and says, "What do you think about the class?" I could feel the blood draining from my body. I never expected him to ask me this question. I paused for a moment and to this day I have no idea how I got up the courage to quietly say, "Mr. Huot, I don't understand why every class is the same. We have the same glove to draw every day. I am actually quite bored!"

When I finished speaking he looked at me and yelled, **"Young lady, there is nothing boring in this world … there are only boring people!"** He then took my many weeks' worth of drawings and ripped them to shreds, threw them on the floor, and left the room. If there is more to the story, I certainly have no memory of it. I was in shock.

You can image with my poor self-image, quiet style, the efforts I made to overcome poverty and make something of myself, this incident was traumatic. It wasn't until years later that I realized he was correct. I was boring and all my perceptions of the world were boring.

Mr. Huot never instructed us to only use pencils, he never said the drawing had to look like reality or rendered like a photograph. I could have brought a red pen or a blue spray-paint can to class. I could have made the glove a geometric, abstract shape. I could have imagined the glove was turned inside out, or being held in a gladiator's hand. I could have drawn another item in room. I could have pursued infinite ideas, but I drew the same thing in every class. The Glove wasn't boring, the class wasn't boring. It was who I was—that was boring!

If you take away or learn anything from this book, remember one thing. Remember Mr. Huot and what he said to me:

**"There is nothing boring in this world,
there are only boring people!"**

I now understand what Mr. Huot meant as he ripped my drawings and threw them away. But I had no idea how a shy, introverted girl raised in a one-room apartment could be anything but boring!

My personality continued to be quiet and shy. No friends to speak of except one girl, Lynn, who I'd met in an art class. We shared a love of contemporary art, and in our free time we would go to the galleries in Manhattan and rave about the new

Minimal Art trend that was being exhibited. This art was incredibly simple. There would be an entire room in a gallery filled with canvases that were just one black square painted on a giant white background. WOW! I loved the simplicity and it inspired me to think that art could be something different, even if it wasn't a realistic portrait or a painting of a bowl of fruit. It was so minimal in design and direct with a strong statement ... it was truly not boring. Amazing that I could now look at a solitary black square and find it exciting, a big contrast to my boring days of drawing The Glove.

Thinking out loud ... if someone hadn't painted or constructed this piece of art, I never would have seen it. This was a profound thought for me, how creative a human could be and do something incredibly different with so little. I found that once an artist focused on something they felt intensely about they repeated it and explored it in infinite ways. So the black square paintings turned into the red square paintings and then became the blue circle exhibit, which resulted in the black square sculpture twenty feet high and never ended its journey of exploration and transformation. It was never boring—it became the artist's style or **Personal Brand Image**.

I remember one day at a gallery on 57th Street and Madison Ave, I was looking at a Minimal Art exhibit with Lynn and I remarked how the sculpture on the wall was unbelievably brilliant. I was amazed at the simplicity and the symmetry. I stared for minutes, gazing at the beauty and style of this art form when Lynn poked me and said, "You know what you are looking at is the cover of the air conditioning duct. It's not part of the exhibit!"

True story that today I cannot look at any air conditioning duct without that memory and a smile for my youthful naivety. My mind made the hardware on the wall into art. I was looking at the mundane metal grid differently than its intention. Two years after Mr. Huot's class and "boring" remarks, I realized that all the creative art I was looking at, past or present, had the same root idea. Take something ordinary, look at it differently every time until you find something extraordinary. Whether it was the shape, the color, the size, it was an endless exploration making a special statement.

Personal Brand Image:

Look at what you're doing until you find something that's extraordinary.

My last semester at Hunter College I was fortunate enough to have Mr. Mac Wells's painting class. Mr. Wells was an American abstract artist and like Mr. Huot, Mr. Wells was exhibiting in the New York City galleries. I loved this class and particularly thought Mr. Wells was a warm and gracious person. He was unassuming, soft spoken, and extremely handsome with his long blonde hair, slim figure, and tight blue jeans. He looked more like a rock star than a teacher. Of course, all the girls in the class had a crush on him. I don't remember if I was one of his fans, but the fact that after forty years I still remember him says a lot about the situation and my feelings.

We were near the end of the course and Mac Wells gave us our final assignment. He told us that for the last class we were to present a **Finite Project**. In other words, something that had a beginning and an end. This was an extremely avant-garde assignment for a 1969 student's mentality. This really meant we could do anything. There were no limits, just a beginning and an end. You could start and finish a painting, start and finish singing a song, dance a dance, give a speech ... all would be acceptable. This was almost too free, too open, too immense for me.

I felt I had a chance now to prove to myself and yes, prove that I wasn't boring. Actually force myself to not be boring. This was a chance that I couldn't overlook. I had to do something extraordinary and memorable for this project. Something guaranteed to be over the top and outstanding. I challenged myself to create an experience that would be unforgettable for the class, Mr. Wells, and me.

The **Finite Project** was weeks away from its due date. I was obsessed with finding the right medium to obtain the impact I sought. Any type of art execution wasn't an option. It was too obvious to do an art project for an art class. I was looking for the unexpected, especially from this shy, introverted student that nobody even knew was in the class. I had to do something brilliant, lasting and make a huge statement. I wanted to be the one to present a visual experience that without me as the creator, no one would ever experience or see it.

I thought about doing something that was guaranteed to make the viewer feel good, feel euphoric. How could I create a **Finite Project** with this guaranteed result? My mind wandered and thought about what made me feel good. My thoughts drifted to the medium of television. I admit I watched my share in television's early days, since we'd waited a long time to afford a TV set. I was immersed in the programs of the 1950s and 60s that were fun and made me laugh. Favorites were comedies *I Love Lucy* and *Laurel and Hardy*. Some of these funny shows gave me a vision of what I would do for Mr. Wells. I must make this a surprise presentation. No plan could be divulged, and not even my one friend Lynn could know about my project. This was the biggest secret for the most important moment of my life and I would keep silent until the day the **Finite Project** was to be presented.

Mac Wells's class was in the late afternoon and I was a nervous wreck all day in anticipation of presenting my work. The class was divided into sections and we were all assigned time slots to share our projects. When my name was called I went to the front of the class, where there was a high-top table for students to present. I honestly cannot remember what any other student showed that day, so I have to believe no one was memorable. I felt every eye in the class on me when I slowly appeared before the students to present my project. Mr. Wells, who usually dressed casually, for some reason was a bit more formal this day. He was wearing a sport jacket with his jeans and collared shirt, looking like he was going somewhere after class. I took a deep breath and decided to move forward with my plan.

I had everything carefully prepared. Without uttering a word I stepped up to the table. Faced the class, reached for a bag which I'd previously hidden under the table. I took out a red checkered tablecloth and flamboyantly draped it over the tabletop. Out of the same bag, I removed a pie plate with a graham cracker crust insert and carefully placed it in the middle of the tablecloth. I then took out a large can of whipped cream, removed the cap, shook it vigorously as I pressed the nozzle to fill the pie crust with the contents of the entire can. The next step was shaking chocolate and multicolored sprinkles out from a plastic container, dispersing these small sweets over the top of my cream pie. Lastly, a cherry was put on top.

I was silent during my pie construction. I lifted the decorated pie and finally spoke. I asked one the students to dip her finger into the pie and taste the cream. I repeated this taste request two more times, until I finally was standing near Mr. Wells. Just as I was about to ask him to taste the pie, which everyone thought was the end to the project, I held my breath and smashed the pie into his face! His long blonde hair was like a magnet to the cream. He was bent over, covered and dripping with pie ingredients. My **Finite Project** was now complete. I fulfilled the requirements: it had a beginning and an end.

The screams from my classmates were deafening. The students in rooms adjacent to Mr. Wells's class ran in to see what the problem was and there was Mr. Wells's head hanging down, shaking off whipped cream, sprinkles, and graham cracker crust. Everyone was so happy. The cheers, screams, laughter, applause, attention, and fame was all mine. Finally, I was not boring!

This special day ended and I was in the locker room packing my books to head home on the long train ride. Another student near my locker, who was packing her belongings, came over to me and said in an excited, loud voice, "Did you hear what happened to Mac Wells? Some student threw a pie in his face!" I just smiled.

All classes were completed. I received an *A* from the famous Mac Wells and graduated from Hunter College with a BA degree in graphic design.

Personal Brand Image:

Do everything possible to never be boring. You can change ordinary to become extraordinary.

Chapter 3

Get a Job

My official college graduation date was January 1970. However, classes were completed in November 1969, before the Thanksgiving holiday. Still living at home with my parents in Sheepshead Bay, I looked for a temporary job during the Christmas holiday. Simultaneously, I was searching for employment until I would find that dream job. My parents needed my financial support. It never crossed my mind to move out and live on my own. In the 1960s a female usually didn't leave her parents' home until she was married. Living with my parents and helping with the finances seemed the normal next step.

I started my job inquiries with department stores near Hunter College. One of my favorite places to window shop was **Georg Jensen**. The Jensen brand is from Denmark and famous for high-quality merchandise and stunning designs in jewelry, silver, and housewares. The New York location was on 5th Avenue and 53rd Street, a few blocks from Hunter College, The Plaza Hotel, Saks Fifth Avenue, Rockefeller Center, and The Museum of Modern Art. This would be such a terrific area to work. Even if the job was temporary, I would be surrounded by the exquisite designs and art that define New York City.

Georg Jensen was hiring for holiday help in their gift-wrapping area and part-time sales for crystal home goods. The interview was scheduled and for this upscale store, I made sure to wear one of my stylish outfits, enhanced by an awesome haircut. My mother had instilled in me that if I was to have a haircut, it should be good. She introduced me to the best of the New York salons, Vidal Sassoon, on Madison Avenue. The style was a stunning asymmetrical, signature Sassoon cut. With my trendy outfit, great haircut, and the advantage of a college degree to be granted in a couple months, I was confident I would get hired. I had the right style and attitude for that store.

My strategy worked. I was hired for the Christmas season in the gift-wrapping area. They trained me in the Georg Jensen standards and I was having fun. All those silver-toned gift boxes and ribbons that needed to be tied perfectly was no challenge. When I wasn't wrapping gifts, I was in the crystal department, selling gorgeous glassware. I realized this was temporary and not a job that would give me a career, but at least I felt and tasted success on my first try.

Personal Brand Image:

First impressions count. Show confidence and dress the part to help make up for lack of experience.

The Christmas and New Year holidays were over and the Georg Jensen job should have ended. However, because of my excellent work and reputation as a conscientious worker, the store manager asked me to stay on for their January discount sales. By February I was job hunting on my own. The painful process of looking through the newspaper ads for employment was a daily routine. I went on many interviews at Madison Avenue companies, carrying my large portfolio, walking up and down the streets of NYC in the freezing cold. No one wanted to hire a fresh grad with no experience in advertising. I was becoming extremely frustrated.

There were no positions in the newspaper want ads that I was qualified for. Then I saw an ad for a "Textile Colorist" at a company called Brewster Design and Finishing, located in midtown Manhattan. They were looking to train beginners. I had no idea what a Textile Colorist did. My familiarity with fabrics was limited to picking out clothes from the "Reduced for Clearance" rack at Saks Fifth Avenue. Since I had no other interviews lined up, I decided to take my inner strength from my pie-throwing Mac Wells experience and be bold enough to get through the interview.

It was a month before my twenty-second birthday. I had no work experience except for a part-time job at a shoe company, counting inventory my freshman year, and gift wrapping at Georg Jensen. Textiles meant nothing more to me than that they formed the clothes on my back. The interview was in the heart of the NYC Garment Center, fashion capital of the world, and a few blocks from the famous Macy's department store. If you've ever watched the Macy's Thanksgiving Day Parade with marching bands and Santa Claus riding on a sleigh-float, they all passed in front on this building that I was about to enter.

My plan was to make sure I looked fashionable for the interview, since this job involved fabric that ends up in clothing. Creating my image as a fashionista was necessary to balance out my lack of textile expertise, lack of understanding of fabric manufacturing and fashion design. I wore one of my trendy 1970s outfits, an attempt to overcome my weak qualifications for the job. There I was in my short, mid-thigh, brown leather miniskirt, white wool bulky turtleneck sweater, knee-high cream leather boots, and my Vidal Sassoon haircut to literally top off the fashion statement. I proudly carried my large black portfolio with highlights of my Hunter College graphic design pieces, an array of bright colored, hard-edged, minimalistic visuals.

I entered the interview room, where two handsome gentlemen, Mr. Jerry and Mr. Wilson, were looking at applicants' portfolios. They were the textile stylists for Brewster's print fabric divisions. Both men wore tailored business suits, neckties, and silk handkerchiefs in their jacket pockets. Smartly dressed in every detail and flamboyant in their mannerisms and attitudes. They studied my portfolio, which obviously had NO textile items. My art examples were all graphic designs—i.e., stationery, business cards, invitations, posters, interior design concepts, etc.

After Jerry and Wilson reviewed my work, they said I was a great candidate for the job.

Textile colorist designed the different color combinations for printed fabric patterns. They actually painted the different color styles (bright, pastel, neutral) on watercolor paper. Yes, all the designs were hand painted with a small paintbrush. Then the colorist traveled to the factory and directed the technical engineers on how to match the colors and aesthetics from the artwork on the actual fabrics.

I was direct with both Mr. Jerry and Mr. Wilson when I told them that my major interest and study was in graphic design. I had never taken any textile or fashion design courses. They could see from my portfolio that the focus of my BA degree was graphic, not fabric. I explained that I was honored to have the job offer and I wanted to understand why they felt I was a good match for the position.

Jerry said that my portfolio was a clear example that I had an excellent sense of color and style, which demonstrated my ability. The visual presentation of my work was well organized, professional, and exceptionally colorful. Jerry and Wilson felt that with the entry-level job, they could use my talent to train me in textile design and manufacturing. In addition, they noticed I had a fashion flair by the outfit I wore to the interview. They never mentioned my haircut, but I knew it cinched the deal!

Did I have a choice as to what to do? Were there other opportunities out there? Was I being pursued by dozens of other companies? I had to accept the job. I needed the employment and any experience I could get. It wasn't necessary to love the job. My thoughts were just like the ones I had about the Georg Jensen job: this would be temporary, maybe six months, until I found a position where I could utilize my graphic design skills. I dug deep in my soul and expressed in a confident, happy voice— although the opposite was true—that I would be honored and pleased have this opportunity.

Personal Brand Image:

Create a strong Brand Image that fits the job, which can compensate for weak qualifications.

Even writing down these memories, I find it hard to believe I accepted this position. I had major doubts about my decision, but decided to take it and do my best. I had every reason to be worried about whether I could succeed as a textile colorist. I wanted the experience and income, then would leave when I had found a job more suitable for me. All my education and life experiences had nothing to do with textiles. If I am paid to do something, I should do it well, even if the job is temporary. Both Jerry and Wilson were willing to take a chance with me, and I didn't want to let them down.

It was a chilly morning on Monday, March 2, 1970, when I walked from the subway station in Manhattan to my new office at 1412 Broadway. The textile division I was assigned to was Lauratex Inc. One of gentlemen who interviewed me, Jerry, would be my boss. He intimidated me, since he was so technically knowledgeable and I was without a clue regarding textiles. He was quite admired and respected in the textile industry, which further made me feel inadequate. I wasn't sure how long my fashionista appearance would help me keep my job.

The office was comprised of a sales staff workspace, a showroom, and a studio for designing the fabric art. I would work in the studio. It wasn't a traditional office with desks or cubicles; it was one large room with floor-to-ceiling windows. All work areas had artist tables, chairs, a set of textiles dyes, paintbrushes, water jars, and porcelain palettes for mixing colors. Jerry had his artist desk too, and four other young ladies working in the studio would be my colleagues: Eloise, Ellen, Eileen, and Elaine! My name was even an outsider on this E-team.

It seemed if I was again an art school student, rather than being an employee. Luckily, Jerry really did intend to train me. He personally mentored and micromanaged me. He was extremely particular about color and how to mix the paint and design color combinations. He drove me crazy with his perfectionism. His fashion flair was outstanding and looking back, I owe so much to Jerry for being hard on me. I felt frustrated that I wasn't as good as the other staff and I was uncomfortable with painting floral designs, since my graphic design focus was mostly on geometric styles. Jerry gave me the tools to be a colorist, but he also taught me the foundation for my future careers.

Personal Brand Image:

Use strong points to enhance and even create the skills you need.

My goal at Lauratex was to be successful and indispensable. I was going to excel in what I do best and make an impression on Jerry. Even though I was still a beginner, I could show I had potential. The first few months was basic training. I was insecure and hated what I was doing.

I watched the other ladies in the studio. They all had Jerry's confidence, especially Eloise. She was smart, fast, outspoken, and had a great recall of small details. Jerry loved her and I made it an objective to copy her efficiency. With my own great memory, I decided to memorize details and facts in the studio. Pattern numbers, printing schedules, customer requests were all in my head. Jerry started to depend on me for data. What I couldn't do well with a paintbrush, I overcame by excelling with business knowledge memory.

Personal Brand Image:

Be recognized as an expert in something, even if you think you'll never need the skills to help create your Brand.

After I became more competent with painting color combinations, Jerry decided it was time for me to go to the factories for onsite fabric approval. This was a milestone. Jerry had to feel comfortable with you to send you to the factories, because any mistakes you made would be costly to the company. The pressure was on the colorist not only to match the painted paper design to the fabric, but also to make a judgment if the final printed fabric looked good enough for the customer to purchase. This assignment at the plant was my crash course on textile manufacturing. If Jerry's studio mentoring was my classroom education, then the plant experience would be equivalent to Textile Graduate School.

My day for factory onsite approvals would start at 7 a.m. at our office building, where I was met by the company driver for either a two-hour drive to Cornwall, New York, or a forty-five-minute drive to Paterson, New Jersey. This is where the fun began. I was a novice at this business, working with men who'd had long careers in manufacturing fabrics. Yet I was given authority to make the final decisions, which meant they would print a thousand yards of the fabric I approved. The longer I took to approve the aesthetics, the more time and money that was being wasted. If my decision disagreed with Jerry or his boss, Miss G, the fabric would be scrapped and redone. A giant waste of time and money, and I would eventually be fired if this happened.

I will never forget the first fabric combination that came off the printing machine for me to evaluate. The head technician, Phil, was the most experienced person at the factory. He had a reputation for being impatient and rude. Therefore, I was extremely nervous when he called me to the office to evaluate the first fabric submission. I had no idea what to do except hold the printed fabric next to the painted watercolor paper to see if it matched. I corrected every color and rejected what was printed. Phil threw down the watercolor paper and screamed, "When you look at fabric you need to know that you will never match each color exactly. This is impossible! You need to look at the whole pattern as a work of art and see if it meets aesthetic expectations. The final customer never sees the original watercolor paper. This is what you need to do!" Then Phil's voice became quiet and kind. He put his arm around me and asked if I understood and said he was trying to help me. This all reminded me of the experience I'd had a few years earlier with Professor Huot. Huot ripped my drawings, but Phil did something worse— he ripped me.

Phil was right. I had to learn to depend on my artistic and designer instincts. If I couldn't visualize what looked beautiful and what would be right for a customer, then I needed to move out of this business. From that day forward I trained myself not to touch the watercolor paper standard. I only used the paper as a guideline. Of course, my success at mastering the aesthetics wasn't a one-day learning experience. A combination of ruthless Phil and perfectionist Jerry eventually improved my decision making.

The head of all the company's design studios, Miss G, had her office in the same building as Lauratex. All the studio heads, who were called stylists, reported to Miss G. This included Jerry and Wilson. Miss G was always critical of everyone and everything. She and the owner of the company, Mr. T, started the business together and she had the final word.

I usually finished work around midnight or later, after a sixteen-hour day at the factory. The company driver was there to take me safely home. Perhaps I didn't get to sleep until 2 a.m., but still I felt I needed to show how loyal I was, to impress Jerry and Miss G, and I made it a point to be at work on time at 9 a.m. the next morning. I was exhausted. The process was to stop by Miss G's office first, to show her the fabrics I'd approved and get her comments.

Usually when I saw Miss G, she was sitting at her desk eating cantaloupe with a scoop of cottage cheese. She barely looked me in the eye, since she was focused on chewing. With a mouthful of the orange fruit and the white, oozing cheese combo, she told me that the fabric was acceptable, but I could have done better. All colors didn't meet her standard. She never looked at me or thanked me for working all night. This was the matriarch of the company, who rarely uttered a kind word to anyone.

I wanted to leave Lauratex. Miss G's attitude was frustrating and the thanklessness of the job was humiliating. The good part was that the salary increased a few times a year. Lauratex was a private company and it was at the boss's discretion to give me a raise. Jerry appreciated me. I supported him with loyalty, precision, and good aesthetics. When I thought I would quit, was at the end of my patience, I got a pay increase and remained at the job. Financial security and the ability to help my family were priorities. The temporary job was lasting longer than I'd planned.

It was April 1972, and I had been employed by Lauratex for two years when I received a phone call at work from my mother. Dad was in the hospital, and I'd better meet her there immediately. My father was a chain-smoker. He'd smoked since he was eleven years old and he was now sixty-seven. Dad hadn't been well for years. Suffering from emphysema, he could hardly walk without breathing heavy afterward. Even when he was diagnosed about ten years earlier with this condition, he never stopped smoking. The US government's "dangers of tobacco" message had only been communicated to the public in 1964. For Dad, this news was too late. There was no cure and our medical support wasn't aggressive to help. We seemed to be in denial of the disease's seriousness and inevitable consequences.

Dad was on oxygen and the doctors said the only thing that would keep him alive was to perform a tracheotomy to open his airway. Looking at my dad's pale gray pallor, I knew we had no choice. Dad had never been ill before chain-smoking caused his severe illness. He'd been an athlete as a young boy in Montreal and now was basically choking to death from the effects of cigarettes.

The surgery was performed and Dad seem to be recovering. The plan was to take him home in a few days. This was a temporary treatment, not a cure. Mom and I went home that night so very sad, but at least Dad had a chance to survive. At 11 p.m. the hospital called, telling me that Dad had passed away. My mother and I were hysterical. We couldn't believe this happened. The doctor informed us that although my father never had a heart condition, the surgery was too much for him and his heart just stopped.

I was only twenty-four years old at the time of Dad's death and totally unprepared to lose a parent. I'd never known anyone who had died or even had a friend whose parents died. All the details for a funeral and burial, not to mention the expense, was never planned. We had no savings except for what I had put away from my salary, which all went toward the funeral costs.

Fast forward to 1976, when my mother died from cancer. The diagnosis was that the breast cancer she had in 1952 returned. Even though she had a mastectomy, the cancer had spread throughout her chest, and it was inoperable. My mom was so brave. She knew the reality of her shortened days and even planned her funeral and what it should say on her tombstone: "**Enjoyed Every Day.**" This is how she felt and that is what is chiseled in stone at her New York gravesite.

My parents' deaths created overwhelming unhappiness for me. I was now twenty-eight years old and orphaned. My adult orphan comment isn't meant to be funny. I had no brothers, no sisters, no boyfriend, and my circle of friends were the folks I worked with. I was alone. No one to phone if I would be home late. Without parents, what will my life mean? All my savings from my job went to pay for two funerals. There was no insurance and all I had was the contents of our apartment, some jewelry, and my current employment.

After nearly six years working at Lauratex as a textile colorist, dissatisfied with my career, as well as distraught over being without family, I was still continually getting salary increases. Being liked by Jerry was important to me, since no one else needed me. I didn't actively pursue looking for a career in graphic design and decided to stay at Lauratex, hoping to focus on being promoted to head stylist in one of the Brewster studios.

Jerry had me in charge of all customer special requests. I worked with garment manufacturers and their fashion designers, executing personalized and exclusive printed fabrics for them. If I was capable of doing this type of independent assignment, why wasn't I being promoted? It seemed that some new staff was climbing the success ladder quickly, but not me. When I approached Jerry about a promotion, he told me that Miss G felt I didn't have the "right style" to head a studio. In the 1970s, that was code meaning I wasn't attractive enough.

It didn't matter what I physically looked like. The point was that Miss G wanted a more attractive persona to lead a studio. I was humiliated, which exacerbated my already depressed outlook on life. It seemed I was at a career dead end. I needed the income from this job to survive, but I didn't want to be at a company that gave the "good-looking" staff the edge for success.

I focused on continuing to be exceptional at my job to fool myself into feeling emotionally better. I also moved out of Brooklyn. Nothing was keeping me there. I was traveling by public transportation daily to work. A three-hour round trip seemed a waste of time, not to mention dangerous for a girl to come home alone late in the evening. I made the big move to a small, one-bedroom apartment in Manhattan in the Murray Hill midtown area, a fifteen-minute walk to my office. Great location to live in, but the novelty of my own place in NYC was wearing off and depression was moving in.

My best friend at Lauratex was Gary Kalman, who worked as a converter for the company, traveling to the factories to coordinate the textile manufacturing. What Jerry taught me about textiles, Gary taught me about music, food, fun, and a happy outlook on life. Gary was a charming, sensitive man. We were about the same age, in our late twenties, when we became good friends. Gary was tall, a bit on the heavy side with a handsome face, and always greeted me with a smile and giant hug. The embrace was comforting, like a brother. I felt safe with Gary. He was my best friend and he confided in me that he was gay. I suspected this, but in the 1970s if you were homosexual, you kept this a secret. No one at work knew about Gary's personal life. I was honored to have his trust and loved him for his humanity, not his sexuality.

When Gary saw how sad I'd become, he insisted I seek professional help. Otherwise he felt I would wind up without a job, living on the NYC streets, carrying my belongings in a shopping bag. He shared with me that he was in therapy for many years and would be glad to give me his analyst's name. Thinking this was a ridiculous idea, I didn't follow up. I wasn't crazy. Only crazy people went to see a psychoanalyst ... a SHRINK! I felt I'd gotten this far on my own, I didn't need any help from a stranger behind a couch.

A few weeks passed and I found myself crying most of the time. I was losing my style and strong attitude, and my work was in decline. My **Personal Brand Image** of a fashionable, competent textile colorist was at risk. I needed help if I was going to keep my job and survive.

Perhaps Gary was right that I was on my way to a new Brand—a homeless bag lady on the streets of New York.

Chapter 4

In Fashion

Gary finally convinced me that I needed professional help to overcome my emotional paralysis. He emphasized that seeing a "shrink" was in fashion and that I shouldn't be afraid to seek help. I made an appointment with his psychoanalyst, Dr. D, on the Upper East Side, a few subway stops from my apartment and office. There are many stereotypes of psychoanalysts and what they look like. In my mind I thought I'd see a bearded Sigmund Freud type or a gray-haired lady wearing a tie-dyed T-shirt and blue jeans, beads dangling around her neck. Neither could have been further from reality. Dr. D was in her late thirties, slim, attractive, stylish, and with great legs she prominently displayed in knee-high dresses and accentuated by shoes with four-inch heels. This was only the beginning of unexpected confrontations with Dr. D.

The inclusion of my involvement with Dr. D isn't meant to delve into the details of each session or be a clinical study of a doctor-patient relationship. My experience with therapy was life changing and enabled me to secure a strong **Personal Brand Image**. Dr. D taught me what no parent, graduate school, or mentor could have. This is why I'm highlighting the work and influence my analysis had in my career, life, and yes, writing this book.

At twenty-nine years old, recently orphaned, I'm depressed and hanging on to an unsatisfying job, in spite of being successful. I'm not seeking other employment, I'm facing a roadblock to expand my career and change my life. Not to mention that I still have the daily ritual of morning vomiting. I sought help from Dr. D to fix all my problems. It was as if I thought she was a magician who would wave a magic wand and all would be okay in a few sessions. What I learned is that the cure would have to come from me, and the journey would be long. After all, it had taken me twenty-nine years to get this place in my life and seek help. It would take years to correct my dysfunctions.

I was in session with Dr. D twice a week. She soon became my role model. I had no one else to look up to. Let me state that Dr. D was no mother substitute. There was no nurturing, no warmth, not much kindness, just tough reality and guidance to correct the damage of my childhood that was crippling me. Dr. D told me that she would cure me if I cooperated and that I would become a well-adjusted adult. The decision was entirely up to me if the analysis would be successful.

I'd rush out of the office, down the subway steps to make my bi-weekly appointments with Dr. D, who didn't tolerate lateness. If I was late it was a sign I was unable to control my life. The therapy process was slow and I want to emphasize that the most important lesson I learned in the first few years was that it didn't matter how I felt about myself or a situation. What was important was acting appropriately. Figuring out what was appropriate was the hard part. Once that was accomplished, you either had to act or not act. In other words, if I hated to go to work, it didn't matter how I felt. I couldn't act out my anger by being a troublesome employee or disruptive at Lauratex. I had to do my job regardless of my personal turmoil.

Personal Brand Image:

Make positive action a habit. Be enthusiastic, make every effort to be perceived as professional and competent, even if you don't feel that way. If you keep acting appropriately, after a while these actions become habit.

I obeyed the doctor's instructions. I was a valued staff member, and I had a great rapport with the garment manufacturers I worked with on customized textile projects. My personality was warm and I was extremely dependable. These fashion designers loved to work with me, since I conveyed great knowledge of textile manufacturing and was recognized as having fabulous fashion flair. I never let my professional contacts know the pain and depression I was suffering. My business style was all about acting appropriately. I saved my sadness and anger for my sessions with Dr. D.

My focus was on being successful, overcoming my personal loss and isolated life. I was a perfectionist at work, and this didn't go unnoticed by one of Lauratex's customers, who worked for a ladies' sportswear manufacturer, **Eccobay**, a privately owned company run by an eccentric man named Mr. H. His head designer, who I had been working with, approached me one day and asked if I would come work for her at Eccobay. I would be designing and buying the printed fabrics for their fashion line, shop the textile market, coordinate and assist with merchandising the sportswear line. She loved working with me and felt I had talent. Her boss Mr. H was aware of my excellent reputation and wanted me on his staff. They offered me double the salary I was earning at Lauratex!

Eccobay was famous for overworking its staff and Mr. H was notorious for his outlandish behavior and unorthodox style. It would be a tradeoff. The temptation of double the salary was like a carrot in front of a hungry rabbit. The money was attractive, but the fact that a company wanted me because of my business success and style was also seductive. This offer, unlike Lauratex's promotion requirements, wasn't based on beauty, but capability, my **Personal Brand Image**. Even though I had no design background, Eccobay's management wanted what I did have: great color sense, style, and expert textile knowledge (thanks to the teachings of Jerry and the factory technician Phil). I accepted the job and became a Lauratex customer, and now they would have to pursue me for Eccobay's printed fabric business. Sweet!

The Eccobay office was across the street from Lauratex. My commute from home was the same walk across town. Eccobay's environment couldn't have been more different from Lauratex's. Mr. H was involved with everything and everyone. All of his direct reports were female and he kept long hours. The days really started at 5 p.m., when Mr. H would return to the office from his day out in the NYC Garment Center, or when he opened his private office door in the late afternoon. He ordered dinner in for all of us and we worked until 10 p.m. or later. Mr. H's chauffeur would drive us home. Since I lived only five minutes away, it wasn't an inconvenience to stay late. After all, I was single, had no family, and was making double salary!

Mr. H was a charmer. He'd sweet-talk us all with his verbal compliments and warm manner, which he turned on and off like water from a sprinkler. Just when you felt safe and cared about with all his compliments, he then became vicious and turned on you. I soon learned that this tactic was his strategy to set you up for an unpredictable personal attack and keep you a prisoner at work. He was like a serial character assassin, so you had to be sharp and aware every second. This is why he paid double salary. In his mind he owned you and he could treat you any way that made him happy.

All the ladies loved him because the pleasant times were wonderful, and the random additional salary increases were at Mr. H's whim, so all the staff put up with his character disorder. I guess I fit in very well. Mr. H paid attention to me and he was extremely nice because my skills served him. Working only one week for Mr. H, I received more attention from him than in the six years at Lauratex from Miss G. With no family at home, Eccobay became my family.

I wanted to learn everything about the sportswear business and fashion design, to please Mr. H more than myself. The twelve-hour days and being exposed to my new boss were the next steps in my career education. It was like being paid to get a master's degree in fashion design and business administration.

No school could have provided the courses or life lessons that I got from the New York City Garment Industry and Mr. H. I made sure I used my excellent memory skills, textile expertise, and bold personality to stand out in his entourage of female staff.

To be clear about what I learned from Mr. H, I must tell a few short stories that even Hollywood wouldn't need to embellish to earn an Academy Award. Mr. H was in his forties, handsome, and a perfect example of a non-boring person with his own **Personal Brand Image**. My Hunter College professor, Mr. Huot, would have loved him!

Lessons Learned from Mr. H

1) Silence is a Valuable Skill

Mr. H's chauffeur would arrive at the end of the day with a briefcase handcuffed to his arm and enter Mr. H's office. The chauffeur stayed behind closed doors for a few minutes and then exited with the same briefcase still attached to his arm. These daily, mysterious rituals were never spoken about.

2) The Boss Makes the Schedules

Mr. H was married and had his two young sons working for the company. Mr. H also had his many girlfriends visiting him in his office. Mr. H and his selected girlfriend stayed behind closed doors in his office. Another reason why our meetings started after 5 p.m.

3) The Boss Always Thinks He Is Right

We were brainstorming the colors for the fall sportswear line, and Mr. H wrote down on a notepad the color **fushia**. I helpfully said the spelling was incorrect; it should be **f-u-c-h-s-i-a**. Mr. H was furious. He argued with me in front of all the staff and pulled a thick dictionary from his desk drawer (this is 1977, so no smartphone to check). He looked up the spelling. It took a few minutes, and then he showed me the dictionary page. Well, Mr. H had taken some Wite-Out, painted over the printed word "fuchsia," and used black ink to replace it with "fushia." "See I am right," he screamed. Winning wasn't an option—it was a necessity for Mr. H.

4) Negotiating Skills

Once a month Mr. H called all the salespeople he was buying textiles from and had them lined up outside his office like cattle waiting for slaughter. Since I was one of the staff buying fabric, he had me sit in on these meetings. It took all day to see everyone. If the vendors left without seeing him, Mr. H would cancel the order. Once they entered the office, the routine began with Mr. H asking for a lower price. Of course they all argued that was impossible. Then Mr. H looked at the contracts, and if his name or the company's name was misspelled, he deducted ten cents per yard from the price. More typos and the price went down another five cents. He wouldn't listen to the vendors' protests and told them to "take it or leave it." They took it and then left!

5) Use Your Imagination

One day Mr. H asked me to go with him to our largest supplier of solid fabrics to meet with the salesperson, EJ, who happened to be one of the few females in NYC textile sales during the 1970s. Mr. H wanted me to learn more about negotiating. This large company was famous and had a huge, highly elaborate, stylish sales office. Mr. H was in his happy mode and flirted with the female receptionist, who asked us to wait since EJ was running late. Mr. H was displeased. You can imagine that Mr. H didn't like to go unnoticed or be ignored and definitely didn't like to be kept waiting.

Mr. H started to pace back and forth in the reception area, while he unbuttoned his tan trench coat and nervously held his unlit cigar in his hand. All of a sudden he clutched his chest, gasped for breath, and fell to the floor! I rushed over to him and everyone was screaming with panic as Mr. H was lying motionless on the marble floor. EJ ran out of the meeting room when she heard the shouting and bent down to Mr. H to help revive him. He opened his eyes and quietly said, "What took you so long?" He then jumped to his feet, laughing.

6) Be True to Yourself

It was another late night working with Mr. H and his all-female staff. We were very tired and Mr. H was looking at the fabric colors that were approved during the week. One color caught his eye. It was a solid beige to be used for pants and skirts. He hated it. If front of all the staff he yelled, "Who approved this color?" Since I was coordinating the solid colors, I raised my hand and said I gave my approval. It was as if a nuclear weapon exploded in the room. Mr. H started to curse me with foul, X-rated language and told everyone in the meeting room that I was a damn idiot.

It didn't take me much time to think about my response. I had never been publicly humiliated, certainly never in front of a team of my peers and other executives I respected. Mr. H did have his dark side but never had his anger focused on me. I stood up from my chair, and every eye in the room was on me as I screamed at the top of my lungs, "Mr. H, you are a **COCKSUCKER** and I quit!"

I ran out of the room and went to my office to pack my personal belongings. I didn't care that I was giving up a big salary. This was a spontaneous reaction to the verbal violence and humiliating attack. The crazy work atmosphere and late meetings I could tolerate, but this incident was unacceptable and represented the opposite of the way I was brought up. Not to mention that Dr. D would never allow me to enable myself to be abused.

Before I could finish packing, Mr. H came to see me. He said he was leaving the office and insisted on driving me home. I refused the offer but he blocked the door until I agreed. The chauffeur was waiting in front of the building in the long, ostentatious black limousine. Mr. H and I sat in the backseat. I was furious and a bit frightened, expecting a shouting match. We were both silent. He unbuttoned his dark blue, pinstripe suit jacket, gently rubbed his star sapphire pinky ring, which was on the hand holding his large, smoking, smelly cigar. He swiftly pushed a button in his armrest, which closed the window partition between the chauffeur and backseat. It was like a scene from a bad gangster movie. For a moment my survival during this short ride to my apartment seemed questionable.

After puffing his cigar then flicking the ashes on the floor, Mr. H turned to me and said, "No one should be talking to their boss the way you did." I replied that perhaps he was correct. However, his attitude, language, and humiliation of me was unacceptable. I felt justified and I wasn't sorry for my reaction or what I said. We were now in front of my apartment building and as I was about to leave the car. Mr. H told me to be at work first thing in the morning and that I had no choice but to be on time. The door shut and the limo left. He never apologized, but I do believe, on some level, he knew I was right and respected me for standing up to him in spite of his seductive nature and high-paying salary.

I was at the office in the morning, on time, proud of myself and hard at work. No one ever mentioned the incident. I knew everyone respected me for defending myself against all the odds. The feeling I had was almost as good as throwing a pie in a professor's face.

My job at Eccobay had now been more than three years of success, education, and survival. After the horrible confrontation with Mr. H, I never felt secure. I knew that at any time he could give me a pay raise and then rip me to shreds at his own delight. Staff turnover was high. Either Mr. H fired you or fearful employees left. The drama was daily and I couldn't have coped without having Dr. D to talk to.

One of Eccobay's competitors was a company called **Donnkenny Apparel**. One day I received a phone call from Miss Leslie, Donnkenny's head designer. I didn't know her, but she invited me to lunch. At that meeting Leslie told me she knew about my success at Eccobay and wanted me to join Donnkenny. She arranged my interview with her boss, Mr. Murray.

This was the second time I was offered a job based on my excellent work reputation. I was proud that I was able to keep high working standards, even though I didn't like my jobs and was dealing with many emotional issues in my therapy. I agreed to meet Mr. Murray to see about another opportunity.

Personal Brand Image:

Consistently present yourself as a professional.

Chapter 5

Breakthrough

I met Murray at his office. He was an older man, in his sixties, and very short; we stood nose to nose. He was straightforward, neither charming nor warm, but did tell me that he'd heard of my great style and business reputation. Murray offered me a job paying double what I was currently earning.

There was no reason not to accept the Donnkenny position. The pay he offered was extremely tempting and working at Eccobay was a daily battle to protect myself from emotional injury. I didn't care for working in the garment business, but if I could gain more experience and earn more money at Donnkenny, while figuring out my career path and life, this would be a win/win situation. I decided to accept the Donnkenny offer, with Dr. D's blessings.

Mr. Murray asked me to start right away, which meant giving Mr. H my resignation and a two-week notice. Donnkenny was a direct competitor of Eccobay and I was sure Mr. H would want me to leave immediately. The next day I gave Mr. H my formal and verbal resignation. He took one look at me and said, "No one leaves me." I told him I wasn't going to change my mind. Mr. H left the room and never to spoke to me again, either in the office or as a passerby on the street. I had "left him" and it was as if I'd never existed.

The long hours and dealing with Mr. H's intense personality gave me an education that I never would have gotten at a formal institution. I look back at this experience and I have to thank Mr. H for showing me the opposite of what I thought were good business ethics. He wasn't wrong, he just used a different way to achieve his goals. His methods did work and he wasn't running for public office, where he needed to be liked.

The reality is, you must do what you have to do to survive. Was throwing a pie in Mac Wells's face that different from faking a heart attack in a public reception area to get attention? Mr. H's methodology was an extreme case and I don't follow his lifestyle philosophy, although there have been many tough situations in my career when I asked myself, "What would Mr. H do?" I believe his non-boring style made him very attractive to work for and do business with. Therefore, I must say he was a great influence on the way I formulated my own **Personal Brand Image**. Mr. H was a performer first and businessman second. The showmanship he displayed to get results was a role model for me.

Donnkenny was only across the street from Eccobay, but it might as well have been on another planet. The atmosphere in my new office was quiet to the point of being dull. There were no days when you worked twelve hours, Murray was rarely involved with the design process, and his presence was almost invisible. Leslie handled all design issues. They left me alone to do my job, since I was hired to raise the aesthetic level of the printed fabric designs. They wanted my Eccobay/Lauratex influence to bring some life back into their fashion designs. I wasn't prepared for this responsibility. I had been in the textile/garment industry for almost ten years, and I did learn the business from some dynamic and smart people, so I was fearless.

I also had three secret weapons:

1. Fear of being destitute if I lost my job

2. Counseling from Dr. D

3. My **Personal Brand Image**.

My private daily life was focused on living the New York dream, visiting museums and getting inspired at art galleries. I didn't have many friends and the few I had were working ladies, who only had time to meet for an occasional dinner out. Hanging out at bars wasn't something I did or could afford to do. In the boyfriend arena I had a few dysfunctional relationships that never lasted, which reinforced my unconscious feelings that I was unworthy. A self-fulling prophecy. Hook up with a bad guy and then you have an excuse not to have a relationship.

After nearly four years of psychoanalysis, Dr. D wasn't about to let me fail at work or life. She told me from day one that she would cure me of what was holding me back from success and give me the tools to lead a productive life in work and love. When would this happen?

Dr. D invited me to attend a group therapy weekend retreat, which was a big change from the twice a week one-on-one sessions I'd been having with her. The thought of being in a group of people I didn't know and locked up with them for a weekend was frightening. The only salvation was that my friend Gary was still Dr. D's patient and was planning to attend. I also understood that Dr. D would never put me in a situation that would hurt me. She must have felt that I was ready for the next step. I went with this reasoning and reluctantly agreed to attend.

The entire time in this group session I felt uncomfortable and feared something was going to happen to me. The group of approximately twenty people were sitting on the floor in a circular formation. Dr. D was is the center of the circle, sitting on the floor as well. She looked so different than when we had our sessions in her uptown New York City office. She always wore her slim-fitting knit dresses and high-heeled, trendy shoes, and now she wore jeans and a blouse for the retreat's casual atmosphere. It was my turn to enter the center circle with Dr. D.

I don't remember all the details, but the group conversation was focusing on me and made me feel sick to my stomach. The same feeling I'd had every morning of my life since I was a little girl. Now, in front of my doctor and all these people, I had this same overwhelming, intense nausea. I told Dr. D and the group that I needed to be excused to go to the bathroom. Dr. D refused to let me leave the group. I announced what my problem was and that I feared I was on the verge of vomiting. Dr. D stood up and returned with an empty bucket, which she placed in the center of the circle near where I was sitting and advised me that if I needed to vomit, it was okay—I could do in the bucket!

I then became hysterical with screaming, crying, and begging her to let me leave to use the bathroom. She wouldn't let me leave the circle and the group moved closer, creating a blockade. I couldn't escape. I was trapped. Dr. D sat next to me. The nausea was uncontrollable. I felt dizzy and tried to leave this circle of entrapment but everyone continually prevented me from doing so. Fear for my life swelled in my mind, heart, and stomach. I became hot, sweaty, and extremely nauseous. I was desperate by now and jumped up with no control over my body. I gasped, choked, and then relieved myself the only way I could—by vomiting near the bucket and all over Dr. D!

Yes, this is fact. I had exposed myself as an unstable individual and violated the doctor-patient relationship and humiliated myself in public. To my amazement I wasn't rejected. On the contrary, Dr. D was covered with my projectile vomit but held me close. The others in the group weren't laughing and they weren't repulsed. They broke the blockade as some cried, others hugged me.

Dr. D remained drenched in my vomit and kept her arms around me. She spoke softly and reminded me of the dream I'd told her about months ago, about a baby drowning in a pool of blood in the bathtub. The water ran quickly and you couldn't turn it off or stop the baby from swirling and being sucked into the drain. Dr. D now asked me, "In that dream, who was the baby?" Without hesitation I replied, "It was me."

Finally, the dream's significance became crystal clear. I was actually sick to my stomach, thinking that my parents didn't want me. The nausea and the euphoric feeling after vomiting took away the anguish of feeling that I was meant to end up as an embryo in a test tube, or flushed down the toilet. My daily hanging over the toilet bowl, waiting to dispose of what was inside me, was my unconscious reenactment of my mother's abortion thoughts about getting rid of me. The dream allowed me to express my pain. I could express my unconscious horror by creating the scenario of a baby being flushed down the drain. My daily nausea symbolized morning sickness and trying to flush the baby down the toilet. Once I vomited I felt better since I was in control, not my mother.

With this group of strangers and with Dr. D holding me close, I looked around the room and there was no one who wanted to flush me down the toilet. I had no reason to feel unworthy. Since that day in the middle of the circle, with the bucket and drenched Dr. D, I have never experienced the vomiting ritual again. I finally was ready to like who I was and to be cured. This episode was a Breakthrough in my life.

Personal Brand Image:

Personal hang-ups are no excuse for failure. Push past them and find a way to discover the root cause and then change your behavior.

I had been working at Donnkenny for two years, without tension or an eccentric boss. Even though I didn't love being in the fashion industry, I had made up my mind to put in 110% effort and see where it took my career. My job was financially rewarding and I was looked at as the expert in textile design, but my private life was unfulfilling and lonely. Dr. D had told me I would be cured when I was happy at work and love. It seemed I had a lot more road to travel before I met those requirements.

To get the best designs for the printed fabrics, it was my responsibility to shop the textile design studios and select the artwork to be printed on various fabrics. This activity was the fun part, since I could get out of the office and visit the different textile manufacturers, who always gave me the royal treatment because of my cooperative attitude.

Personal Brand Image:

Project a positive attitude, and you will benefit in life and business with what you get back from those interactions.

It was a freezing cold day in February 1981, and I had an appointment with the Head Designer of Texfi Industries, June Anderson. The walk from my office was brutally chilling as I passed by Bryant Park on 42nd Street. Braving the cutting wind, I arrived at Texfi, where Miss Anderson was waiting for me. Being in the same room with June was like visiting an art museum. Everything about her screamed with creative energy. Her dress, jewelry, and hairstyle were avant-garde and fun. She hardly took a breath before her next idea came out of her mouth, her desk drawer or the pencil in her hand. She was a design magician. June was an attractive woman in her early fifties, and her skin was a transparent porcelain vision, which just made her naturally bright red, curly hair look even more glamorous. She looked very much like the actress Billie Burke, who played **Glinda, The Good Witch of the South**, in the famous 1939 movie ***The Wizard of Oz***. All that was missing was the magic wand, and I'm sure she had one of those hidden in her desk.

I was sitting in June's office looking through art sketches, trying to select some designs, when the telephone rang. June quickly answered the call. I really wasn't paying attention to her, but after a few seconds she said, "Okay I'll get that information for you. Just talk to this lady for a few moments and I'll be right back." June handed me the telephone and said, "Here, talk to this guy while I get something for him."

Surprised with a phone shoved in my face, I said, "Hello." The gentleman on the phone introduced himself as Mel, the Los Angeles sales representative for Texfi. His voice was a warm baritone and he talked about living in California, being divorced with three children, and how he was originally from New York City. I only spoke a few words about what I did for a living and why I was at Texfi working with June.

Mel mentioned that he'd be coming to New York for a sales meeting in April and would like to take me to dinner. This was about the last thing I expected. Although I'd never make a date via phone, he was June's sales rep and not a total stranger. I figured he wouldn't follow up on this "blind date" proposal, which made it easy for me agree to meet him. It seemed low risk for a date occurring. June soon returned, taking the receiver from my hands and starting her lively chatter with Mel.

June reassured me that Mel was a really nice guy, and it was a great idea to have dinner with him. That's all she said. No gossip about his past, not even what he looked like. I didn't worry because the chance that I would hear from him was small. Actually, I hoped he wouldn't call me since the circumstance of having met on the telephone was strange.

A few days passed and I received a phone call at my office. It was Mel, letting me know that Texfi's sales meeting was arranged and he would take me to dinner on April 22 at 8 p.m. He advised me that he would pick me up at my apartment and call me when he arrived in New York to confirm the time. He didn't ask, he just told me the plan. I was taken off guard. This was still February and a guy from LA I'd never met had spoken with me for less than five minutes on the telephone and was arranging a dinner date with me sixty days in advance. I knew this was basically a business meeting, but I thought it was rather aggressive.

I figured that he wanted to meet me for business reasons. I hoped Mel would cancel. I didn't want to spend a few hours with a man I didn't know, who would be going back to LA forty-eight hours after our dinner date. What was the point?

Wednesday, April 22 arrived and I received a phone call in the late afternoon. It was Mel. He had just arrived from LA and found out his boss was holding a team dinner that night, and all the sales representatives needed to attend. He apologized that he had to cancel our dinner date. I was thrilled! I didn't have to go through the ordeal of a meeting a textile salesman from California.

Textile salesmen were stereotypically classified as low class. This is more truth than fiction, since I'd worked with many salesmen for over ten years. I told him I understood the situation and I was sure our paths would cross sometime in the future.

No sooner did I hang up the phone and kick off my shoes to relax when my phone rang again. It was Mel. He'd thought it over and decided he didn't want to change plans. He'd be at my apartment at 8 p.m. and was sorry for the confusion. My worst fear would be ringing my doorbell in a couple of hours.

It was a mild evening in April as I nervously went about deciding what to wear for this dinner date. Spring in NYC is the nicest time of year and quite a contrast to winter's freezing cold, snow, and sleet. For this dinner I wanted to be professional looking and modest. The last thing I wanted was to be seductive or imply anything other than having a business dinner. I chose an outfit that I'd gotten at a bargain price, designed by Koos Van Den Akker, a Dutch-born, New York City designer, famous in the 1980s for his clever use of patchwork appliques. I coordinated it with a black turtleneck sweater and black leggings. The result was stunning and none of my skin was showing except for my face, ears, and hands!

It was 8 p.m. and the doorbell rang. I held my breath, promising myself that no matter what, I would smile, be courteous and professional. I opened the door and there was Mel, smiling from ear to ear. He was six feet tall, with a full head of dark brown hair, green eyes, very slim and extremely handsome. He resembled a young Roger Moore, who'd played James Bond 007. Mel wore tight denim blue jeans and a plaid shirt open at the neck, with one gold chain peeking out. To complete the outfit he proudly displayed a short tan leather jacket and great-looking brown cowboy boots.

My apartment was rather unique because it was on the eighteenth floor of a high-rise building in midtown Manhattan. It had giant windows with an amazing view of the NYC skyline and the Empire State Building. My walls were painted dark purple, the furniture was white with clear glass and chrome accents. Very cool 1980s modern.

Mel asked me to select my favorite restaurant for dinner and I chose a chic Chinese restaurant called HSF, a short walk from my apartment. HSF was very trendy-looking and had delicious food that was a cut above the imitation Chinese food usually found in NYC. We ordered two glasses of Chardonnay and as we were sipping and sharing stories, Mel looked at me and sincerely said, "You have a beautiful nose." I must explain that my nose is large and far from beautiful. However, it suits my face and I, like Barbra Streisand, would never change it. My immediate comment was, "You like the nose … you buy the face!" This was my perfect surprise response and kicked off an amazing four-hour dinner date.

We ended the evening back at my apartment to continue our conversation. Mel told me that he was attracted to me and wanted to stay the night. The gorgeous guy I'd just had a fantastic dinner with is sitting in front of me, telling me I was attractive, which made it tempting to ask him to stay. I knew he was leaving for California in two days, so there was no way this could be more than just dinner date. I declined the offer and explained how I felt about the situation and warmly thanked him for his kind words. Mel understood and was gracious as he left. We walked to the elevator and he gently kissed me goodnight.

The elevator doors closed and just like in the movies, it was The End!

Back in my apartment, I flung myself on my bed and wondered if I'd made the right decision. In the morning I felt awful and helpless about what to do. Rather than brood or act out, I called Dr. D for an emergency phone session. I told her what had happened and all about Mel and how sad I felt that I would never see him again. Dr. D told me to wait one day and then call him. What? Call a guy I'd only known for a few hours, who lives three thousand miles away, and tell him I like him?

After four years of analysis with Dr. D, I'd learned to take her instructions seriously and act appropriately. I did as she suggested, although I felt extremely uncomfortable taking any action. I waited a day and called the Texfi office. The receptionist paged Mel. His cheery voice answered and I could tell he was genuinely happy to hear from me. He was leaving in a few hours for the airport, returning to LA. I told him I had a wonderful evening and thanked him for dinner. Without planning, the words burst from my lips,

"Mel, I think I have a **crush** on you!"

Silence for a few seconds, and then he told me he would write me and said goodbye. Another reminder that there was no email or smartphone communication in 1981. I couldn't believe I was so bold. But that was the truth—I had a crush on him. I had nothing to lose and he should know that I thought he was a gentleman. Receiving a letter from a guy you hardly knew wasn't going to happen, but at least he didn't laugh at me.

A week later I received the following letter on **United Airlines** stationery.

Here's the text and a copy of the original handwritten note from Mel.

4/24

Hello,

I am on my way home and thinking of you. I feel happy to have heard you tell me that you have a crush on me. (Because) To tell you the truth I have a crush on you too.

I want to get to know you and I want to hold you in my arms.

Would you come to L.A. and spend time with me? I am taking my vacation 6/1 - 6/15. What do you want to do?

You are special to me. I have a feeling about you that makes my head light, my blood rush and yet I feel serene because I don't feel pressed or intimidated by you and it feels so good. Come.

Sincerely,

would you come to
L.A. and spend time
with me? I am
taking my vacation
6/1- 6/15. What do you
want to do?

You are special to
me. I have a feeling
about you that makes
my head light, my blood
rush and yet I feel
serene because I don't
feel pressed or intimidated
by you and it feels so

Good. Come.

Sincerely

Melvin Goodman Bazerman

UNITED AIRLINES

4/24

Hello,

I'm on my way home
and thinking of you. I feel
happy to have heard you
tell me that you have a
crush on me. ~~Because~~
To tell the truth I have
a crush on you too.

I want to get to know you
and I want to hold you
in my arms.

Chapter 6

After the Letter

Ladies and gentlemen, you read the letter I received dated April 24, 1981, and postmarked April 24. Mel mailed it when he landed in LA. This wasn't an ordinary guy, and now I'm even more impressed with him. Admit it—you read the letter a few times with disbelief. This isn't your typical male response, not to mention the geographical distance, which was a lot to overcome in 1981. Anyone would think twice about traveling three thousand miles for a date. I must have done something positive to attract his attention, with my openness, bold attitude, and style. Perhaps it was my apartment's purple walls or the fact that I wasn't boring.

Personal Brand Image:

The same attributes that help you in your career can work in you private life as well.

I was at ease with myself, so Mel felt that comfort as well. Only after many years of psychoanalysis was I able to feel good about who I was. Perhaps now I could let someone else see the good in me.

I'd been to Los Angeles in 1978 to visit my friend Eloise, who I'd worked with at Lauratex when she lived in NYC. I'd toured all the attractions and I loved the continuous great weather. However, I was a devoted urban NYC gal and LA wasn't a place I dreamed of living.

How could I be interested in a man who lived in California? A place I felt was devoid of culture, filled with avocados and sprouts layered between tomatoes on whole-grain sandwiches! What could possibly result from a second date across the country? My expenses for a week of fun and then back to NYC was irrational. My instinct told me not to travel to California, but instincts aren't always correct. I needed to arrange a phone session with Dr. D to clarify the next steps. She was correct in suggesting I call Mel and tell him how I felt. I didn't want to lose Mel, but I was scared to death to lose my NYC comfort zone.

I shared Mel's United Airlines letter with Dr. D. In her usual style she was calm, void of any emotion in reaction to what I thought was an amazing letter. Her silence at the other end of the phone was chilling. But she was my psychoanalyst, not my girlfriend. A few uncomfortable, quiet moments later she asked me what I wanted to do. I told her I wasn't going to California and explained my long list of fears—i.e., no culture, no job prospects, everything is spread out, and I didn't know how to drive a car! I even remarked that Mel was too handsome.

She quickly replied in a straightforward, uncaring voice, "There is nothing wrong with a man that is handsome, and if you decide not to go to California you are still more than welcome to stay with me, since you'll have nothing else to do!" What? Is this my fate, to be an old woman living with a caretaker? How ridiculous it was for me to reject Mel because he was handsome. Those few words from Dr. D rattled me. How could I pass up a chance?

Eloise living in LA was a safety net if this second date didn't work out. I scheduled my vacation for six days, to coincide with Mel's vacation. We wrote weekly and this written exchange between us became a collection of love letters. Each letter from him was poetic and increased in exhibiting tenderness, dispelling the hard salesman stereotype.

The following is a short description of my date with Mel in LA. I know when you read my overview you will think I am exaggerating the events to make a point, or sugarcoating the story for the purpose of creating a more interesting book. I have no need to enhance any details. I therefore feel it's necessary to add this statement for the record and let the truth speak for itself: **The following events of my second date with Mel in June 1981 have not been changed, exaggerated, or fictionalized.**

My second date with Mel started when I exited the airplane at Los Angeles International Airport and saw Mel's handsome, smiling face. He remembered that my NYC apartment was painted purple (who could forget?) and he greeted me with purple roses. The driving route he took to his condo was the long, scenic tour via the winding Pacific Coast Highway with a view of the glorious sunset. Mel prepared dinner, a delicious homemade pot roast, almost as good as my mother's cooking. This was a preview of the impressive experiences that awaited me in the next few days.

Mel planned adventures for us in California, but they weren't the usual tourist attractions. We went to Union Station in downtown LA to look at and appreciate the building's Art Deco design. Then there was a night for the operetta *The Pirates of Penzance*, with a dinner at a funky Chinese restaurant in Chinatown. The last two days Mel planned a drive to Rosarito Beach, Mexico, which is about ten miles from the California border, where he rented a beach house.

It all seemed dreamlike, especially after our third day together, when Mel hinted that he was in love with me. This seemed bizarre, to have this declaration after just a few days. I always found ways to meet the undesirable men. Why should this be different? I thought a good guy wouldn't want me and, like my parents, would want to abort me. I'd now had many years of psychotherapy to make me an emotionally healthier person, who felt worthy of a good relationship. Secretly, I called Dr. D to tell her of Mel's probable proposal. She said, "If you do not know what to do ... then do nothing."

I adored him. Every day was like a perfectly directed scene that could have been scripted in any Hollywood movie. I tried not to think of the reality of the geographic distance and all the roadblocks that would confront us. The morning that we planned to leave Mexico we spent relaxing on the beach. The weather was stunning and Mel had the radio on, Elton John singing **"Big Dipper"** as we sunbathed on a blanket by the water. In the middle of this song, Mel turned to me and said he loved me and wanted to marry me.

What could I say? I was leaving the next day for New York and I'd only known Mel for five days. I remembered Dr. D's advice. "If I did not know what to do … do nothing." I turned to hug Mel and said, "Maybe." That was my version of doing nothing. I needed time to think. This wasn't a small matter and he deserved a sincere answer.

I left the next morning with Mel's understanding that I would give him an answer to his proposal soon, and with that promise he placed the gold chain he was wearing around my neck. I was very touched and I have to say so very much in love. At that moment I held back from saying the big YES. I was thirty-three years old and Mel was forty-three. He'd been married twice before and had three children. His sixteen-year-old daughter lived with him. Would Mel's third time be the charm?

I called Dr. D as soon as I arrived back in NYC and told her the week's events. She listened to all the details of the California Second-Date Saga and the speedy proposal, then asked me one question: "Is there any reason you can think of not to marry this man?" In my head I was ruminating on all the small, insignificant negative thoughts I'd been having. I was afraid to reply. Dr. D boldly said that the offer to move in with her was still open. That did it! I decided to accept Mel's proposal. There was one requirement. Dr. D insisted on meeting Mel before I could confirm the plan to marry him.

Think about this demand she made. I have no parents, no siblings, and only a few friends. Was my version of Mel delusional? There had to be a "court of last resort," a joint session for Mel and me at Dr. D's Park Avenue office.

What did I have in NYC, other than a financially rewarding job and a great psychoanalyst, who I talked to on the phone fifty percent of the time? What would hold me in NYC other than a bad attitude? Dr. D wasn't about to set me up for failure. The point of analysis was to become well adjusted and function in life, being happy in work and love. I wasn't happy in either at this time, so I wasn't cured. Would Mel think I was crazy if I asked him to come to NY and meet my psychoanalyst? Was this a deal breaker?

That night I called Mel and told him that my "maybe" reply turned into YES, and I would marry him on one condition. He knew I had no family, and I asked him to come to NYC and meet my psychoanalyst Dr. D in a joint session. Mel was so thrilled to have a YES answer that he was pleased to cooperate. He'd also been in therapy for about four years with a doctor in LA. After his two failed marriages, fathering three children, and being a bachelor for seven years, I could understand that he had a lot on his mind and needed someone to help with life's vicissitudes. Therefore Mel didn't feel that meeting my psychoanalyst was a strange request. I think he welcomed the sanity check.

Two months later in hot, muggy August, Mel arrived in NYC for a week. The first business at hand was to meet with Dr. D. I was so happy to have her involved to reinforce my decision. On the other hand I was scared to death of Dr. D's straightforward, intimidating attitude. This wasn't like meeting my parents, who would be warm, welcoming, and gracious, since they wouldn't want to upset me. Dr. D was the judge, jury, and executioner if needed.

The session with Dr. D lasted forty-five minutes and I hardly spoke a word. Dr. D interrogated Mel as if she were a combination of a police detective looking for a confession and a five-star army general going into battle. I was in a panic but sat quietly. She wasted no time and went straight to asking about all his marriages and children. What he said and what he didn't say were being continuously scrutinized and questioned. The session was over and Mel was still intact, with both his head and soul. He held me and kissed my hand during the interrogation. Dr. D didn't jump up and down with joy, but graciously told us our session was over and gave us her professional smile as we left her office. If Dr. D felt the marriage plan should be cancelled, she would have verbalized this. The fact that there was a smile from her and that Mel survived the ordeal was the confirmation we needed.

As soon as the door closed, outside her office Mel collapsed against the wall and told me he now knew what a prisoner of war feels like in the torture chamber!

The shock waves of my engagement rippled around everyone that knew me. They couldn't believe I'd accepted a marriage proposal from basically a "stranger" and was moving to California in a few months. All my friends, colleagues, and few distant relatives wanted to see the man who proposed to me so quickly. I planned a party in my apartment to proudly present this exceptional guy who'd won my heart. To say the least they were all impressed with Mel's extremely handsome presentation, charming personality, and his obvious adoration for me.

The wedding was held outside in the afternoon sunshine, by a waterfall at the Calabasas Inn, Woodland Hills, California, on November 29, 1981. At the end of the ceremony I jumped for joy and shouted, "I got him!" Mel started to spontaneously sing "You Are My Sunshine."

Champagne brunch followed the ceremony.

Personal Brand Image:

Being bold in your career also works in your love life.

Chapter 7

The Wild West

From my fortress apartment on the eighteenth floor in midtown Manhattan, I am now living in a condo near a lake, in a somewhat rural area of Los Angeles called Calabasas, Spanish for pumpkin. I needed to find a way to continue with my career and learn to drive a car. Not sure which was the most traumatic. Then there is the hard work of making sure I have a happy marriage with a man I've only known for few months. It was the same feeling as my first job, taking a position in the textile industry without any knowledge of the business!

My last name changed to Bazerman. I thought that my husband's first name, he preferred to be called Mel, was an obvious cover-up for the awful birth name of Melvin. I never would have picked a name like Melvin for my son. What were his parents thinking? I was proud of my new husband being a master of all things romantic and dynamic. I felt that there was nothing he had to hide—if his name is Melvin, he should use it. The day I had this revelation I would never call him Mel (the fake name) again. A few days after our wedding until the present day, my husband's name, boldly in your face, the real guy, is Melvin. Yes, it's all about the **Personal Brand Image**, and making a statement about who you are really is important.

Living in California didn't change the fact that I was still in psychoanalysis with Dr. D, in New York, via telephone. The formality of marriage isn't the happy ending you see in storybooks or movies. It's the happy beginning that needs to be retained and nurtured. I don't think most people are prepared for the compromise and caring that is needed when you live with another person. All aspects of my life were different, and to deal with numerous unknowns I needed the support of a professional, to give me the edge for a successful relationship with Melvin. We never let any problem go without resolution.

Personal Brand Image:

Whether in work or love, fix the issue before it becomes a problem.

Finding a job matching my talents in the textile or garment industry was surprisingly difficult in LA. I was used to New York's fast-paced business and the higher New York salary. What I was finding was a laid-back attitude in business and the type of career I had in NYC didn't exist in LA. The companies here were smaller and usually the owners did all the designing themselves. I was unemployable, unless I wanted to take a job with no challenge and less than half my NYC salary. At thirty-three years old I had no career opportunities.

Being a full-time housewife was novel for a few months, but not what I saw myself doing long term, and we needed additional income if we were to have a baby. I'd never loved the textile or garment industry, it was never my career aspiration. They were only my temporary jobs. So perhaps I could pursue something that I really had a passion for. My personal success in psychotherapy and a desire to help others inspired me to ask Dr. D if she thought I had any potential to become a psychoanalyst. She thought this was a valid idea and suggested I contact one of her colleagues in Westwood, California, who was head of the **California Graduate Institute (CGI)**, a school where I could study to get my master's degree in psychology.

I started classes at CGI on a part-time basis. The courses we engaging, my classmates were from diverse backgrounds, and the subject matter was fascinating. I was really well prepared for CGI. You might even say my undergraduate work was from my own therapy with Dr. D, which enabled me to obtain good grades and a great understanding of the subject. Even if I never finished the degree program, the life lessons I was learning and the student interactions gave me tools to deal with people at work, in the street, or with my husband.

Melvin's career had always been in textile sales. After graduating from high school he took an entry-level job with Abraham Silk Company in New York. This company was a Swiss textile manufacturer, who saw Melvin's potential and enrolled him in a training program to learn the business in Zurich, Switzerland. He lived in Zurich for three years. What an unusual opportunity for a young man in the late 1950s. This led to his sales career, with travels through Europe, South America, and the US, which contributed to his broad scope and maturity. Eventually it brought him to LA. All this after growing up in the Lower East Side of New York. He never had the money to attend college, but he had global experiences that surpassed the curriculum for a college degree.

Darling Melvin had an idea: we should take a risk and start our own business. He'd been a textile salesman for over twenty-five years and was very knowledgeable in fabric manufacturing. He was interested in developing, manufacturing, and selling a unique fabric that stretched and could be used for swimwear and the emerging bodywear/aerobic industry. The fabric was a knit made with cotton and spandex. Now, in the twenty-first century, even jeans and T-shirts contain spandex. But in the 1980s making this fabric was an expensive, rather new process. Melvin had connections to knit, dye, print, and finish the fabric. The plan was that he would find the customers, I would design the fabric, and we would both handle customer relations and production. It would be our own business. I thought we had no other option, since I couldn't find a good-paying job. After all these years, Melvin deserved a chance to have his own business.

Personal Brand Image:

No need to follow the crowd—be an Entrepreneur.

We made a great Mr. and Mrs. team. We picked the name **PhD Textiles, Inc.** since I planned on continuing graduate school at CGI and getting my PhD in psychology. Textiles would be a way to build our net worth and enable us to afford to have a family. I could eventually obtain a career that grew from studying psychology.

We started the business from our car trunk, overflowing with fabric samples and piece goods to be delivered. We went everywhere together. We drove to downtown LA and did our rounds, visiting the knitting mill, the dyeing and finishing location and the print factory. We went to customers, showing our line and marketing our **Brand** and as a creative, caring team.

Our **Personal Brand Image** of a working newlywed team intrigued our customers and gave them that "feel good feeling" when they saw us holding hands. Melvin's sharp wit with my fashion flair made a winning combination. The customers loved us more than the product we were selling and gave us business because they wanted us to be successful.

The product was unique and well priced, and our follow-up customer service was unbeatable. We eventually moved from our car trunk to an office in LA, a small room we decorated with two desks, two chairs, and a vase of fresh flowers.

It is now 1985. We'd been married four years, PhD Textiles was growing, and I was still attending CGI graduate school at night. It was nonstop busy and the 24/7 workday was never ending. When you work, love, and live with your spouse/business partner, there's no downtime. Especially if your approach to the business came from opposing corners. Melvin was the aggressive, manipulating salesman that would twist and turn the truth to get orders. I was the one focusing on the aesthetic perfection and fabric designs. Sound like a good balance? The beginning was good, but eventually we became frustrated with each other's working style.

I was usually the one to answer the phone and talk with the customers. One afternoon I received a call from a bodywear manufacturer checking on their order. The customer told me that Melvin informed them that the fabric would be delivered in a week. My reply was, "This is not possible. Melvin hasn't even ordered the yarn for knitting!" The customer was furious and threatened to cancel the order.

Melvin was in the same room and grabbed the phone from my hand when he heard my comment. He smoothed it all over by charming his way out of the situation, claiming that his darling wife had incorrect information. Seriously? I'd told the truth and Melvin was lying. How was he going to deliver the fabric if it hadn't been manufactured yet? We had a cash flow problem and sometimes we couldn't purchase the yarn for knitting in time to meet the promised delivery date. Melvin would make up a story to hide the problem. He called what he was doing "creative waiting." This was the sales business. Not much different from being a politician who tells his or her constituency a story that doesn't make them look bad, an explanation that will get them re-elected, or in this case, a reorder. If I couldn't manipulate the truth, Melvin suggested that I look for my own job and not work with him. Did my husband just fire me?

I couldn't work this way. Sure, in NYC I'd watched Mr. H lie to everyone, but that wasn't my style, to routinely misrepresent situations. This wasn't how I wanted to **Brand** myself. The truth in my own business would rule and get good results. Evidently the sales approach for textiles to garment manufacturers was based on telling customers what you think they want to hear. They don't want to know the truth. They would rather just yell and scream when the deliveries are late, since that is part of the business plan. I could be married to a ruthless textile salesman who adored me, but the essence of being a storytelling salesperson conflicted with my trusted **Personal Brand Image**.

To escape working with Melvin, the next day I began exploring my options in the *California Apparel News*, a local newspaper for the LA fashion industry. Scanning the list of what I might qualify for, I spotted an ad from **Mattel** for a "Textile Analyst." I knew Mattel made toys, but I wasn't sure what their product line was. The title of Textile Analyst brought back memories of fifteen years earlier, when I was looking for my first job and replied to an ad in *The New York Times* for "Textile Colorist."

I had nothing to lose by contacting Mattel. It was rather funny that I didn't have a résumé/CV. When I first started job hunting in 1970, I was a fresh grad with no credentials. I applied for jobs with my physical portfolio. I'd obtained my Eccobay and Donnkenny positions based solely on my reputation. I never had a written résumé. Now I am applying for a job with Mattel, and the procedure was to send a résumé to Mattel's human resources department. I was anxious to move on and no longer work at PhD Textiles. I loved Melvin so much, but the pressure of working with him and trying to keep the sales pitch going wasn't enjoyable.

I decided to formally apply to Mattel by writing on bold red graph paper, which I thought looked unique, using a black calligraphy pen. I wrote in my best handwriting,

"Dear Mattel HR, I have no idea what a **Textile Analyst** is, but if it has anything to do with fabric and fashion design, I have 15 years of New York Garment/Textile Industry experience. I am currently an entrepreneur in my own textile manufacturing business in California.

With this expertise I am sure I am able to handle the job."

I listed all my New York careers and PhD Textiles ownership as my work history. I wanted to show my style and confident attitude. Visual impact was important, as well a good reason to make my résumé stand out from the black-and-white typed pages of my competition. Of course, not knowing how to type or owning a typewriter was also great motivation to be different. A few months later Mattel contacted me with a date to be interviewed with the manager of the Soft Goods Engineering group, Nancy Harrington.

Personal Brand Image:

Even something as mundane as a résumé can be made to stand out with style and be part of your Brand.

It was August 1985, and my interview was scheduled at Mattel headquarters in Hawthorne, California, about three miles from the LA International Airport. The location might as well have been on the moon. This was an area in California I wasn't familiar with. The thirty-two mile journey from my home was stressful and almost made me forget that I hadn't been on a formal interview for fifteen years. I didn't know what to expect.

I definitely recollect meeting Nancy Harrington. Nancy was a beautiful, blonde-haired lady, a few years younger than me. She was dressed conservatively, in a tailored jacket with a small bow necktie neatly placed under her blouse collar. Smart looking, but not a trendy fashionista, as I would have expected for a New York fashion business interview. I was dressed in some of my stylish business clothes from New York, a flashy, 1980s metallic design on a purple sweater. We talked and I shared my past experiences, including the reason I was looking for a job. I confessed I couldn't stand working with my husband and this is why I was seeking employment. Telling the truth was refreshing.

Nancy explained that the position of Textile Analyst was in her department, **Soft Goods Engineering**. The majority of the projects were for Mattel's #1 Brand, **Barbie**. Design teams in Hawthorne created all the fashions for Barbie, as well as all the girls' toys. These designers used fabrics that they bought or garments they acquired of the latest trendy human clothing. They would cut up and reuse the fabrics to create fashions for an eleven-and-a-half-inch Barbie body. When the doll fashion designs were finished, the Textile Analyst was consulted to evaluate if the clothing could be manufactured in mass production, calculate the cost, give cost reduction ideas, state any safety concerns, and provide sewing method advice.

The final fabrics were sourced from Hong Kong, Taiwan, Japan, Korea, and China, where the manufacturing of Barbie dolls and the sewing of the fashions were completed. In the 1980s Mattel had factories in China, Taiwan, and the Philippines. The Textile Analysts in California communicated with the Hong Kong office and requested a sample of the design, which would be mailed to Hawthorne for comments and final approval for production.

Nancy's description of the process seemed like a rather bizarre, complex series of events to make doll clothes. The fact that I'd never had a Barbie, or even touched one, made it seem even more unreal. Barbie entered the toy market in 1959, when I was eleven years old, and by then I wasn't playing with dolls anymore. So to think about all the fuss made to execute these tiny fashions seemed humorous to me. I had no idea how dolls were manufactured, and the Asian countries Nancy mentioned were a geographic mystery to me. Asia was never more than a mention in school, except what I knew about the Korean and Vietnam Wars. Of course, New York-style Chinese food was a frequent meal, but its origins for me were Chinatown.

The procedures Nancy talked about made no sense to me and the long-distance communication to Hong Kong sounded inefficient. I made no comment—after all, I'm the one being interviewed. Nancy asked if I would mind working for her, even though she was less experienced than I was. What a shocking and honest question from her.

Nancy had been working at Mattel for only eighteen months. She had a BA in clothing and textiles from San Diego State University (SDSU) and her MS in textiles from Cornell University. She taught textiles and clothing construction classes for five years at SDSU, was a merchandise manager and buyer for The Highlander men's clothing store while teaching at SDSU. This was an excellent academic/technical background, but not fashion design experience. She was looking to add that skill to the Mattel Soft Goods department. With my experience, I would be the only one on her staff who had actual fashion industry knowledge. Clothing for Barbie was miniature versions of what was being made in the women's fashion industry, so having someone on staff who'd worked in this industry made sense.

This job offer was totally out of my expectation of how to execute. Sort of a familiar situation at the start of all my jobs, although I knew much more about what the Mattel job required than I ever did for any of my New York positions. The attraction for me was that this was the toy industry. Perhaps the lying, foul language, and manipulation tactics of the garment/textile industry wouldn't occur at Mattel. The salary was much less than what I'd earned in New York, but the benefits were good, and the company was stable and famous. At best, this was another temporary job. I still hoped to complete an internship program in graduate school to earn my master's in psychology.

Nancy Harrington was so warm, friendly, and straightforward, I felt I could actually enjoy working for her. We'd make a good team with her more academic side to fashion and my textile design, development, and manufacturing expertise. We could have some fun making toys!

I accepted the job offer.

Personal Brand Image:

Emphasize your strengths, which will lead you to the next step.

My first day at Mattel was August 19, 1985. I had no idea how I was going to be effective as a Textile Analyst. I had made up my mind to follow the same strategy working in New York. I needed to present myself with all my professional expertise and style. I couldn't walk into Mattel with an attitude of "Oh dear ... I've never held a Barbie doll!" or "I have no idea what anyone is doing!"

The first thing I did was to dress appropriately. Most LA work environments, even in the 1980s, were relaxed and casual, and the dress code matched that atmosphere. I kept my trendy New York clothes and used this opportunity to wear and flaunt my **Personal Brand Image**. I was told that I knew more about textiles than anyone at Mattel. I needed to emphasize this to compensate for my lack of knowledge about toy manufacturing and not knowing the reason Barbie was such a popular toy.

Mattel had its own six-story building devoted to Mattel design, development, engineering, and the headquarters for their executive team. You couldn't miss it from the freeway, with the large, familiar red logo on top of the building. I spent the morning with a group of other new staff, attending Mattel's human resources orientation program. Lectures about rules, regulations, benefits, an overview of the company's history, and I was issued a badge with a photo ID. Rather a nice beginning of the day, relaxed and informative. It was lunch time when we left the orientation room. Nancy Harrington, my new manager, was waiting for me. She was there not only to welcome me, but also to take me to the cafeteria for lunch.

It was like being back in school, with a class in the morning, then lining up with a tray at noon, selecting a hot lunch, and taking a seat in the open community area with your teacher, who happened to be your new boss. After lunch I was introduced to the rest of the Soft Goods Engineering team—designers, engineers, and the executives that were part of the Girl's Toy division.

The Design Center tour was like a fantasy. So many dolls. Barbie was everywhere, on the tables, lined up on shelves, on desks, stacked in offices, hanging out of drawers, and in display cases. Barbie was clothed and unclothed, dressed to perfection or headless and ready for design options and revisions. The small clothes, the pink fabrics, the tiny shoes, the miniature purses, fashions accessories, and jewelry were glittering everywhere, as if this were a Tiffany & Co. that only sold pink treasures for Barbie.

A designated department did the face paint and hairstyles only, and sewing machines were clicking away with staff sewing the small dresses, swimsuits, gowns, little gloves, and socks to fit Barbie. Sketches were being drawn, fabric draped on models just like in the fashion industry, except the small, eleven-and-a-half-inch models being fitted for their wardrobe were made of plastic and didn't complain about so many tedious fittings!

To this newcomer, it was truly Santa's Workshop. If it weren't so warm in LA, I would've thought I was at the North Pole. Absolutely amazing to see so many staff creating doll prototypes for Barbie, her family, and friends. I still wasn't aware of the power of the Barbie Brand and couldn't comprehend the seriousness of every detail for a doll.

In a matter of moments, at the age of thirty-seven, I would hold and play with my first Barbie doll. Nancy showed me to my work area and gave me a new Barbie fashion project, to evaluate the sample fabric proposed for production use. I was holding a prototype of an idea that the designer wanted. There I was, Barbie doll in hand, trying to put on her pantyhose to analyze the fabric construction. You might laugh, but let me tell you it isn't an easy task to pull thin fabric over tiny plastic legs with pointed itsy bitsy toes, when your fingers are bigger than the doll's legs! My first attempt was embarrassing and I struggled with frustration that I couldn't accomplish this activity. This was definitely a setback in my career path.

Since my doll-dressing skills needed improvement, my plan was to win over my new colleagues with my textile expertise and good attitude. The first few weeks at Mattel were educational and fun. The atmosphere was relaxed, with dolls and toys endlessly spread throughout the Design Center. The process to get a doll designed, developed, and into production was usually at least eighteen months, most times longer. You can imagine that the submissions back and forth from Hong Kong and waiting for the mail to arrive was one of the biggest causes for delay. Another was what I called "design by committee," the evaluation and approval process in every category of design proposal, marketing strategy, hairstyle, face paint, accessories, packaging, safety concerns, and the list goes on. There was a specialized department for every category and layers of people evaluating items that needed coordinated approval to set a target date for production. To me it seemed more complex than building a rocket ship.

This lengthy process was opposite to that of textile and fashion business. Usually it was the boss who had the final say, during a meeting or on a casual walk by your desk. No committees. Then the fabric or garment went into immediate production, since it needed to catch the seasonal markets—i.e., spring, fall, holiday, winter, and summer—before the trends were over. It was an express train that always needed more engine power. Mattel, on the other hand, was on a local train, with more stops randomly added when someone thought a detour was necessary for sightseeing. You never knew when you would arrive at the final destination or if the train would be derailed.

I would come home and complain to Melvin that this was a ridiculous business. I was having fun surrounded by toys and doll fashions, but I didn't understand how the atmosphere at Mattel could be so relaxed, with so much time being wasted over things like what color should Barbie's gloves should be. They were the largest toy company, but the slow pace was time lost and money thrown out. Sure, the staff was always joking and enjoying designing toys, but this was a business, not high school. Once again, the philosophy was creativity by committee. I was serious about expediting my assignments and making or beating deadlines. That effort wasn't a priority at Mattel, although Nancy and the design team appreciated what I was doing. It was a daily frustration for me and I was trying to adapt to this work style, which was in extreme contrast to the working style in New York or with our own PhD Textiles.

I loved Nancy Harrington as my boss. She was warm, caring, and very smart, and gave me the time I needed to learn the process. We became good friends on and off campus. Cafeteria lunches together and an invitation home for dinner to meet Melvin made our relationship feel more like that of sisters than colleagues.

I told her that sometimes I didn't have enough work to do and she said it wasn't a problem. That happened often. The roadblock was usually in the design group, where the creative ideas started. Winning design ideas don't appear by magic. Therefore, the product flow moved at a snail's pace. I didn't have much to do when the roadblock signs were displayed and rather than invent busywork or claim to be bored, I took action. Taking my lesson learned from Mr. Huot, the situation wasn't boring—I was boring.

I had to reinvent myself at Mattel and during the slow times took the opportunity to mingle and bond with my design and marketing colleagues. This was the "art of customer service." I would use this skill to advise the designers on fabric options, explain the fabric manufacturing processes to educate them on production capabilities, and yes, even recommend a good color for Barbie's microscopic gloves. This resulted in my becoming a partner with the designers' efforts, without intimidating anyone. Within a few months they appreciated my input and I can honestly say they loved working with me.

Personal Brand Image:

Be aggressive to network and be creative. The payoff will follow.

After nearly six months of working at Mattel, the daily job wasn't challenging. I felt underwhelmed with the slow pace and small workload. The quiet office chatter was deafening compared to the cursing, screaming, and pressure to meet deadlines in the New York offices. Everyone at Mattel was so polite that it was painful to be in this quietly dull environment. No outrageous bold emotions were visible or audible. I even asked one of my new colleagues in design, Susan, who was from the East Coast, if she would yell and curse for a few seconds so I would feel at home. She was happy to oblige and this was an energizing chance for her to shout a few foul words.

Meanwhile, Melvin was doing extremely well with our entrepreneurial adventure at PhD Textiles. He was truly a one-man show, or as he explained it, "a one-armed paper hanger with an itch." He had moved the business from the downtown office to our condo's spare bedroom, to save money and travel time. Melvin was working 24/7, since the office was in our home and there was no way to escape the work. Here I am at Mattel, underloaded with assignments, going to grad school a few nights a week, and there is darling Melvin, nonstop running the business. We talked about the imbalance and the fact that we missed each other.

Melvin wanted me to quit Mattel immediately and go back to work with him. For PhD Textiles to grow, either I had to come back to work with him or he needed to hire someone to help him. He could no longer handle the load himself. The result would be that what I earned at Mattel would be used to pay Melvin's staff. It was common sense what I needed to do to make PhD Textiles successful and reinforce the foundation for our business future together. I would resign from Mattel.

Chapter 8

Resignation

It was clear, my reasons were appropriate, and I felt fearless as I was about to meet with Nancy Harrington to resign from Mattel. I would have overcome my aversion to the slow pace by being extraordinary at Mattel, but PhD Textiles's business growth and giving my husband support was paramount in my mind. I couldn't let Melvin down.

Nancy was in her office when I warmly told her how much I appreciated what she and Mattel had done to train me for this job. I was honored that I was given an opportunity work in the toy business. However, my loyalty was to my husband and he needed me back at our business; therefore, I was giving her my resignation. Nancy was surprised. She took a few moments to think and then looked at me in her academic teacher manner and said, "I don't want you to quit. You are the only one in this department that has been in the textile and fashion industry. We need you. Let me make you an offer. Why not work for Mattel as a consultant? You could identify your own days to work and be paid by the hour. No benefits, but the hourly wage would compensate for what you would lose. I don't want you to leave. Please give this some thought."

What a flattering comment from Nancy and an offer I never could image was in my future. Working my own hours? Making some additional money? This opportunity could be fabulous or send me into a black hole of too much to focus on. I thanked Nancy for even considering this alternative work schedule and told her I would give my answer the next day.

My mind was racing. Why couldn't Nancy just accept my resignation and we could all move on? I didn't want PhD Textiles to suffer if my attention wasn't one-hundred percent in the business. On the other hand, I had a low workload at Mattel and in reality, with a bit of New York Attitude I could do my full-time job in two or three days a week without an issue. Melvin needed to hear all the options, and we would decide together.

After updating Melvin, he said without hesitation, "Take the offer! If you can call your own hours for a few days a week, why not give it a try? If this arrangement does not work out you've lost nothing since you already resigned. The money is good, so go for it." Melvin is always the risk taker. Hey, Mr. Prince Charming proposed marriage to me after only five days, so his response shouldn't have surprised me.

I accepted Nancy's consultant offer and committed to complete all my assignments regardless of this shorter work week. She was thrilled and I was pretty happy with this decision. My resignation was official, I was off Mattel's payroll, and now an employment agency was issuing my paycheck. I officially had a temporary job.

Personal Brand Image:

Be flexible and see beyond the conventional.

I found myself working at Mattel two or three days a week and I charged through the projects like a bulldozer. Held up by the usual design roadblocks and the delays from Hong Kong, I used the waiting time to be in everyone's office, plowing through the details. The times I was waiting for information to be passed to me and creating work for myself became a day off from Mattel. With this strategy, every day was fast paced. It felt good that I was contributing my expertise and it was being appreciated.

Nancy recognized my efficiency and she always found opportunities to thank me. I wasn't any smarter, I just knew how to expedite. In New York if you didn't meet deadlines you most likely would lose your job. In LA and for sure at Mattel, the relaxed working attitude left a lot of room for accepted delays and anticipated errors.

After a few months of working part time, Nancy asked me if I would consider taking a three-week trip to Hong Kong. I would be working at the Mattel office, evaluating fabric submissions and meeting with textile companies to discuss how to speed up the approval process. They were in a crisis to get these approvals completed and there was no one else to send overseas. Nancy pleaded with me to accept this assignment.

Well, I almost fell out of my chair. Hong Kong? Three weeks away from Melvin in a place on the other side of the world. This is crazy. I'm not a full-time Mattel employee. How could I be away from PhD Textiles for three weeks? The whole point of being a Mattel consultant was so I could be on my own schedule.

Nancy advised me that Mattel would pay all expenses and I would receive a flat-rate fee for the assignment, since I'd be working nonstop for three weeks. I thought, "I do not want to go. This is too far away. I have not traveled much and I have never been separated from Melvin during the five years that we have been married, I need him with me." My international travel was limited to Canada and Mexico, and my passport had expired years ago. Everything going through my mind was negative. I couldn't think of any reason to take this assignment. And of course, Melvin wouldn't let me go.

I rushed home to our condo and hugged Melvin like I was never going to see him again. Explaining every detail of Nancy's request to travel to Hong Kong, I didn't see a surprised look on his face. He said, "Go to Hong Kong. This will be a great experience for you. Think of how much you will learn about the textile and manufacturing business in Asia. I will be fine for three weeks." Melvin never ceased to amaze me with his pioneering spirit and logic. All the reasons I gave for not going, Melvin found more reasons why I should definitely go.

Still unconvinced, I had one more reality check, the Dr. D feedback court-of-last-resort. I was feeling uncomfortable at the thought of going to Hong Kong. If it were up to me I would refuse the offer and stay safe at home. I told Dr. D about the offer from Mattel and my feelings. She said, "Don't be ridiculous. I have been to Hong Kong—it's exciting, a wonderful cosmopolitan city. No matter how you feel just go."

I was emotionally immature about traveling and it seemed that Dr. D and Melvin had a healthy outlook. The decision was out of my hands. A couple of weeks later, after scrambling for a new passport, planning, and reading about Hong Kong, I was on my way for the twenty-hour flight to Hong Kong via Seattle because there were no direct flights to Hong Kong in 1986.

I boarded the plane with tears streaming down my face. It was all I could do not to start making whimpering noises as I took my seat in business class. I put my head on the small airplane window and wept. I was scared of the unknown and not having Melvin with me on this trip made it unbearable. The work assignment and trip's goal wasn't an issue. I would be in Asia in a few hours. I imagined myself like a lost child in the jungle. I was totally unprepared.

It was mid August, Hong Kong's hottest and most humid month of the year. The worst time to travel there, if you're not used to nearly one-hundred percent humidity. I exited the plane at 7 p.m. and looked for a taxi to get to the Hilton Hotel in Central Hong Kong. Since Hong Kong was a British colony, all the signs were thankfully bilingual. I had no idea what I was doing. Mattel only supplied me with general information and I was basically on my own. Nothing was familiar and the Chinese folks were staring at me because Western tourists were uncommon.

Finally I found a taxi. I clung to the seat as the taxi swerved on the narrow roads, wondering if I would ever make it to the hotel. I didn't allow myself to enjoy the remarkable nighttime views of one of the most fabulous skylines in the world. The only comfort I got was when we drove past a 7-Eleven store. Something so American, and there it was in bright neon lights.

When the taxi stopped at the Hong Kong Hilton Hotel, the doorman rushed to help me out and escort me to the hotel entrance. I was about to be submerged in the famous Hong Kong customer service experience.

What I remember most about my first morning in HK was the hotel staff's attention to detail and the guests' comfort. I was in the Hilton lobby café, having only coffee and toast because I wasn't hungry enough to order a full breakfast. My cup of coffee was presented by three servers all wearing white gloves. Number one brought the cup and coffee pot, number two poured the coffee, then number three asked if I needed anything else as she placed the cloth napkin on my lap. As a foreigner in HK, I was respected and elevated to receiving the royal hotel service.

After the relaxing coffee service, I took a ten-minute taxi ride to the Mattel office, an old building in an area called North Point. This was an industrial neighborhood right near Victoria Harbour. I had no idea what to expect. Now it was daylight and I could see the crowded streets with cars, double-decker buses, trams (trolley cars), and pedestrians moving in every direction non-stop. It was like looking at ants swarming over a sugar lump. After exiting the taxi, the aroma in the air was anything but sweet. The odor of sewage from the waste in the harbor water, along with the extreme heat and humidity, could knock you unconscious if you took too many deep breaths.

The Mattel office entrance wasn't impressive. Could have been any industrial office, with a dull gray atmosphere and papers stacked high on desks and nothing to distinguish it as a toy manufacturer, except for the few doll items around the facility. If I didn't know that I'd traveled twenty-four hours to get to the other side of the world, nothing in the office was remarkably Asian—except the staff.

I was going to work with Lawanna Adams. She was from Mattel's California office and on assignment in HK to oversee the fabric sourcing. Lawanna was a striking-looking, sixty-year-old woman, with bright red hair and a fabulous energetic attitude. She had been with Mattel since the 1960s, traveled extensively to their manufacturing facilities in Japan, Taiwan, China, Malaysia, and the Philippines. She conducted sewing audits, instructed the workers on manufacturing efficiency and how to meet the aesthetic requirements for sewing Barbie fashions. Lawanna was quite happy to have me in HK. She made me feel comfortable and welcome in the office. She knew that the fabric approval backlog was huge and needed my help.

There were at least three months of fabric submissions waiting to be evaluated. These samples were from many vendors for the same fabric items and needed immediate comments to the vendor for improvement or approval and actual samples sent to California. The overload was too much for the HK office to expedite in a timely fashion. Production delay was the result. I had to review them and compare them to the standard sent from Mattel. This was ridiculous. I wasn't a robot. You couldn't just look at one small swatch and say *yes* or *no*. These were projects I'd never seen before, and I had to understand the end use and entire doll aesthetics.

Yes, I was the right person for the job, but I lacked complete information. There wasn't even a photo of the whole toy. This was a time-consuming, meticulous undertaking and I could now understand why Nancy told me this would be a three-week project. I wasn't happy with the situation. I was working in the dark, and the effort I would put into ensuring a perfect outcome was in jeopardy. How could the HK office know what was in the realm of acceptable, since there was no complete fashion standard in the office as a basis for comparison? They weren't just in the dark—they weren't even in a room with electricity!

Even though Mattel was a part-time, temporary job for me, I was determined to make sure I finished my assignment and didn't disappoint Mattel or Nancy. I dug in my heels and started the long process of evaluating fabrics, using my design instinct and positive attitude to get me through this nightmare.

Personal Brand Image:

A horrible job isn't an excuse to fail, but an opportunity to be a hero and reinforce your trusted Brand.

I was locked in the office every day evaluating the textiles, trims, and soft goods accessories, except for a few trips to meet local vendors to review their manufacturing capabilities. After each workday, Lawanna or her office manager, David Tsui, took me to dinner and showed me Hong Kong's sights at night. During the weekends there were day trips to the most notable tourist spots. Mattel HK staff hospitality was impressive and very touching. I was never treated so well in any other working situation, so once again the royal HK treatment was evident.

I experienced all the available transportation methods— trains, ferries, buses, and trams. Over and under Victoria Harbour and then up and down Victoria Peak. The extremes were obvious. Wealth next to poverty, high-end restaurants and five-star hotels near open-air markets where they were slaughtering chickens and pigs. The animal body parts would lie out in the hot, humid open air, ready for someone to purchase and cook for dinner that night. The memory of putting glittering pink tights on Barbie's tiny legs now seemed sophisticated compared to stepping over bloody pig hoofs.

I wasn't a world traveler, and I'd been warned about the local food and hygiene. "Don't drink the water and only eat cooked food" was on my mind. The last thing I needed on this assignment was to become ill. The heat and humidity were awful. After only one step outside the air-conditioned office interior I was dripping with sweat. The food choices near the office were terrible and I was afraid to experiment, so I stuck to a limited menu mostly of rice, steamed vegetables, and hot tea.

Keeping care and caution in mind, one weekend I went shopping by myself at Stanley Market. Stanley was an open-air market that was originally for the convenience of the British Armed Forces stationed at nearby Fort Stanley. This market had cheap prices on a variety of items—food, clothing, souvenirs—and some beachside bars and pubs. A great location and low prices for larger-sized clothing for the British, which soon brought the Western tourists for shopping and drinking pleasures. It was an old and dirty place, but the amount of local Chinese goods and Western clothing for export was amazing. The prices seemed like a giveaway, so the journey there was worth it. I was so happy to be out of the drudgery of the office and walking by a rural, small beach with great shopping. I really didn't care about the severe heat and humidity.

After a few hours of roaming through the market, I was really hungry and thirsty. Places to eat were limited and none of them met my hygiene standards. I have no recollection of what I ate, but before I could do more shopping I was feeling a bit sick and needed a bathroom immediately! Well, there was no Macy's department store or hotel to run into to use the bathroom. There was only the **Stanley Public Toilet**. I had no choice but to use that facility. That building, like most in Hong Kong, had no Western toilets. Concrete cubicles with holes in the ground lead to a trough that carried the sewage underground into Stanley Bay. I closed the door, but there was no place to hang my purse or shopping bags. I was in survival mode and held them by the straps, with my teeth, as I stood over the hole in ground. I will spare the reader anymore details since you can image my situation, with no air conditioning and no proper sewage removal. Luckily I was advised to always carry pocket-sized tissues, since most toilets didn't provide any toilet paper. A bit of good luck for me.

As soon as I recovered from this episode I cut my leisure trip short and headed for a taxi, returning to the salvation of my air-conditioned, beautiful hotel room. My lips would be sealed as to what I went through during my weekend adventure. As a result of my own ignorance my comfort level was at an all-time low, but I had a job to finish and I still had another week to complete the task.

I met Ron Drwinga, the vice president who ran Mattel's sourcing office. He had been on assignment in Hong Kong since 1970 and was gracious enough to invite me to his home for dinner with his wife Linda, and to the **Hong Kong Country Club** for the best Chinese food HK could offer. The hospitality really impressed me. I wasn't a permanent Mattel employee or a high-ranking executive, and for the VP to go out of his way to share his home and treat me so special was heartwarming. Sure, I was a guest, but I was also one of the few who traveled to HK to represent Mattel's California design team. Most of the staff didn't want to make the trip to a place that was perceived as having limited Western conveniences and was considered a hardship post for anyone assigned there. I'm not dismissing the fact that I was a respected envoy from Mattel headquarters. However, I do believe that my presence was a novel event for the manufacturing and engineering folks.

The three-week visit to Hong Kong was nearly over and I was desperate to go home. I missed Melvin so much that my heart was empty. We had limited communications. The phone calls to the US were extremely expensive and we only spoke once a week. Being homesick for Melvin and American familiarity was making me anxious. I was tired of being locked in the office and feeling that at every turn I would either be lost in this foreign place or food poisoned! My departure day couldn't come soon enough to release me from working like a robot.

The job was complete and my HK adventure was over. Yes, I'd met great people, I was treated like an Empress, and I saw sights that most people from the West could never image. I was lucky to have this once-in-a-lifetime chance to see another world that was so different and filled with thousands of years of history. Now I could say I'd been to HK and move on with my life. It was a place that didn't interest me at all.

Back in Melvin's arms, feeling safe, I told him that I never wanted to go to HK again unless he had some desire in the future for a vacation and we went together. Otherwise it wasn't worth the effort. Of course, I wouldn't tell Nancy or anyone at Mattel how I felt. All Mattel needed to know was that I'd completed the challenge and would give them a full report of the workload and vendor status. My personal feelings about HK were irrelevant. The chance that I would ever go back was remote. I just kept the negative feelings to myself.

Nancy was very happy with my accomplishments. I never updated her about the system inefficiencies and communication delays that I'd witnessed. I felt my work with Mattel wasn't going to be a career, and to actually do something about the communication problem between HK and LA was a major project. I was new to the toy industry and only a consultant working a few days a week. Who would take me seriously if I recommended corporate restructure improvements for a multibillion-dollar company? I decided to let this "Problematic Dragon" rest.

Chapter 9

Change of Plans

It was early in 1987 and I was still routinely commuting to Mattel a few days a week while helping Melvin with PhD Textiles. Classes at graduate school for my master's in psychology were complete and I needed to do an internship program, working with patients, to receive my degree. On the way home from Mattel one evening I was delayed in a traffic. This was usual for my commute but on this day it was particularly slow to get home. I sat for two hours in the car, for a trip that would normally be forty-five minutes. I started to feel a sharp pain in my stomach, but continued the drive for another hour. Finally, I reached the supermarket near our condo, where I needed to stop to pick up dinner supplies.

I stepped out of the car and as I placed my foot on the concrete, I started to hemorrhage. This event wasn't an anticipated monthly occurrence. I got back in the car and drove home. Melvin took one look at me and insisted we go to the hospital emergency room. We were both extremely concerned that something terrible was happening. When I saw the doctor, he said he thought I might have a tumor and asked us to wait for the blood test and ultrasound results.

After a thirty-minute wait, the doctor came out smiling and said, "Congratulations, Mrs. Bazerman—you are twelve weeks pregnant! You should go home and schedule an appointment to see your doctor."

This news seemed impossible, since I had no signs that was I pregnant. I couldn't believe I was three months pregnant and didn't know it! We'd been married for nearly six years and wanted to have a baby, but the circumstance of this discovery was a surprise.

The next day I went to my gynecologist in Beverly Hills, fearing the worst since bleeding in this manner wasn't normal. Dr. Kadner told me that I was indeed twelve weeks pregnant and to expect a baby sometime around November 13. However, I was thirty-nine years old and having some bleeding issues, so there was a possibility of losing the baby. He instructed me to go home, relax, and put my feet up. If I lost the baby it meant Mother Nature was taking care of any problems, and there would be another chance to get pregnant in the future.

I told Nancy I was under doctor's order to stay home until my condition improved. This was absolutely the best news, to know that we would have a child, but I was also terrified that the blessing would disappear. I was afraid to move so I just sat on the couch. After about a week of my confinement and resting, the bleeding stopped and I was back at work. The doctor's instructions were not to strain myself and I shouldn't lift anything heavier than a Barbie doll! This would be easy to accomplish.

I'm nearly forty years old and the baby's doing fine. The test results were in—I was having a baby boy. It was the end of September and Nancy asked me if I felt well enough to go the Mattel factory in Mexico to give the engineering staff a lecture on textiles. Although I was pregnant, I was still six weeks away from my delivery date and the doctor advised that it was no problem. Melvin would drive me the few hours across the US border and we would return home that evening. I felt well and I was flattered that Nancy asked me to speak to the Mexico team.

I didn't expect the factory to be so warm. I was overdressed for sure. I lectured for ninety minutes in the heat and humidity. After a factory tour we were ready to head back to California. This was the first time I'd ever spoken in public. Surprisingly, I was really good and not a bit nervous. I even amazed myself. I think the training in New York, working with the intense, rude, and obnoxious men from the garment industry, was basic training that prepared me to have a fearless attitude toward public speaking.

I was back at work the next morning to tell Nancy the results of my trip. Early that afternoon at Mattel, I didn't feel well. I had no idea what it was like to have a baby and I ignored the discomfort in my stomach. However, I was concerned that something might be wrong. I called Dr. Kadner and he said to come to his office. I couldn't connect with Melvin (reminder—we didn't have mobile phones) so I decided to drive myself the twenty miles to Beverly Hills from Mattel's office. I knew Melvin would panic, but I had no choice. I was feeling very strange.

Dr. Kadner examined me and confirmed the baby was okay. He advised me, once again, to go home and put up my feet and relax. I drove myself another twenty-five miles home to Calabasas. Melvin was there, nervously waiting, stressed out of his mind from worry. We sat together, talked, and hugged until we were so tired we fell asleep. My sleep didn't last. I was awake most of the night with stomach discomfort. I didn't want to wake Melvin just to complain about something I was probably imagining. However, by 6 a.m. the pain was horrible and I couldn't stand it any longer. I finally woke Melvin and told him what was going on. He said to me, "Darling, you have never had a baby. I have had three children and I am telling you: you are in LABOR! Get dressed and we are going to the hospital!"

It was true. I was in labor. Now the waiting game began. After thirty-six continuous hours of the same pain that billions of women have experienced, and many chocolate Snickers bars for Melvin to ingest, I prematurely gave birth to a healthy, five pound, seven ounce baby boy at 2:40 a.m. on October 3, 1987. **Haris Marc Cristopher Bazerman**. Yes, three given names to cover all those we wanted to honor. Yes, the spellings are correct as written.

Once again, **Personal Brand Image** at work. Can't give the kid a boring name!

Because I wasn't aware of my pregnancy until the twelfth week and I gave birth six weeks early, it seemed that I had a short time to enjoy my pregnancy and all the attention I would get. I didn't eat or drink much in Mexico, wanting to avoid any ill effects from the potential lack of hygiene of the local food. It may be that this caused darling Haris to want to escape to a better environment. I was dehydrated. We will never know, but this was the first and only time I saw an early delivery from Mattel production.

Since I was a consultant and not a Mattel employee, I wasn't entitled to any maternity leave or medical coverage. The need for a **Change of Plans** became obvious. Melvin and I had no family to help us, so it made sense for me to stop working at Mattel and stay home with our baby. Mattel was a short-term, temporary career for me. At this point Nancy and I were good friends and I knew she would continue to be in my life even if I didn't work for her.

The timing of yet another departure from Mattel was interesting. In 1987 Mattel's profitability was down and they were undergoing corporate cutbacks and layoffs. Inevitably, the cost-saving policies would have limited or discontinued the engagement of outside consultants. My employment most likely would have been terminated anyway. Nancy and Mattel were unhappy that was I leaving. However, it would be a cost reduction for the department and they took it in stride.

As naive as I was about knowing whether I was in labor, I was more naive about how much attention a new baby needs. I thought babies slept most of the day. I expected to have all this time to take care of PhD Textile business, devote quality time to Melvin, and watch Haris peacefully sleep in his crib. I was entirely misinformed. No complaints, but as a new mom, I was never able to get out of the house or pay attention to anything other than Haris until after 2 p.m.

When Haris was almost eight months old I got a call from Nancy. She told me that Mattel layoffs and cutbacks were complete but she couldn't hire anyone. All new hire requests were frozen. The company restructuring was in progress and the Soft Goods Engineering workload was increasing. With no ability to hire permanent staff she was only able to hire temporary staff to handle the workload. I could feel it coming—she asked me to work a few days a week again to help her out.

Intriguing offer. I didn't want to work at Mattel, and I already had so much responsibility taking care of Haris, helping Melvin at PhD Textiles, and having a life. The positive side was that I enjoyed working with Nancy and it was extra money. Having a baby with no medical insurance to back us up and expenses incurred were a financial strain, so extra income would help. I was flattered that Mattel wanted my talents and was supportive of my new mom situation. However, I had no one to take care of Haris and in 1988 Mattel, like most companies, had no day care facilities. This offer was nice but impossible to even consider.

I thought seriously about Mattel's offer. Melvin and I agreed the additional money would be helpful and actually take some of the financial burden off of him. He suggested that if I went back to work a few days a week, he would take care of Haris on those days. Melvin was working from home and with his flexible schedule, taking care of Haris was feasible. The days he needed to travel to customers he could either take Haris with him, or I would stay home that day.

I couldn't believe Melvin's offer. Sure, he is The Dad, but this is a rare guy, who wanted to be a part-time house-dad. As I'd learned since the first day we met, the unexpected is what I should expect. You gotta' love him even more. I thought this was at least worth a try, to see if we could both manage and make this a win-win situation. **Change of Plans**. I accepted Nancy's proposal and went back to Mattel on my own schedule, while Melvin took care of Haris.

You can image our crazy schedule. I have to say it was really fun and so wonderful to know I had a husband who could handle anything. The best was when Melvin needed to go to a customer in downtown LA and would take Haris with him. The customers couldn't believe that there was a guy selling piece goods, carrying a baby with him, changing diapers in the car trunk or on a customer's showroom table, and at the same time making a sales pitch. If I didn't know better I'd say this was an ingenious selling tool for PhD Textiles, and the increased orders were the proof that a cute baby with his working dad deserved to get the order.

We were in blessed chaos. Melvin was unbelievable and I was completing five days of work at Mattel in three days. Haris benefited by having two devoted parents involved with every detail of his life. I would have to say it must have been very stimulating for Haris to be "working" with his dad and not just lying in his crib like other babies. This went well for another six months, and then Haris was no longer a baby, but an active toddler who wanted to do more than look at factories or be confined inside a fashion studio. We needed to change our plan again.

Melvin and I were lucky to find young lady, Ela Rimon, formerly from Israel, who'd served time as a soldier in the Israeli army. This was a comforting safety factor and she came highly recommended. Ela would come to our house to take care of Haris. More like having a live-in teacher who provided him with formal playtime and focused on his early education. I saw no end in sight for my part-time job. I decided another **Change of Plans** was needed and quit Mattel to be home with Haris. Hopefully I would have time to complete an internship for my psychology degree, the real career I wanted to pursue.

Nancy had confided in me that she was thinking of leaving the Soft Goods Engineering group. She was unhappy because she didn't see any career opportunities in SGE department. Her boss frustrated her and she was ready to go. There was a new department being created at Mattel, called Vendor Operations. Mattel's factories were focused on manufacturing the core Brands—i.e., Barbie dolls and Hot Wheels toy cars. Outside contractors or vendors manufactured Mattel's many other products. Business was growing and Mattel was restructuring to gain more control over the supply-chain processes, by approving vendors to regulate price and quality.

Nancy wanted to be part of this new Mattel organization. I could understand, with her background being more on the technical side, this position would utilize her knowledge. She would be traveling to Asia to meet and qualify fabric vendors, as well as insure they adhered to Mattel Corporate Responsibility guidelines. A huge task, and Nancy was ready for the challenge.

It looked like I was severing ties with Mattel at a good time. One of the main reasons I was back at Mattel was Nancy. She wasn't only a great boss, she was also a woman with common sense and high ethical standards. Without her as my boss I most likely would have shortened my Mattel assignment, even if I didn't have Haris as my primary concern. Looks like this would be a mutual business separation.

It was clear to me that when Nancy left the Soft Goods Engineering group I would leave Mattel. To my surprise Nancy said, "Why don't you apply for my current job? You can have a permanent position at Mattel and run this department. You are qualified since you have been in a working relationship with Mattel for nearly four years. You would not have to be trained. I will recommend you for this position."

This was a pattern I needed to break. Every time I wanted to leave Mattel, Nancy was there to lure me in, like a small fish hungry to bite on the baited hook. It was a nice thought from Nancy, but this job had no attraction for me. I definitely didn't want a career in the toy business!

I was quitting Mattel. It was firm in my mind that I was **not** going to have another **Change of Plans**.

Personal Brand Image:

A trusted Brand attracts opportunity and gives you options.

Chapter 10

Repeat Performances

Melvin was neutral about whether I should apply for Mattel's Soft Goods manager job. We had Haris to think of as our first priority. Of course, the most comfortable thing for me to do was not return to Mattel. Having learned my lessons well from Dr. D, I know that being comfortable isn't always the right path. I arranged to have a phone session with her. We discussed what I thought were the pros and cons of Mattel employment. Before I could complete my list of negative issues, Dr. D interrupted.

"What is wrong with you, Mrs. Bazerman? Don't be silly. Apply for this job. Take the job … you can eventually become Vice President! "

I thought her reaction was typical Dr. D pushing the limits of what's possible. I'm a novice about toy manufacturing and Dr. D thinks I can be Vice President of this Fortune 500 company. What a joke. Perhaps she was having a lapse of psychological insight. Or she was bored that day and wanted to make me crazy for her entertainment. I really didn't want my role model, my mentor, who had saved me, inspired me to marry Melvin, and helped me raise a well-adjusted son, tell me to take a job that I wasn't qualified for with hopes of becoming Vice President!

This wasn't the only therapy session I had about the Mattel topic. I resisted Dr. D's advice for weeks, but after talking through why I was so angry and unwilling to even apply for the job, I realized it was my fear of failure. What if Mattel rejected my application for the manager position? This would prove that in all my careers I wasn't really worthy but was only lucky. Was my trusted **Personal Brand Image** not strong enough? I pulled myself together and remembered my decision to throw that whipped cream pie in Mr. Mac Wells's face and my continuous efforts to prove that Mr. Huot was wrong.

This current situation was the same. I had to apply for the job and act professionally appropriate. If I think I am a loser, guess what? I will lose. If Nancy thinks I can do the job and my reputation as a consultant has been first class, then I'm going for it. My hat is in the ring for this Mattel job.

Personal Brand Image:

Feeling comfortable will limit success, since challenges aren't comfortable.

Based on Nancy Harrington's recommendation, my textile expertise, fashion design background, and reputation as a Textile Analyst, I was rehired by Mattel for a full-time position on July 1, 1989, as Manager of Soft Goods Engineering (SGE). Now I have the manager's pay, the benefits, and the opportunity to be an effective leader. In the nineteen years that I'd worked in my four careers, I'd never had any staff reporting to me. I'd never been responsible for a department. I'd never had any leadership training or business school education. But it was too late to feel unqualified—I had the job.

Nancy was right. Her former boss Mr. J, now my boss, wasn't inspirational to work with and lacked great management style. He had been with Mattel for over thirty years. Looking back, I believe he had other priorities and perhaps had no patience to mentor me or get too involved with SGE details. The Vice President who oversaw our department was Mr. Lewis, who was a smart guy focused on returning to life as a flower child. He looked the part, with a full head of long, dark blonde hair and a huge mustache. He was causal, relaxed and had that bohemian attitude. Since I don't have any hard facts on why he was so relaxed I will just leave it to the reader's imagination.

Mattel provided no management training and managing people is the most difficult job of all. It was as if I was plucked from a tree and expected to have good flavor, even though I wasn't ripe. My only hope was to do what I had done before, which is to excel in what I do best until I can figure out how to swim in the sea with no life jacket. I was on my own and the ride looked rough, but I was determined to be outstanding.

Personal Brand Image:

Find something to be great at so the negatives will go unnoticed.

My textile knowledge and fashion sense is what impressed Mattel. I made sure that the designers all had my support and can-do attitude at their disposal. I could have earned a Miss America Congeniality Award for my cooperation and teamwork. The goal was to set an example for the small four-person staff that reported to me and create a team that could get things done in spite of the corporate bureaucracy. It wasn't long after I took over as manager that my VP, Mr. Lewis, asked me to give a lecture on textiles to the Design and Development teams. About eighty to one hundred staff would attend. He wanted me to share my textile knowledge to help them understand the different manufacturing techniques' processes, limitations, and potential. The objective was to give the staff a better understanding, which would lead to more creative soft goods execution. I agreed this was a great opportunity to help the company.

What was I thinking? I'd never spoken in front of a large audience. The only other time I'd stood up and lectured was for Mattel in Mexico nearly two years earlier, when the physical heat and stress caused me to go into labor and give birth to my son. I needed to find a strategy on how to capture the attention of these creative and technical groups, which would include a cross section of design staff and executives. I had to come up with something to hold their interest. This would be my introduction to Mattel as part of the management team.

How could I take a technical subject and make it interesting and memorable? I had promised myself twenty years earlier in college that even though the subject might be boring, **I would not be boring**. Mr. Huot's comments were echoing on my mind. This situation was similar to the **Finite Project** assigned by Mac Wells in my senior year at Hunter College.

I felt exhilarated. I could repeat that 1969 performance and use the pie throwing to catch my audience's attention to make a point. The creative staff would love a visual example, rather than a blackboard with a series of notes. I could hardly stand my internal excitement. Although I'd gotten an *A* in college for that project, this was the real world and I was being paid to do a job. Never mind a failing grade—I could get fired.

I decided to create the cream pie only as an example of the many ingredients for textiles. I wouldn't throw the pie, I would just use it as a metaphor to bring attention to the different processes fabrics go through before you have a useable product. It would be an example, a recipe for textile manufacturing. I would then break down the ingredients and compare that to the different textile processes. Pie making versus fabric making. This presentation would still be interesting without throwing the pie.

It was the day before my presentation. I was at my desk, finishing writing the details for this event when Mr. Lewis interrupted me. He took a step into my office and with a big smile on his face he said, "Hey, Bazerman, are you nervous?" (He always called me by my last name.) I replied no, that I was ready for the lecture. Lewis smiled again and said, "Well, Bazerman, I will tell you something that will make you nervous. I will be at your presentation tomorrow and I will being sitting in the front row and I will **not** be wearing any underwear!" He chuckled and quickly left the room. I couldn't believe what he'd said to me.

At the time I never thought he meant it as sexual harassment, but only wanted to make me uncomfortable, a joke. In 1989 the sexual harassment terminology was rarely used. I don't think I even heard that term as a workplace issue. I was shocked that a Vice President of Mattel would talk to me so rudely, with possible sexual implications. I was furious. At that moment, I thought that if I decided to actually throw a pie at my presentation, it would be at Mr. Lewis. I wasn't going to let him get to me. I left the office and on my drive home I pondered if I should proceed with "Vice Presidential Pie-Target."

My big day to make a lasting impression at Mattel arrived. I wore one of my New York fashionable outfits and was excited to start the lecture and see the result of my first public speaking as a new Mattel manager. I was surprisingly calm. This was laid-back California, a toy company with a great group of creative people who already respected me. The attendance was large, with over eighty staff quietly taking their seats. I was at ease, ready to educate and attempt to make myself an indispensable colleague.

A few minutes before the scheduled start time, in walks—no, in swaggers—Mr. Lewis. He was dressed casually in a T-shirt and jeans, with his long hair softly flowing in rhythm with his swagger. He grinned in my direction and headed for the front row, just as he promised, and sat in the audience directly opposite to where I stood. He nodded and smiled at me as he rested his hands in his jean pockets. I was furious that he was trying to make me nervous and confirming his threat to me, his "I will not be wearing any underwear" bullshit.

Reminiscent of my Hunter College Finite Project, I covered the lecture table with a bright red tablecloth and proceeded to take out my ingredients from a shelf beneath the table. First the graham cracker pie crust was revealed, and then I briskly shook the large, chilled can of whipped cream. The surprised looks on everyone's faces were fabulous and invigorated me to complete the show. I stopped my performance and told the Mattel group that I was comparing making a pie to creating fabric. That many ingredients were needed to make a pie look good as well as taste good. It also took many processes to make fabric look and feel good for the end use. I continued to take out chocolate and multicolored sprinkles and candied cherries. I dramatically filled the empty pie crust with the entire can of whipped cream, poured the sprinkles over the white mountain of cream, and then added the cherry on top. My pie was finished. I then explained that if I didn't add the right ingredients or bake the crust at the correct temperature, the pie would be ruined.

Mr. Lewis made it easy for me by sitting, as promised, in the front row. All I needed to do was to take one step forward, and I said, "Similar to a pie, if one of the processes in making fabric was not done correctly, the fabric could literally blow up in your face!"

I then quickly shoved the pie in Lewis's face! There was cream, cherries, and sprinkles flying everywhere! The scream-ing-laughter from the shocked Mattel teams was loud and overwhelming. I felt I had just won a championship game and the gold medal was mine. Mr. Lewis was covered with cream and he was a complete mess. If I got fired, so be it. I wasn't going to be intimidated by this VP!

To Lewis's credit he did laugh, and I was once again famous for doing the unimaginable, for breaking the rules, for thinking differently—for not being boring. You might say I established my professional credentials with Mattel and my boss that day.

After everyone recovered from the cream pie performance, I did follow up with more practical textile manufacturing details. I knew my audience of designers had no patience to dig too deep. They just wanted to know the general guidelines. All of which seemed to be overshadowed by my attempt at vaudeville and targeted revenge on Mr. Lewis. I never told any of my colleagues about the sexist remark that Lewis had made, which motivated me to actually throw the pie. Nor did I mention to him the reason behind his being selected as the pie recipient. Mr. Lewis will find out now, if he reads this book. I didn't get fired. I got praise and a reputation for being bold. This performance remained a success and set the high standard for all my future work at Mattel.

Personal Brand Image:

When doing the usual won't achieve your goal, break the rules.

Mattel management left me alone to do my job. I always wondered if the reason for lack of direction was complete trust or fear that they'd be the next pie-in-the-face target. I was used to working on my own and just expediting a project. This was the opposite of Mattel. No one person or team had the authority to complete a project. You had to interface, share, and evaluate before you could move to the next step. Then you have to wait for information from the team in Asia to continue. In my opinion there was little independence or risk taking, and sometimes the process was out of control.

It was January 1990 and I had been a full-time manager for six months. I put a hold my graduate school internship since there was no time in my schedule. Haris was two years old and I rushed home daily to have dinner with him. Melvin was overloaded with PhD Textiles business and being home early to pick up Haris, who now stayed at Ela's house for day care. I kept thinking of when I could stop working at Mattel and spend more time with Haris. There was no date I could identify as my second resignation from Mattel, until PhD Textiles was more established and more profitable.

My relationship with Mr. Lewis was very good, considering the pie episode. He was a good sport and respected me for what I did at his expense and what I was accomplishing at Mattel. He asked me, without putting his hands in his pockets, if I would go to Asia and attend a fabric quality meeting at one of Mattel's production factories in Kuala Lumpur, Malaysia. The trip would include a stop at another Mattel factory in Taiwan, then on to Hong Kong to evaluate the soft goods submission backlog. In addition, Mr. Lewis wanted me to give a presentation at the Malaysian factory. All of Mattel's Asia factory general managers and staff would be attending. My lecture's focus would be Barbie fashion aesthetics and fabric quality concerns.

I didn't want to endure the hardship of the long flight and a bit of fear of the unknown, traveling to different Asian countries for two weeks. I had no choice but to agree to make this trip, since I'd already established myself as a person with unique communication skills and I was perceived as fearless. This was a good opportunity for me to understand Mattel's manufacturing process and reinforce my **Personal Brand Image** at the company. I had no desire to return to Hong Kong, a place I found to be a difficult environment. Melvin was supportive and happy to take care of Haris. This man never ceased to amaze me with his Rock Star Powers.

The first stop was Mattel Kuala Lumpur (MKL), for the fabric quality meeting. I was traveling with three other colleagues from Mattel California.

The general manager of MKL and meeting facilitator was Mr. P, originally from the United Kingdom, who was a charming, strong-headed Brit. He was tall, thin, and dignified looking. His British accent was a pleasant distraction from the fact that he was really annoyed that so many fabric production problems were causing manufacturing delays. I'd only been on this job for six months, and I had no idea what I walking into. There seemed to be a red target painted on my head. After a warm welcome the reality set in that this meeting wasn't going to be any fun for me. No design representatives ever came to MKL and now they had me, a captive audience. I was going to be the recipient of built-up years of aggravation. Once I realized what I was up against, I immediately turned off my defensive, polite position and changed into my New York Attitude—"I Will Be In Your Face In A Minute If You Attack Me" mode.

I'd never had any experiences with group confrontation, and looking back on this episode I will say I wasn't very political or diplomatic. I could deal one-on-one with a difficult boss, like Mr. H in NYC, to make my voice heard. However, I was a new, untrained manager and didn't know how to persuade a group of about fifty (mostly male) colleagues to accept my point of view. I had more textile manufacturing experience than all the attendees combined and understood that the complaints they were highlighting were normal for the industry. Mr. P and his team were asking for the textile manufacturers to deliver perfect fabrics consistently, with no defects. It was like a child asking that every spoonful of chocolate chip ice cream put into their bowl would contain twelve pieces of chocolate.

The situation was similar to what I was trying to explain when I made the whipped cream pie at Mattel California a few months earlier. Fabric manufacturing and pie making weren't an exact science and any small deviation in the process could result with a product that blew up in your face! Of course, I couldn't repeat what I did to Mr. Lewis with this group. They didn't seem to have senses of humor and their egos couldn't handle being covered with cream. I needed some other avenue to win them over.

I had already angered Mr. P with my direct explanation that his expectations for perfect fabrics were unrealistic. I brought some fashion accessories to use as props for a discussion on Barbie aesthetics. I thought to redirect my presentation efforts and turn it into a performance, not just to make my point, but to make a statement that could win Mattel's engineering teams' attention and hopefully admiration. It would be difficult to destroy me if I had their respect.

My presentation was about Barbie aesthetics. I was dressed professionally in a modest, short purple skirt with a coordinating purple sweater, purple high-heeled shoes and no trace of any jewelry. I slowly walked to the podium and every eye in the audience was on me. The Mattel engineering staff seemed to be waiting for me to say something provocative or argumentative, and then they would have a reason to verbally attack my concepts. I was the only person from California design team, and I was also the only female presenter. This was new meat for the hungry tigers.

I smiled as I surveyed the audience and without speaking, I picked up a bag that I'd previously placed in back of the podium. I dramatically started to remove items from the bag. I took out a thick, glittering rhinestone choker and secured it around my neck. Next I removed four rhinestone bangle bracelets from an organza pouch. I raised my arms and boldly put two of them on my left wrist and the other two on my right wrist. I opened another pouch and took out a pair of long, rhinestone drop earrings and attached one to each of my otherwise undecorated ears. The audience was restless and talking out loud, wondering what I was doing as I silently proceeded with this visual dress-up display.

I continued to dress myself with a purple metallic shawl that draped around my shoulders and a small, rhinestone-encrusted purple clutch bag to add to the fashion statement. With my final deep dive into my supply bag, I took out a large, princess-style rhinestone tiara. With a slow, deliberate wave of my hands and giant grin on my face, I placed the tiara on top of my head to complete the ensemble. I then stepped away from the podium, walking toward the audience like Miss America taking her first bow after being crowned, and paraded around, finally speaking:

"I was dressed very plain and now, with adding jewelry and matching accessories, I have completed the look of a Fashionista. Please let me know if I look terrific." Audience applause followed.

I said, "This is the objective that our design team is looking for when a Barbie fashion is created. Just like for humans, Barbie must have fashion perfection because she is not just a doll—she is a fashion icon! This is why when Barbie is in production, the details are so important to retain the look, the same as what would be expected from a Paris fashion model or a real princess. Nothing less will get the customer's approval and a purchase for Barbie."

This may not sound very extraordinary. However, in 1990 Mattel's engineers in Asia had never been exposed to any dynamic presentation styles, only charts, graphs, and statistical data. In contrast to the usual information style, I was ready for a Hollywood Academy Award by the time I placed the tiara on my head. This was my statement and performance that made everyone feel good. I was bold and entertaining. They had fun. They understood my message. I had their respect.

Personal Brand Image:

Make your point without being dictatorial, demanding, or angry. Be different and get the audience's attention.

After Malaysia I traveled to Taiwan to visit another Mattel Barbie factory and local fabric suppliers. I don't remember much about this short Taiwan visit but I do remember the food was fabulous. The Taiwanese love seafood. Smelling the fresh fish brought back memories of growing up in Sheepshead Bay. The Taiwanese restaurant served a multi-course meal of all fresh seafood. These underwater delicacies were accompanied by giant bottles of Taiwanese beer, poured into your glass by special servers whose only job was to keep diners' beer glasses full.

There were lobsters, crabs, clams, squid, and many kinds of fish being displayed before me. I recall when the final shrimp dish came out, overflowing on a large platter. One of the local Mattel employees told me this was their favorite dish, "drunken shrimp." I assumed the shrimp had been marinating in an alcoholic beverage overnight to enhance the flavor. My colleague told me that the shrimp were still alive and literally being drowned with boiling hot Chinese wine. When I looked at the masses of shrimp, they were jumping on the platter, struggling with searing intoxication. The idea was to eat them as they were dying and feel them pulsating in your mouth before you started your chewing process. I was speechless as I watched my Taiwanese friends participate in eating this unique shrimp recipe. I personally waited until the shrimp drowned in the wine and were peacefully at rest before I dined on them.

The last part of the trip was a repeat performance in Hong Kong, to evaluate hundreds of fabric submissions. I was staying at the JW Marriott Hotel located in the central part of the Hong

Kong Island. An underground path connected the hotel to the Hong Kong Metro train system, which I used for my daily commute to the office. This was convenient because the Mattel office had moved from the Watson Estates in the industrial northern part of HK to Kowloon, across Victoria Harbour in Tsim Sha Tsui. Quite an improvement over what I'd seen in 1986. The new location was in a huge, modern office building. The first three levels were a shopping mall with a couple of restaurants and many luxury name-brand stores mixed in with some local shops.

Mattel occupied a few floors in that building. I was once again going to work with Lawanna Adams, Director of the Textile Sourcing and Development (TSND) department. I was hoping that some process improvements had been made since my prior visit, to make this a more pleasant experience. Lawanna's assignment was as an expatriate, but she only wanted to stay a few years in her position, since she was sixty-two years old and widowed. Lawanna was Mattel's first overseas female executive and she was awesome, with her fabulous attitude, experience, and willingness to mentor the local staff.

She confided in me that a lot of what she was doing on the product development side was new to her and perhaps she wasn't prepared for the task. Her group worked with my California staff to create sewn prototype samples of Barbie fashions for toy show sales, which required more of a creative eye than just the ability to duplicate. The mail communication between the US and HK was mediocre at best, and the slow, inaccurate process frustrated Lawanna.

I was now full-time, permanent staff and exposed to the methodology and processes of Mattel's Design and Development office. As a result I had a very good knowledge of design and marketing expectations. The HK sourcing group, TSND, had nonstop inquiries about the products and fabrics they asked me to evaluate. I was reviewing all the fabric submissions and answering questions when I realized this team was working with little direction from California, and with little knowledge of requirements.

HK received swatches with no explanation, no details, no intent of end use. This situation was worse than what I'd observed three years earlier, since HK was now sewing samples that needed to look aesthetically correct. However, the direction they received was either inadequate or nonexistent. If I were HK staff and received this type of information, I couldn't execute the requirement. I was appalled that this mega toy company had such a weak communication process and such a dysfunctional approach to soft goods development for their largest Brand, Barbie. To make matters worse the HK office didn't ask the right questions. Obviously incorrect samples were submitted and shouldn't have been sent to California for evaluation.

The lack of understanding on both sides of the Pacific Ocean resulted from inadequate clarity and not knowing how to ask the right questions. What a waste of time, to work in a circle of redundancy due to poor communication. I had no idea that the process to develop fabric and sewn samples was so backward. Why should this be happening at the #1 toy company? This was an incredibly eye-opening moment for me and I was embarrassed to represent the Mattel California office that was responsible for the chaos.

Chapter 11

More Proposals

The situation in HK had deteriorated since my visit three years earlier. Upon my return to California I was filled with enthusiasm to fix the process dysfunctions that I'd observed in HK. I was ready to write down the issues and propose action to resolve the problems. Even though I had no long-term plans to remain at Mattel, I couldn't keep quiet while time and effort were wasted, the current normal between California and the HK offices. The fact that Mattel had been in business over forty-five years and I was new to the toy industry, as well as a novice at business management, didn't deter me from evaluating and advising what was right for the company.

Personal Brand Image:

When confronted with a crisis, if you remain silent, you are part of the problem. Don't just complain—offer a solution.

My solution to the disaster that I could foresee was based on my previous experiences working in New York and in my own PhD Textiles business. I had never written a business plan and I didn't know how to be politically correct with my advice. The nearly twenty years that I was employed in one of the most competitive, cut-throat industries in New York and in LA became my "official credentials" in lieu of an MBA degree. My **Proposal** to Mattel management was commonsense steps on how to accomplish speedy and cost-effective soft goods development.

In 1990, the eighteen-month development process was acceptable to Mattel management. The end result was good, so the waste of time and added expenses for delays were ignored. Barbie was the #1 fashion doll in the world and had little competition. Therefore the long lead-time for development wasn't seen as a problem. Mattel's relaxed atmosphere reflected the fact that they were profitable in spite of this dysfunction. There was no incentive to change. If no one noticed or cared that the system was broken, why fix it?

The most efficient way to resolve the time and money wasted, as well as improve the product, would be to authorize a HK team to approve fabrics and fashion production for Barbie. California would keep designing, and HK would execute the designs from sketches or a sample until production. In short, eliminate the global approval process and improve the onsite aesthetic capability near the manufacturing source.

That was the simple version of my **Proposal**, and it seemed obvious how make these changes. Sometimes an outsider with a new way to look at things can see the light through the thick fog of habit. The old ways are easy to follow since you don't need to expend effort to revise anything—you just repeat what worked before and hope for the best.

I'd been sent to HK to evaluate a fabric submissions backlog. No other staff was willing to go to Asia and subject themselves to a long flight, an unromantic location, risky food choices, hot humid weather, and long working hours. If I hadn't witnessed the clumsy work process in HK, I might have followed what Mattel did in the past. After all, they were the leader in doll manufacturing and must know what they're doing.

Personal Brand Image:

Common sense isn't always obvious. Put the problem in simple terms to find the reasonable solution.

If Mattel were a small, private company, my **Proposal** would have gone directly to the person in charge. Approach the boss and see what he or she thinks and then make it happen. However, large corporations have multiple layers of bureaucracy, just like governments. Mattel had its own hierarchy and I was about to step into the arena of a "Congressional Barbie Battle."

Mattel protocol was to submit my written **Proposal** for Hong Kong Soft Goods Design and Development (HKSG) to my immediate boss, Mr. J. I thought he would realize my **Proposal's** value and take action. He never responded to my recommendation and seemed rather distracted at the office. My feelings were confirmed a few months later when he resigned after his long career at Mattel.

My new boss was Bonnie Gretz, who had been with Mattel for twenty-five years and was manager of the Product Development team, which tracked projects from inception to production. Bonnie was loyal to Mattel and a fair individual. She had no expertise in soft goods but was interested my **Proposal** for HKSG and decided to bring it to the next level, her boss—the famous, unpredictable VP, Mr. Lewis.

A few more months passed and no one in management commented on my **Proposal**. Later that year, Mr. Lewis decided to live out his dream of making pottery. He left Mattel and moved to Hawaii to begin his artistic career. He resigned and swaggered away from the pressure of heading the Girls Engineering Department. No wonder my **Proposal** was lost in the shuffle of bosses quitting Mattel.

I couldn't control Mattel's politics and chances were that before new management was in place, I might resign again. My personal priorities hadn't changed. I might not be employed at Mattel by the time management finally considered my **Proposal's** validity. I just moved forward with giving 110% effort to insure Barbie's fashions were high quality.

The organizational effects of Mr. Lewis leaving Mattel resolved themselves by the end of 1990. Mr. Don Hartling, who headed Boys Engineering and had worked at Mattel over twenty-five years, was assigned to be the VP of Girls Product Engineering and Development. The only thing Don Hartling had in common with Mr. Lewis was that they were engineers. Don kept to himself and was always appropriate with policy and people. He was the kind of guy who wouldn't sit down to have coffee with you or casually chat, but he was the man you could depend on to be an approachable, straightforward gentleman.

In August 1991, over a year after I'd written my **Proposal**, Bonnie Gretz presented my HKSG suggestions to Don Hartling. At that point I had put the whole idea out of my mind. I was discouraged with Mattel and their slowness to react to obvious dysfunction with HK's product development process. This lack of organizational action convinced me to look for the opportunity to resign again and move on. I was powerless to initiate any major changes in the workflow with HK, to reduce Mattel's cost and improve efficiency.

The approaching 1997 handover of HK back to China was a never-ending concern for Mattel. They were heavily represented with various offices in HK and manufacturing in China. Mattel was preoccupied with looking at alternatives, in case China changed the regulations and operating procedures for US companies. This was the perception not only of Mattel, but also of the HK staff, wondering what the future would hold under "Communist Rule." As an insurance plan, other options for manufacturing in Asia were being considered, including Indonesia.

The final plan was to open a state-of-the-art fashion doll manufacturing facility in the developing location near Jakarta, Indonesia. The sophistication of the supply chain there was unknown, especially for the textile industry, and Lawanna Adams was asked to investigate textile sources in that region. By 1991 Lawanna was no longer living in HK. She'd returned to Mattel California headquarters and managed the TSND group long distance. During this year of Indonesia vendor evaluation, I joined Lawanna to check out Indonesian fabric opportunities. This trip was only two weeks away from Melvin and Haris, who promised to patiently wait for me to come home and get ready for Thanksgiving. I hated to leave my boys, but I'd committed to make Mattel successful, part of my **Personal Brand Image**. My impending resignation from Mattel was always on my mind, so this would most likely be my last trip to Asia.

I met Lawanna in HK and then we flew to Jakarta to start our adventure assessing the textile supplier availability, in an effort to support the almost completed Mattel doll manufacturing facility. We had no idea where to start the search. Lawanna basically used a phone directory to identify potential suppliers. They were all at different locations. We needed a driver if the factory was close by, or we arranged short domestic flights on small planes to visit nearby territories. Pretty adventurous when I look back at what we did. We were unaware of the risks for two Western women traveling alone in remote areas near Jakarta. We moved without hesitation, or more appropriately, out of ignorance, to identify the reality of what the textile vendor base was like.

In contrast to HK, Indonesia was in the dark ages. It had the beauty of Hawaii with volcanoes, gorgeous vistas, and lush tropical foliage. However, it was stuck in a time warp of a third-world country. It had great potential, with infrastructure, natural resources, and a large workforce. The capitalist attitude was relaxed and the customer service was almost nonexistent. The vendors we visited weren't very interested in working with Mattel. They mainly produced large quantities of textiles for the Indonesian domestic clothing market. Mattel wasn't big business for them, since only small amounts of fabric could be made into huge quantities of fashions for Barbie. It didn't take much lace to make a Barbie blouse collar.

It was obvious that the new Jakarta factory would have to depend on the fabric supplies from HK, China, Taiwan, or Japan, until the local vendors became more sophisticated and technically advanced, and found profit in low-quantity Barbie orders.

Our next visit was to Seoul, Korea, where Mattel had a small sourcing office. Lawanna wanted me to meet the key vendors they used, to get an understanding of their diversity and capabilities. Seoul had sophisticated, artistically focused people. The textiles Mattel would buy from Korea were all special or fancy novelty fabrics. They were masters of designing unique fabrics and I was impressed with the Korean culture and commitment to doing their creative best.

The night before our last day in Seoul, one of the vendors invited us out for a traditional Korean dinner at a local restaurant. Since it was winter in Korea, we sat on a heated floor with food served on a low table. The vendor ordered all the traditional foods, with lots of cooked, spicy cabbage known as kimchi. This local experience was colorful and flavorful, although as usual, I was cautious and only ate cooked food.

Then huge amounts of raw lettuce were served. You were supposed to fill these leaves with cooked meats, then roll up your selected protein in the lettuce and eat it with your hands. I didn't want to insult my host by refusing the food. I said I was no longer hungry. Lawanna was sitting next to me, shoving all the delicacies with the lettuce into her mouth. She raved how good everything was and insisted I try it. I figured that Lawanna, who was old enough to be my mother and an experienced traveler, would give me sound advice. I proceeded to taste all the various meat combinations with the cold lettuce wraps.

It's a well-known fact that the first thing you're warned not to do when you travel in a foreign country is don't drink the water and don't eat raw food! Lettuce is like a time bomb of bacteria, with the water that is used to grow it and then more water used to wash it for consumption. Within ten minutes after I returned to the hotel, I was terribly ill. I felt so bad that I had to turn off all the lights in the room and lay down on the cold bathroom floor. You can image the rest of the events.

Lawanna arrived at my hotel room early the next morning to take me to another vendor. When I opened the door to my darkened room and she saw my pale face, disheveled clothing, and bent over posture, she was shocked. I told her how sick I was and that I wouldn't be able to leave my room to join her for the day. She was worried, with good reason. I was like a zombie! She said, "Well, I ate the same food, and I'm okay!" Lawanna has been traveling in Asia for over thirty years. Her body probably adjusted to all the foreign bacteria years ago. With her immunity and cast-iron stomach, she didn't worry about the hygiene. Too bad I hadn't realized this the night before, while I was inserting lettuce into my mouth.

Lawanna stopped by my room that evening to check on me. She had a gift to say she was sorry about insisting I eat the lettuce. I didn't blame her—it was my stupidity. The gift was a beautiful wooden box with Korean calligraphy hand-painted on the cover. Inside were six carved celadon, turtle-shaped chopstick holders. Lawanna told me that the turtles symbolize long life. I loved them. I still have these turtles in the original box and I smile when I look at them, since they mark a special milestone of learning not to eat raw lettuce in a foreign country.

After spending a day in complete darkness in my hotel room, I was ready to go back to HK for the last part of my trip. This was my third time visiting HK and working at the Mattel office. I was aware that the pile of fabric submissions would be waiting for me. I knew the solution to this tedious approval process, an onsite team, was in my **Proposal**.

A couple of days before I was scheduled to leave HK, I received a phone call from California from my boss, Bonnie Gretz. Nothing unusual. I expected a call for an update on my trip status. However, Bonnie never asked about my trip. She proceeded to tell me that she'd had a meeting with Don Hartling, and the **Proposal** that I'd written over a year ago, regarding creating a Soft Goods Design and Development group in HK, had been approved by the CEO, Jill Barad.

I was delighted. At last, this would be the start of changing Mattel's business environment. It seemed that the Barbie Brand was growing, the business climate was changing, and delivery schedules needed to be shortened. My **Proposal** was now ready to be implemented. Mattel management realized that this onsite HKSG group would be a step to shorten development time and cut expenses by moving activities and some jobs to HK.

Bonnie asked me to meet with Mattel human resources representative Judy Saylor when I returned to California. Judy would explain the details of an overseas assignment. Surprisingly, I was offered the job to head this team! Mattel wanted me to move HK as soon as possible for a temporary assignment. This was not my plan.

I was perplexed. The **Proposal** was my recommendation for a business process to correct the long lead times and confusion. I had no intention to head this team and the last thing on my mind was to move to HK. I told Bonnie I was flattered by the offer and would speak with her in a few days when I was back in California.

After fourteen years of psychotherapy, I was no longer Dr. D's patient. She felt I was now a "healthy, functioning adult" and could handle all situations. If I needed her I knew she would be there for me. I resisted calling her. Instead I placed a long-distance call to Melvin. I explained the overseas assignment offer and that if I accepted the position, he and Haris would be moving with me to HK.

I went into my monologue of how we could never live in HK. It was dirty, crowded, polluted, and had horrible weather and poor hygiene. What would Melvin do about PhD Textiles? Haris was only four years old. What about school for him? How could I lead a Chinese staff? Melvin stopped me from continuing my ranting, and even though he'd never been to Asia he said, "What's the big deal? It will be an adventure for a couple of years. I have no problem closing down PhD Textiles. I can always reopen it when we return to the US. You can focus on creating this HK team and I will do everything else in HK, including caring for Haris. Take the offer and don't worry. I love you."

I really thought this extreme move would be out of Melvin's comfort zone, since it certainly was out of mine. I sent a message to Judy Saylor and made an appointment to see her upon my return to Mattel California.

I'd never met Judy Saylor before and was anxious to discuss the details of what Mattel was offering me to move to HK. Judy was a very beautiful woman with stunning silver-gray hair, even though she was only in her forties. She was tall, well dressed, and greeted me with a smile and warm handshake. Judy wasted no time explaining Mattel's policy for staff assigned overseas. She took out a document and read the list of what I was to expect if I accepted the assignment in HK, including a promotion to director.

She went on to tell me that I shouldn't worry about any-thing—"Mother Mattel" would take care of me. She advised that in the next few weeks, after Chinese New Year, I was to go to HK with Melvin and Haris to look for housing, check out the schools, and confirm my acceptance of this expatriate assignment. Mattel wanted to relocate me as soon as possible, and this trip was to make sure I felt comfortable with the offer and the living conditions for my family. I had no idea about Mattel's corporate policy for staff being relocated to a foreign country. This all seemed like a dream. The door to a new opportunity was open.

After finding out the details of the Mattel compensation for this assignment, I spoke with Don Hartling. I said that when I wrote my recommendation for this HK team, I wasn't expecting the role to be mine. I was surprised about the offer. I asked him why I was chosen. Don told me that this was a new vision, to have Barbie soft goods approval authority transferred to HK. Mattel needed a strong person who was respected by the design team. There was no other choice than Paulette Bazerman for the HK Director to make this project a success.

As Melvin always says, "If ten people tell you that you are drunk, even if you never had a drink, you should probably lay down."

The Mattel HK expatriate offer was beyond my expectations, not to mention off track from my career and life plans. Melvin, Haris, and I arrived in HK in early February 1992 to familiarize ourselves with the housing choices, schools, and lifestyle. No work assignments this trip, just a week of exploring. Melvin was so happy with everything he saw and experienced. He was amazed at the cosmopolitan atmosphere, the vibrancy of the people, and super-high energy level that was everywhere. "What's not to love?" was his mantra. He never commented on the dirt, pollution, or crowds that I saw. He loved everything.

Haris was only four years old and he thought we were at an amusement park. The taxis, trains, trams, and ferry rides were larger than life and he was happy with all the new visual entertainment. The apartment was selected, the international school was perfect, and our tour was fun, since I had my boys with me. PhD Textiles was closed, my graduate school internship was on indefinite hold.

This was the city I'd never wanted to return to and now I was seeing HK with a different set of eyes, through my family. I knew I had to act appropriately and most importantly, I could never show signs that I was actually scared out of my mind!

I accepted the Mattel Director of HKSG position. The Bazerman family would be relocating to HK on April 3, 1992, the Chinese Year of the Monkey.

Personal Brand Image:

Big opportunities can be scary. Don't be chicken—take them on.

Chapter 12

Way out Far East

My life was total chaos in March 1992, after Melvin, Haris, and I had returned to California from our HK "look-see" trip. Judy Saylor gave me an acceptance letter, which was nothing more than an informal document letting me know Mattel's financial responsibilities for housing, Haris's school, taxes, and living allowances while I was on assignment in HK. This was only valid if I wasn't doing anything derelict or criminal. The letter wasn't a contract; it was basically identifying me as an at-will employee. In other words, I could be terminated at Mattel's discretion for any reason and lose the benefits. There was no mention if Mattel would offer me another position back in the US, nor any time given as to when the assignment would be completed. Mattel was committing to huge expenses by leasing my HK apartment for two years, paying for our furniture storage in LA and moving costs for the items we wanted to bring to HK. They had an investment in me and I had my **Personal Brand Image** as a strong leader to maintain.

I never wanted to live in HK and in my mind this unknown, foreign place was just a stopover. Basically, this was an official way to say I had another temporary job.

The news that I would relocate to HK and train a team responsible for onsite Barbie soft goods approvals received a mixed response from my Mattel colleagues. The executives that approved my **Proposal**, as well as the design and marketing teams, were thrilled with my assignment. Because of my relationship with them, I was trusted to make decisions in HK to improve the process and insure that Barbie's fashions were gorgeous.

On the other side, the SGE group in California projected very negative energy toward me regarding my relocation. They didn't think I could change the process in HK, and in some ways they hoped I wouldn't change it, because their positions would become less important and possibly nonexistent. Perhaps they were right and this could eventually mean Mattel job losses in the US. This was a political situation I was prepared to tactfully neutralize and hopefully eliminate. I couldn't succeed if I had a team in California that would sabotage my efforts. I just added this to my long list of what I had to overcome.

After the many goodbyes, dinners, and spontaneous parties, we were packed and ready to leave LA. Melvin closed up our PhD Textiles business and told his customers he would return in a couple of years. Haris partied with his friends at preschool and was oblivious to the stress of the move. This was all fun for him. He was on an adventure, would have a great new school, and Dad would be home with him while I worked.

We arrived in HK and quickly picked up the fast-paced rhythm of the city as we departed the plane. I had an entirely different outlook upon arrival than on the previous trips I'd made to HK. All those other visits were wrapped with the deep sadness of being away from Melvin and Haris. I had my own imagined terror in a culture, in which I had no idea how I was going to survive alone. The major HK complaints that I talked about for years were now non-issues. Home is where your family is, and my family was with me in HK. Therefore, starting on day one of our new life in Asia, HK now seemed to be covered with lucky gold dragons instead of dirt, pollution, poor hygiene, and noisy crowds.

The plan was to go directly from the HK airport to The Great Eagle Hotel in Tsim Sha Tsui, Kowloon, a few blocks from the Mattel office. This hotel would be our temporary home because our new flat (the term for apartment) wasn't ready for us and our personal belongings from the US were arriving on a ship in a few weeks. The flat was across Victoria Harbour on HK Island, a thirty-minute public transportation journey via a ferry sailing over the harbor or a train riding under the harbor. Then a short taxi ride up the hill to our new home.

Victoria Harbour is HK's lifeline, wide enough for ships to dock, and is the main picturesque tourist attraction, with extremely beautiful views that capture the famous HK skyline. The majority of housing on HK Island is high-rise buildings, or as this New Yorker would say, skyscrapers. HK is a compact city out of necessity, with only 420 square miles and seven million people, it's slightly smaller than New York City. The British had colonized HK for over 150 years and had a scheme to limit the release of land for housing. Therefore the demand was always higher than the supply, and property value escalated to beyond imagination, making real estate in HK some of the most expensive in the world. Our new flat was in a prime location on HK Island called Mid-Levels. We selected this location because it was convenient for me to commute to my office and only a ten-minute car ride to the Hong Kong International School, where Haris would be attending primary school.

The building we selected to call home was on famous Old Peak Road and had just finished construction, which meant we were the first tenants. When we'd visited two months earlier, Mattel's real estate agent showed us flats that were within the Mattel budget. The standard for HK buildings in 1992 was below our expectations. The flats weren't westernized or modern and sort of had an institutional atmosphere, with exposed pipes, wires running along the floors and walls, and absolutely no aesthetics. However, when we entered Queens Garden, at 9 Old Peak Road on the eighth floor, we were overwhelmed with the contemporary style and modern, Western features. The flat was on three levels, with floor-to-ceiling windows in each room and a stunning view of the HK skyline and Victoria Harbour.

Most local residents lived in small 400-800 square foot flats (larger than my Brooklyn one-room). By HK standards our new home was huge, at over 2,000 square feet. Of course, the rent for a flat like this was huge as well, the equivalent of US $6,000 per month plus management fees.

Mattel recognized that it is overwhelming to move to a foreign country, far away from everything you're familiar with, and didn't expect work to go well if your home life wasn't up to US standards. In 1992 Mattel's US staff had no desire to move to HK. Mattel had to make the offer attractive. Mattel's expense to support me and my family would be worth it if my business assignment succeeded. This is why I say that Mattel made a big investment in me, and I felt obligated to give them the best result possible and prove I was worth all the privileges that came with this HK position.

Personal Brand Image:

To maximize what you get from a job, maximize what you give to it.

Melvin and Haris had planned a day of exploration to see what the real HK was like, since Haris didn't start preschool for another week. As I've noted many times, Melvin is extremely spontaneous and I did worry that he was over his head, on an adventure in a foreign city with a cute four-year-old boy. My last words to Melvin as I left the hotel room for my first day on my new job were "Don't lose the kid!"

I slowly walked the few blocks from my hotel to the Mattel office. Even though the walk was short it was filled with fascinating sights of modern high-rise glass buildings, waste-collection vehicles with shirtless men loading debris from the late-night activities, glass being chopped into pieces to fit into the garbage truck, and the strong scent of tea and fresh-baked bread filling the alleyways. All very entertaining and stimulating, turning up my energy level that was already on high anxiety. I had visited this Mattel office a few months earlier and selected the location for my team, in a small corner of the Mattel office on the eleventh floor.

The vice president of that organization was Mr. Ron Montalto, also an expatriate transferred from Mattel California a few years prior. I hadn't met Ron before. His personality was extraordinary. He was about my age and though I'm unsure how tall he is, my five foot two inch self was like a small seed in the grass next to a fully grown palm tree. Ron was an extremely intelligent manager and negotiator. Before his career at Mattel he'd been a lawyer in Atlanta, Georgia. His ability to twist words and manipulate everything he touched to reach his goal was truly a work of art to admire. My New York Attitude was activated every time I engaged with Ron.

Ron Montalto was like my landlord at the office, not my boss. My new department was part of Design and Development. Ron was there with his staff only to support my administrative needs. He was the guy you wanted as your friend if you were to survive at Mattel HK.

There was another Ron in HK to help me. This was Ron Drwinga, the gentleman I'd met on previous HK trips, before the Mattel organization expanded. Mr. Drwinga was a few years older and only a few inches taller than me. Ron Drwinga had started at Mattel in California in 1965 as an industrial engineer. By 1970 he was one of the pioneers to be transferred to the HK office as manager of finance.

Mr. Drwinga tells an interesting story about how he was a costing engineer when he worked in Mattel California, before being transferred to HK. His financial background was limited, as he'd explained to his Mattel management. He could balance a checkbook, had only three postgrad courses in Accounting 101, and was unsure he was qualified for this new HK position as manager of finance. Ron's boss assured him this wasn't an issue and that the accounting in HK was under control. The opposite was true. When he arrived in HK the budget balance sheets didn't balance and the year-end statements were three months late. Welcome to HK! (I advised Ron he should write his own book.)

Twenty-two years later, Ron is still in HK after his "on-the-job training" experience, which resulted in his success at every assignment, and he was now the Regional Controller and Director of Human Resources in HK. Therefore, Ron Drwinga was my go-to man to help me set up my HK office. He was my role model for how to accomplish goals with limited knowledge or any precedent in Asia.

I inherited six staff from another department and it was my responsibility to teach this group how to get it right. These six HK employees, transferred to HKSG, seemed shocked to be faced with an American, Caucasian, female boss who had only spent a few days over the past year in HK. If I'd been from another planet, with green skin and fangs, I would've received the same welcome. I reported directly to California, which caused my HK colleagues to think I'd be a loose cannon rather than a competent leader.

Not everyone at Mattel HK was fluent in English, so a language barrier prevented me from easily communicating. I had to speak slowly, with simple vocabulary, and repeat my comments multiple times. Even then I wasn't sure my meaning was being understood. The majority of people in HK under the age of forty spoke basic English, since HK was a British colony and English was the official compulsory language in schools.

My six new staff were all young HK women skilled in soft goods engineering, cost calculating and sewn sample development. This was the start of my plan to develop and approve Barbie fashions. The new staff was politely welcoming, but seemed intimidated by me because I was a foreigner who was there to teach them something new. They were anxious and insecure about the future of the department and security of their jobs.

My other Mattel colleagues were either local HK staff or fellow expatriates. I do mean "fellow," since I was the only female expatriate working for Mattel in HK and Mattel Asia in 1992. The guys perceived me as a weak woman in charge of what they considered insignificant Barbie fashion aesthetics. This role of "aesthetic authority" was unimpressive to the many engineer-degreed men of Mattel. In addition to being the new expatriate, my job description was unclear, and my male peers didn't respect me. I knew I would never be one of the "good old boys." This opinion didn't develop out of the air, based on my own insecurities. This opinion was based on clear examples of what I had to deal with, and the enormous effort I expended to change the way I was perceived.

The vice president and general manager of the Mattel HK (MHK) manufacturing facility in China was another US expatriate, Mr. John McMullen, who'd headed the factory since 1976. John was a few years older than me and well respected for his long assignment in Asia and leadership role. He was extremely outspoken and opinionated, so much so that it was easier to like him for his remarks than find fault. John seemed to have no respect for me. He was ready to argue with me no matter what I said. On my last HK trip in November 1991, before I was offered the HK assignment, I was in a meeting with John and about fifty other staff. John publicly argued with me and shouted, "I would rather suck on a lead pipe than work with you!" So you can image how he felt when I showed up in HK a few months later to be one of his Mattel partners. I refrained from saying, "Pucker your lips, John!"

The relationships with the other executives and my peers were secondary to getting my team created and trained. I decided to adopt a "wait and see" strategy, until I learned the reality of the working environment and how I could best establish my **Personal Brand Image** as a boss, not just an employee. I had a vision, but no step-by-step plan of how I was going to make my **Proposal** successful. I'd worked at Mattel California, but I had no mentor, no detailed process to implement, no experience leading a team to handle my expanded scope of unfamiliar responsibilities. Most importantly, I lacked passion for the famous Barbie doll, which I still felt was just a piece of stupid plastic! I had New York Attitude, textile expertise, a good memory, a great eye for aesthetics, the intense desire never to fail, and yes, one more thing: the ability to focus on what I do best until it's a success.

The plan was for me to hire another three staff to make HKSG a fully functioning team. You can have all the great recipes for cooking a gourmet dinner, but if you don't have the right ingredients available, the end result is tasteless and your customer will take their business to another restaurant. If the new staff didn't have the special skills, personality, and passion, I wouldn't be able to create a great banquet for my Mattel California customers, and the business would fail.

The role of a secretary in HK is very different than what we think of in the US. This position is more of an assistant. Especially in the case of an expatriate. I needed someone with fluent spoken and written English ability, as well as the added responsibility to support personal arrangements for my whole family when needed. This was a top priority, to find a secretary with skills to help me start the business and a personality to fit with my Western style.

It was only a matter of weeks until I interviewed Bobo Choi, a Chinese woman in her late twenties. Although born in HK, Bobo was a Canadian citizen who'd recently returned to HK with her lawyer boyfriend. Bobo was about five feet nine inches tall. She towered over the petite Chinese women and me. More noticeable than her impressive height was her physical beauty. Bobo was gorgeous, like a *Vogue* magazine model, with her long black hair, perfect Hollywood appearance, and fashionable style, including high heels that made her about six feet tall.

Bobo was technically qualified and as a Canadian citizen, she was fluent in English. What most impressed me about Bobo was her aggressive almost "New York Attitude." It was important to me to have a strong assistant at my side, to compensate for my incredible lack of knowledge about HK and to translate into Chinese my intentions rather than just words. I hired Bobo immediately.

The next day I got a phone call from Bobo. She told me that she needed to change her English name from Bobo to Nicole. The English names of the HK Chinese are either chosen for them by a teacher or relative, or they randomly select a name for themselves. Therefore you can come across unusual names like Cinderella Wong, Queenie Wu, or King Lee! When Bobo called me to change her English name, I wasn't surprised. Nicole arrived the next day and before I could escort her to the office, she let me know that she'd consulted her fortune teller and the name Nicole wouldn't bring her good luck. So her English name was now Norma. I did mention she had attitude.

Norma (yes, that name remained) was hell on wheels and I loved it. She walked—no, strutted—into the office and her physical beauty was the talk of the office. Her high energy level, charm, and outgoing personality were exactly what I needed to kick off the new era of my management style. The malaise due to the recent organization changes and my arrival were sobering, and Norma helped me make the statement that HKSG wasn't business as usual!

Personal Brand Image:

The people you hire must be a reflection of your Brand and have the ability to implement your visions.

Two other key positions were needed. The first was a sample room supervisor. HKSG would be making sample fashion prototypes. They needed to be sewn not just with technical perfection, but also with specific aesthetics for Barbie. Sewing a fashion for an eleven-and-a-half-inch doll is much more difficult than sewing human clothing. The small details that make the fashions more realistic need to be sewn with both skill and an eye to understanding how to improve the aesthetics for samples as well as mass production. The aesthetics had to be the same for one handmade showroom sample and for 100,000 units for production.

Every lump, bump, or twist will be noticed if the clothing doesn't fit properly. The HKSG samples were to be used for toy show samples and package photos. They had to be top-of-the-line perfection. When you buy clothes for humans, they're usually selected on a hanger in a boutique. Imperfections are only noticed when you actually try on the clothes. However, Barbie's clothes are already dressed on the doll and must look perfect on the tiny plastic body, especially the samples that serve as the production standard.

I had no problem teaching Barbie aesthetics, but I had no production sewing knowledge. I don't know how to sew. I only took one sewing class in high school. I therefore needed a supervisor who had a garment manufacturing background, spoke English, and was willing to learn.

Mattel's Barbie fashion development was unique. The chances of getting someone capable from the toy industry was close to zero because Mattel was the leader in fashion dolls. I did what any manager would do in the same situation—ask her secretary for help. I told Norma what I needed to get the job done. Norma thought for a minute and recommended someone she knew was perfect for the position.

I interviewed Jessica Choi the next day. Jessica was in her late thirties, dressed very conservatively and rather quiet, mostly due to her English not being totally fluent. She had experience supervising a sample room and proficiency with embroidery techniques. Something about Jessica that made an impression with me. She had an intense passion for the sewing business and a soft, caring manner. Jessica really wanted the job, and her warm personality compelled me to have her as part of my team. I felt she would care for every Barbie sample that touched her hands. This was exactly the type of staff that would make us successful.

She started the next week and kept her English name as Jessica.

The second key position was textile engineer (TE), similar to the position I had when I'd started at Mattel. I needed a TE to work with the fabric vendors and interpret the sketches or samples from the California designers. This person had to be fluent in English, have good communication skills, be a textile expert, and be open to my mentoring on how to do the job.

This was another difficult position to fill and even after asking for Norma's help, she had no recommendation. However, one of my colleagues, an expatriate assigned to the HK office a few months before I'd arrived, had an idea. Since some of his team's work had been transferred to my new group, he offered to transfer one of his staff to my team.

There was no question in my mind that I wanted Miss Winnie Kwok, one of the senior Mattel staff, to transfer to my team. I had met Winnie in California when she'd visited Mattel on a short work assignment a couple of years earlier. I took her to lunch and was impressed with her excellent English, friendly character, and great work ethic. When I arrived in HK on my new assignment, it was Winnie Kwok who'd invited me to a traditional dim sum (dumplings) lunch on my first day.

Over the years I'd worked with Winnie long distance and knew how smart and effective she was. She would be perfect. I made her an offer to join my team and she graciously declined. She didn't want to take on the challenge and was happy with her current position. My persuasive speech was useless. Winnie wasn't crossing over to my team. I literally begged her with the promise of a better career opportunity but Winnie wasn't interested. My first failure on the new job.

There was another qualified person at Mattel, Mr. Midas Ho. He was a well-educated young man is his late twenties, technically competent, and I thought I could train him since he didn't have much Mattel experience—in other words, no bad habits. I had a more convincing influence with Midas and he agreed to transfer and take the TE position.

With nine persons on staff, we were ready to develop seventy-five Barbie fashions. These were the fashion accessories sold without a Barbie doll, the less high-profile soft goods items and my opportunity to prove my **Proposal** was correct. The key words to remember are "ready to develop." The staff was in the office, but not even close to being ready!

Personal Brand Image:

Ready or not, just do it. Being wrong is better than doing nothing.

Chapter 13

Riding the Dragon

HK was similar to NYC, and at times I felt I was back in the Big Apple, with the addition of incredibly delicious Chinese food. When I was a young girl, my dream was to someday marry and live in a NYC penthouse with a grand view. Well, my dream came true. I married a handsome, loving man who is the rock star of my life. And I was living in an apartment with one of the most fabulous city views in the world. Yes, I finally got my penthouse—I just never thought that I would be the one providing it, in Hong Kong.

During weekdays, my daily routine at 6 a.m. was to grind the coffee beans, brew fresh coffee for Melvin and me, prepare Haris's lunch and pack it for him to take to preschool, then dress in my carefully coordinated ensemble and finally head out the door.

Our building had a shuttle bus that transported tenants to the ferry terminal. I was joined on the shuttle bus by six to eight expatriate men wearing business suits, who were making the same trip to the ferry. I was usually the only woman boarding the bus at 7 a.m. Melvin would be standing on the curb with Haris and six to eight women, obviously the wives of the gentlemen on the bus with me, huddled next to them.

These expatriate men couldn't believe that I was the working spouse and my husband was staying at home like their wives. Melvin waved goodbye, smiled at the men on the shuttle bus. In return they chuckled with envy that my husband was in a T-shirt and shorts on a hot, humid day while they were wearing formal suits and silk ties, sweat dripping from their brows.

The less than ten-minute bus ride down the hill connected me with the entrance to the **Star Ferry**. This is an amazing public transport system and the ride is one of the most fun things to do in HK. The **Star Ferry Company, Ltd.** was established in 1898 to transport people across Victoria Harbour. Depending on nautical traffic this is a ten-minute journey, sailing from Central HK to Tsim Sha Tsui, Kowloon, in a double-decker, wooden, three hundred-seat passenger boat. This was the most relaxing part of my day. There are many ferries in this fleet, all conveniently named describing stars—i.e., Morning Star, Rising Star, Solar Star, Twinkling Star, etc. The boats weren't modernized, just kept in pristine condition with wooden flooring, wooden seats with metal frames, and a wooden gangplank that was manually lowered or hoisted to enable passengers to enter or exit the ferry. A brief note here about this "wooden gangplank," which had one-inch wide, raised wooden strips running horizontally across the plank to help your feet grip. Sort of like the plank a pirate would make you walk before you fell overboard and drowned in the sea!

It was as if I were a time traveler sailing the harbor one hundred years ago. For a few minutes I would meditate and be so very alone in a sea of hundreds of people commuting to work. Great therapy for a reasonable fee of twenty-five cents. What an amazing bargain in this astronomically expensive city. After exiting the Star Ferry gangplank I then had a short walk to my office building, adjacent to the ferry dock. The whole exercise in traveling from home to Mattel was thirty minutes.

As was my habit to dress professionally every day for the office, I always wore a tailored jacket, a short skirt, and fashionable high-heeled shoes. One morning the rain was very heavy, and I didn't have much open-air walking to do. However, when the gangplank was lowered for the passengers to exit/enter, I was unavoidably exposed to heavy rain and needed to walk carefully on the gangplank. The unusual amount of rain drenched the ferry exit and as I stepped on the plank I immediately lost my balance on the slippery surface. I fell hard, with both knees onto the wet wooden surface. Just like NYC, no one helped me up and the other passengers hurried by me as I managed to stand up and move to my seat. After the shock of what happened I looked down and saw that both my knees were bleeding. Because I was wearing a skirt the injury was completely visible. I also had no tissues to absorb the blood that was running down my legs into my shoes.

I hobbled to my office, overwhelmed with pain and embarrassment. My knees really hurt and I couldn't manage to walk to the bathroom and wash myself. With my head on my desk, I waited for Norma to arrive. Luckily for me she was early. I saw her enter the office and I motioned her to see me. As she came closer I pointed to my knees and she jumped back in shock. Bravely I told her I was okay, but I needed something to the wash off the blood and cover my knees. We had no first-aid kit so Norma went into emergency mode, took a piece of cotton fabric from the storeroom, and wrapped my knees to stop the bleeding while she got some water from the bathroom. I sat in pain with this T-shirt fabric below my skirt as part of my fashion accessory. Lesson learned on how to walk the plank carefully!

The new staff was hired and I arranged to have a department meeting meant to present the year's target goals and inspire. I had no plan as to what I was going to say. I wanted to be culturally appropriate and not start off with any shocking statement or visual display that might be entertaining, but would completely alienate a team already intimidated by my mere existence.

We all gathered in the conference room and in a soft-spoken manner, I discussed the challenges we had and the training needed. I emphasized that together we were a team and I wanted everyone's input on how they felt we could achieve the goals. The team effort was part of the Mattel California culture and this philosophy is what I was bringing to HK. I wanted the staff to be part of the decision planning, to insure their commitment to the new process.

I asked my nine staff, comprised of the six transferred Mattel HK members and the three new hires, for their comments and ideas. Looking around the room, there were blank stares and silence from everyone. I now truly understood what the expression "dead silence" meant. I felt as if I were going to die! No comments, no changes of expression, no movements except for the slight heaving of their chests when they inhaled and exhaled as a sign of life. Even Norma was quiet. If I were a standup comic you might have said I'd just laid a bomb and needed to be taken off stage immediately, never to return. Struggling to keep my composure, I told the team they should think about my update and give me feedback when we regrouped the next day.

Needless to say I was very surprised. As I entered my office I was wiping the tears from my eyes and taking deep breaths to avoid making hysterical sounds. I would have had more reaction from children in a kindergarten class on their first day at school than from these professional adults. I was mortified. What did I do wrong?

From my past HK trips and over the previous few weeks I'd observed that the HK people were very hard working and had quiet personalities. Formality and loyalty at work was respected and I didn't want to overwhelm them, since they were already considerably overwhelmed by this "Female American Expatriate Boss." I was at a loss as to what I could do. Each day I went to the office there was only politeness—no feedback, and no emotion. I had no connection with my staff. I felt that being on location in HK was no different than working long distance in California. I was unprepared for this response. I cannot say it was negative; it was just indifferent.

For the first time in the twenty-two years of all my careers, I had a lack of communication with my colleagues. Communication is one of my strengths and now I seemed to be failing at my own specialty!

I was over being teary eyed. I was now depressed.

I told Melvin that I didn't think I could overcome the problem. I couldn't imagine being at this job for the next two years, where the result would be complete failure. Melvin was supportive, but he had no idea either as to what I could do. He had faith in who I was. The problem wasn't me—it was a HK cultural issue. I had no mentor to ask for guidance and seeking advice from Mattel California would only make them think I was a poor leader. I'd never considered the Asian cultural factor when creating this team. The HK work concept wasn't teamwork focused, but instead focused on individuals doing their own jobs well to please the boss. I had to reverse the situation. My team lectures meant nothing to them.

For the next few months I explained to my staff the basics of how the California designers created the Barbie fashions and the aesthetic requirements. These lessons went on for weeks because I had to show many visual samples, repeat the directions many times, and ask Norma to translate into Cantonese to be sure everyone understood. This sharing was educational and I was accomplishing something. Applying the aesthetic theory is very difficult. After all, it is a philosophy of art and beauty, a subjective balance. When the item is looked at, it should give the viewer a good feeling. This concept is difficult to teach and depending on the individual, it could be impossible to understand.

Designing and developing clothing for Barbie is an art that changes with fashion trends. However, we can still appreciate a dress on Barbie from the 1960s because it has a certain style, balance, and excellent execution, all of which make the viewer feel connected with Barbie. The same principle as when a meticulously dressed man or woman walks into a room and gets noticed by everyone. Cultures around the world all have different ideas of what is aesthetically pleasing. My goal was to make the HK team understand what characteristics made Barbie fashions appealing to Western customers. Most importantly, to girls three to ten years old. The HK staff was unaware of Western styles and what would sell in Mattel's main consumer market, the US.

The office's quiet atmosphere didn't improve. Staff only spoke to me when work was involved. I was isolated and unhappy. After a couple months of being frustrated, I decided to try a different approach. What did I have to lose? The mood at work couldn't be much worse. Since I was the director I decided to "direct," take authority and tell the staff what to do on their projects. The team consensus approach wasn't working. I realized my staff was in preschool as far as knowing what Mattel needed. Just like in school, the teacher sets the rules because young children have no experience with how to conduct themselves.

The Chinese highly respect their teachers and never confront them. The cultural differences between the US and HK were obvious and I had overlooked this in my **Proposal**, particularly with regard to training time needed. This was why my team wasn't verbal with me—they were respectfully waiting for direction from their teacher. I wasn't going to get input from them. In addition the staff was insecure about their English language skills, another factor I hadn't considered in my **Proposal**.

Personal Brand Image:

Analyze problems rather than stay frustrated.

My staff never called me by my given name or surname. They called me *Loban*, which loosely translates from Chinese as "old boss." When I found out what Loban meant I thought it was insulting. In all my American jobs I'd never addressed the person I reported to as "boss" and certainly not with the rude phrase "old boss." Every morning when I arrived at the office I was greeted with *Jo-san, Loban* ("Good morning, old boss") from my team, as well as other Mattel staff who didn't even work for me. I soon learned that this wasn't disrespectful. On the contrary, it was a sign of respect. The Chinese look to the boss as a teacher and being old in the Asian culture means you have knowledge. The staff was letting me know they respected me and wanted me to "boss" them—that is, teach them my knowledge.

I now realized what my job was in HK: direct the team to reach the goals. I decided to really live up to my director title and actually **direct** everyone.

My **Personal Brand Image** had been voluntarily silenced for months. The person I was in HK wasn't the same person who used her special Brand of individuality to become successful. What Mattel HK needed was a team that the California office could relate to and eventually trust with decision making. The aesthetics would take years to grasp and the way to assimilate into this US company was to understand the US aesthetics and demonstrate to the California designers that HK was aligned with their intent. On the other hand, I needed to assimilate in HK as well and be a DIRECTOR not just a "temporary expatriate visitor."

I had to change my approach and return to the **Personal Brand Image** that had gotten me this job, before I became my worst nightmare: boring!

The days of "we are a team—let's share our ideas" were officially over.

Chapter 14

Wonder Woman

There was no choice. Without any executive experience to draw from, I rekindled my New York Attitude and moved right into transforming myself into a **Wonder Woman**. It was just as if I were walking the perilous 1970s NYC streets as a single girl, being a target for robbery, fighting poverty, and avoiding violence. In NYC I lived looking over my shoulder and walking quickly. I was aware, as I was now with my new job, that at any moment I could be attacked or perhaps even worse, unemployed.

I didn't know how to accomplish getting those who worked for me to be independent thinkers. The only tactic that worth trying was to put my **Wonder Woman** performance into action. Yes, I did have many bold metal cuff bracelets to create the image, and I actually wore them as a physical statement to encourage the perception of magical power and to psychologically make me feel strong. My performance was a daily display of "I can do anything and if anyone upsets my staff I will obliterate them."

I was no longer going to be a quiet observer getting used to my new environment. Instead my environment needed to get used to me. No gun, knife, or pepper spray needed—just New York Attitude projecting a positive, can-do spirit. The lesson from Dr. D to act appropriately for the situation, no matter how I felt emotionally, was exactly the reason I decided to display extraordinary **Wonder Woman** powers. I had to be bigger than life, even though I felt small, inadequate, and underqualified to be the director of Hong Kong Soft Goods.

Wearing my stylish rhinestone-studded jacket and thick silver cuff bracelets to my next staff meeting, I told everyone that I would work with them individually, so I could review and direct what they were doing, in addition to the weekly group lessons. I directed the team not to evaluate anything on their own until it was reviewed with me. I really didn't expect or want to do this, but during my few weeks on the job, I'd observed that everyone was at a low competency level. They were all technically capable, but had no feel or understanding regarding Barbie aesthetics and feared making independent decisions.

Technical textile engineering from a HK school didn't give my staff the needed skills for aesthetic concepts, or the eye to judge what was fashionable for Barbie. The small, twinkling details and meticulous color matching that humanized Barbie had never been a priority in the educational curriculum. Not to mention that almost everyone in HK was dressed in black or gray from head to foot. I stuck to wearing bright colors, bold jewelry, and rhinestones to set the tone for what was to come.

Personal Brand Image:

Lead by example and exaggerate to make your point.

Even with all my work experience and having lived in the US, it took me months to understand Barbie aesthetics when I started at Mattel. The challenge now was to convert from sketches or handsewn fashion samples into manufacturable Barbie clothing and approve them for mass production. We would only consult with California if we had a problem. I needed to make sure this first HK collection met or exceeded all standards. Although this was still a honeymoon period for my team, I wasn't going allow any errors to break the confidence that Mattel California gave to me. I micromanaged everything.

I observed that the staff only felt comfortable when asked to match or copy. Matching a standard versus making a decision when something looks good are two different concepts. In some respects I could relate to what was happening. When I'd started at Mattel I had no idea how to evaluate fabrics for a doll. What was all the fuss about? She's just a piece of plastic! I couldn't understand why a little girl would care if the clothes fit or looked real on a doll. It's just pretend.

I was missing the point. The more realistically Barbie was dressed, the more attracted the girl was to purchase the doll and dream she could be like Barbie, a career woman. In other words, Barbie ignited the imagination. If the fashion wasn't stylish or realistic, the girl wouldn't identify with Barbie and the dream ended. Barbie's fashion was the main attraction and my staff needed to learn how to see and feel the aesthetics, not just copy a sketch.

The burden was on me to review hundreds of fabric colors. Meet with vendors to explain the requirements. Analyze every fashion for fit to make sure Barbie was perfectly dressed. Sharing my critique was part of the training so my team could understand, by my example, how to evaluate projects. The result was a long line of staff outside my office door every day, all day, waiting their turn to meet with me. It looked as if I were giving away prizes and everyone lined up to receive the gifts.

I had no time for my own communications. Due to the 16 hour time difference, I left voicemails for the California team from my home after dinner and reading to Haris before his bedtime. Back in the office in the morning I spent the first couple of hours listening to my voicemail updates from California and replying either by recording a message or calling them directly.

I proceeded with my plan to direct everyone on every detail of their projects. This meant I was never alone in my office. I needed to review, coach, and write down in English what they needed to do, and explain my meaning in multiple ways to be sure they understood the concept. A ten-minute discussion for fluent English speakers would become a twenty- to thirty-minute explanation. Every person received my undivided and kind attention, which hopefully made them feel more confident to make their own decisions in the future. If I couldn't get everyone passionate about our mission and their job, then the vision I had would be extinguished.

You would think this hovering over my staff would cause them frustration or produce feelings of inadequacy. On the contrary, the reaction I got was positive and for the first time the staff appreciated this training. I was **Wonder Woman** in action, protecting them from the evil forces of failure. Without detailed guidance Mattel California would tell them their decision making was wrong. This would be discouraging, to say the least, and unproductive. I had to build confidence even though I was doing most of the work myself, by reviewing and advising on every detail for everyone.

My staff was more comfortable replying with short answers, since English wasn't their primary language. This brief style of speaking and writing seemed rude, and I decided it was best for me to be the only one to directly speak with Mattel California. To avoid misinterpretation and to make the California designers feel confident with HK capabilities, I wrote all my staff's communications. Then they would send the messages or documents to the US, using the dialogue I'd written. They signed their names as if the words were their own. Yes, this could be considered deception, but I felt it was a learning experience and prevented California's unnecessary criticism of writing style and potentially ruining our morale.

Of course, this never would've been an acceptable management style in the US, but I wasn't in the US and the HK team was supposed to have the same methodology as Mattel California. This was a long-term education program and I had to go into emergency mode. My intention was to have the end justify the means.

Personal Brand Image:

Set a high standard by your own example.

One part of my life was involved with the intense activity to organize, train, and inspire HKSG. This was secondary to my main assignment of making sure Melvin and Haris were adjusting to life in HK. I knew Melvin would acclimate to almost anything, with his pioneer spirit. I wasn't worried about him. Four-year-old Haris was my major concern. We'd changed everything familiar to him. He was young enough to adapt, but all he'd known of his California life was no longer available. Everything would be different—his home, friends, school, and even food took on a new look and definitely a new taste. We did our best to keep Haris's life stable and focused on being dependable parents.

I'm not sure how secure Haris felt when I asked him for a big favor to help me with a problem.

It was only a few months into my job. Mattel California was adding a rush project and requested my team's help to expedite development to meet the production schedule. This was exactly the type of assignment that would provide a great example of how to smoothly implement a project and highlight that the HK group was capable. A new Barbie doll was being introduced and it wasn't your ordinary Barbie. This doll was thirty-six inches tall and meant to wear clothing that could be shared with a real girl. It was appropriately called **My Size Barbie**. This was a "role-play doll" that had a fashion transformation feature, where the costume could be changed from a pink princess gown into a glittering, fluffy, pink ballerina tutu.

We had developed all of the fashions but needed to confirm that Barbie's clothes would fit a human girl three to ten years old. We did have a mannequin the size of an average ten-year-old American girl, to evaluate how big the costume should be to stretch and fit a child. But the mannequin couldn't tell me if the costumes were comfortable to wear and to play in. If the size didn't accommodate both Barbie and a little girl, there absolutely would be customer returns and bad publicity for Mattel. We had no test lab in HK and I had no access to American-sized girls to use as fit models. We only had a few days to approve the soft goods to stay on schedule. I really wanted to make this rush project successful and show Mattel California that my team could handle any request.

Out of desperation to expedite the assignment, I asked Haris if he would be my "fit model" for the My Size Barbie doll. He was nearly five years old now, with a slim build and could represent a seven- or eight-year-old little girl. I could at least have some input on how the costume fit on a human. I thought this was a reasonable idea.

Haris was outraged and refused to help me! This was the worst possible request I could ask of a little boy I was trying make feel secure in his new environment. I did what any resourceful **Wonder Woman Mother** with New York Attitude would do. I begged him and offered him a new **Teenage Mutant Ninja Turtle** toy if he would help me. Haris agreed to my bribe on two conditions—I couldn't take a photo or ever tell anyone about him wearing Barbie clothes! He insisted that not even his dad could see him, and he made Melvin stay in the bedroom behind closed doors. I agreed to the secrecy. (I can only imagine how Haris is feeling right now at twenty-nine years old, reading this incident in his mother's book.)

Haris was a Prince not a Princess to do this for me. As agreed, Haris and I, with Dad locked in the bedroom, held the fit session at home in the privacy of our living room. It was all I could do not to laugh at the sight of my handsome son in a glittering, pink, full-length gown/tutu and pink ballet slippers. After he put on the dress I asked him in a serious, professional tone to move, walk around, and give me feedback about the comfort level. Haris adapted to his job and was able to tell me the fabric was scratchy and uncomfortable on his arms, and the elastic was too tight, which hurt him. A mannequin couldn't give this feedback. This was exactly the information I needed.

Wonder Woman Mom probably wasn't very wonderful in making Haris part of this work assignment. I was so happy to have my son involved in my first urgent Mattel project and grateful for his secret assignment cooperation. I now officially take the opportunity to put into print and publicly apologize to Haris Marc Cristopher Bazerman for any distress or humiliation I caused him as a **My Size Barbie** fit model.

Personal Brand Image:

Do whatever it takes to get the job done, without being a criminal or a monster.

Chapter 15

Change

I was quickly learning that a **Proposal** is only a plan or a suggestion based on what you know at the time you make the **Proposal**. It will need to be updated and changed when the unexpected happens.

Culture Shock

While my intense staff training was underway, the ladies in the sample room, where Jessica Choi was supervising the sewing of Barbie fashions, encountered personal health issues. Jessica was suffering from coughing and throat problems, and one of the senior staff reporting to her was diagnosed with breast cancer. One by one the sample department ladies were becoming ill and visibly concerned about their work space atmosphere. Jessica advised me that the sample room location was a problem and the staff was worried. She claimed that the room had bad luck, which was causing the illnesses. Jessica told me that the sample room must have bad **feng shui**.

I thought this was ridiculous. How could a room be bad luck and what is "feng shui" anyway? For a better understanding of the Chinese culture I asked some colleagues about feng shui, which literally means "wind and water" and is a method of harmonizing humans with the environment. It's the interpretation of how to balance man with nature and his surroundings. I initially dismissed this as worthless superstition, but the illnesses in that room were increasing and the mood in the office was fear. It certainly was a fact that the sample room staff were becoming ill and my other staff, in another room, didn't have any health issues. I was in a part of the world that for centuries had believed in and practiced feng shui. Considering the ancient method and the current problem, I had to do something.

My only reliable source to keep me balanced between Mattel and Chinese culture was my colleague Mr. Ron Drwinga. I trusted that sharing this issue with him wouldn't result in laughter, ridicule, or dismissing my inquiry. Ron was patient with me as I shared the bad luck rumor details and asked for advice. Ron leaned back in his chair and smiled. Not a smirk, but a comforting, friendly don't-you-worry smile. In a calm voice Ron told me I needed to hire a "Feng Shui Master" to evaluate my office location and environment. He had no idea how to find a reputable Feng Shui Master and advised me to contact Mattel's HK human resources manager for support.

I think the HR manager thought it was crazy that an American would be asking for such assistance. I admit I was uncomfortable pursuing this service, but it seemed this was my only option to insure my staff would show up for work. I wanted good health for and good attitudes from my team. In addition it was important that they understood I respected the Chinese culture and wouldn't ignore their concerns. HR researched my request and about a week later told me that they couldn't find a trustworthy Feng Shui Master within budget. The famous Masters were too expensive to hire.

I was frustrated for sure and in those days there was no internet search available to locate a Master. I did the next best thing and went to my secretary Norma. After all, she'd had three different names before she settled on the lucky Norma, a choice recommended by her fortune teller. Norma absorbed every word I told her about our department possibly having bad luck and that I wanted a Feng Shui Master to evaluate the situation.

First thing the next morning Norma was in my office with the business card of a Feng Shui Master.

Au Chun Ho

Prosper Bright Life Consultant Limited

He was to be addressed as Au Sin San (Mr. Au). Norma arranged for him to be at the office on Saturday morning, when no one was working, to insure our privacy. She would be with us to translate because Au Sin San spoke no English.

I didn't know what to expect as I nervously paced, waiting for Master Au. I arrived early and waited for Norma to escort Au Sin San to our meeting. Norma, casually dressed in jeans and a T-shirt, was refreshingly gorgeous, like she'd just completed a photoshoot for Calvin Klein.

Mr. Au's appearance was painfully thin and he was dressed very formally in a Western suit with a shirt and tie. He was about thirty-five years old and spoke no English, although I suspected he understood some English phrases, since he was a young HK guy. No matter, his strong Asian demeanor was enhanced by his nonstop Cantonese chatter. If he spoke English, it wouldn't have had the same impactful authority.

After the polite introduction and head-bowing exchange, Au Sin San asked for my birthdate, as well as the exact time and location. It seemed that because I was the *Loban* (boss), my luck and my Chinese zodiac sign had a lot to do with my department's luck. The Chinese zodiac is similar to Western astrology in that it has twelve categories, but the Chinese categories are named after animals, one for each year and repeating in the same order every twelve years. I was born on March 9, 1948, in New York City at 9:40 a.m. My birthdate means I was born in the **Year of the Rat**. This was important to know since my energy would influence my department's fortune. Another boss born in another year would have a different influence. From his briefcase, Mr. Au pulled out a large Chinese compass, and he proceed to intensely study the numerology as he slowly walked around the main entrance of the department and my office, the key points of *chi* (pronounced "chee") or energy. This is a fundamental Chinese concept referring to the air or breath in all things—humans, mountains, desks, plants, buildings, etc.

He traced a path all over the office with his compass and eventually reached the room with issues, the sample department. He instinctively focused on that room. Norma didn't know the details of the office illnesses, so Au Sin San had no advance notice this room had problems. He spotted the desk of the woman who had cancer and told us she was ill but would be okay. At one desk he even noted that the lady who sat there was pregnant (she was). He had a comment for each desk and all the comments were true! Au Sin San finished his walk around and shared that the sample room had bad energy and the entire office could have improved fortunes by adding plants and lucky charms, and moving some furniture. If we did all this our luck would be good, health would improve, and business would prosper.

An hour later the Master's analysis was done and Norma had her list of items to purchase and what office items needed to be moved. As instructed by Norma, for his consulting fee I'd prepared a red envelope with cash inside and held it firmly with both my hands to show respect, as I bowed and offered the payment to Au Sin San. He bowed in return and received the red envelope with both his hands and graciously smiled as he backed away.

This event was truly amazing. All his suggestions focused on balancing the office with nature, resulting in an inward flow of positive energy. This wasn't magic. It seemed to be common sense with a Chinese flair. On Monday I called a meeting to inform my staff that I'd consulted a Feng Shui Master to inspect the office and we were making his recommended changes.

Knowing the perceived problems had a solution was part of the cure. The staff was thrilled. They were so very appreciative and the warm looks they gave me, with their smiling faces, filled me with emotion. I think they were most impressed that a Westerner actually supported a traditional Chinese custom and showed respect for their culture. The idea that the environment would be in balance encouraged a positive attitude. My staff and colleagues all knew I went above and beyond what was in the Mattel rule book. The feng shui **changes** were all implemented that week.

Personal Brand Image:

Adapt to the culture you're engaged with. The respect gained is above expectations and adds to your trusted Brand.

Mattel California Soft Goods Engineering (SGE)

SGE would support me from California, with information needed to execute our project. We agreed it was best for Jessica Choi to spend a few weeks in California, learning the requirements of sample making and pattern engineering. She would be working with Miss E, the head of the sample department. Jessica had never been to the US. Her English was okay but not fluent. She obviously was concerned about her mission and I reassured her that this was a great opportunity for her educate herself and make our team successful. A few HK staff worked in California and they'd make sure she saw the tourist sights and entertained her after work. There was nothing to worry about.

Unfortunately, my prediction couldn't have been more wrong. I was ignorant of the attitude and manner that Miss E would have with Jessica. I assumed there would be a student-teacher relationship and allowances made for Jessica being from HK, her limited English and newness to Mattel. I was unaware that I was delivering one of my lovely new staff, one with great potential, to humanity's dark side.

Miss E was a woman is her forties who always conservatively dressed and proudly displayed a distinct, over-hairsprayed, dark brown, mature hairstyle. She had the look that was typical of a lady who ran a factory sewing department and the attitude of a technician rather than a designer. Ironically, she was no fashion icon, yet she was given authority over the aesthetic quality of Barbie fashion samples. She ruled her department with an iron fist. Rumor was that the staff was frightened to death of her, and that she constantly threatened them with losing their much-needed jobs if they didn't follow her direction. I assumed that the stories were indeed only rumors. This was a toy company! I spoke with Miss E many times while Jessica was in training and was told that Jessica had a lot to learn, but everything was going well.

After more than two weeks in California, Jessica returned to HK. She entered my office hysterically crying and told me that she couldn't do this job. She wanted to resign immediately! I consoled and hugged her. She was nervously shaking as if she were a young child who'd had a really bad day and was scared. I wouldn't accept her resignation because she was very creative and I was sure she could master the skills and aesthetics.

Jessica refused to believe me and proceeded to tell me how horrible Miss E was to her. Every day Miss E was cold, hard, strict, and unfriendly. According to Jessica, nothing that she did while she'd worked in California was correct. Miss E found fault with everything Jessica did. She'd yelled at her and never clearly told her how to improve her work. Then Miss E would tell all the staff how inadequate Jessica was for the job. She'd had a miserable two weeks. Jessica wouldn't have called me from California, since she believed Miss E was right. After all, Miss E was her "teacher" and it is Chinese custom not to question your teacher.

To put it mildly, I was outraged and felt it was my fault for not investigating if the gossip about Miss E being a dictatorial, horrible woman was a reality. Mattel management seemed to overlook Miss E's style. They thought it was part of her being a "perfectionist." I would say that Miss E was indeed a perfectionist, in making sure everyone else looked bad so she could become the bright star by comparison.

If only I'd realized Miss E's intentions, I never would have subjected anyone to such humiliation. I convinced Jessica to stay on the job and told her I would personally train her to the best.

However, I didn't anticipate the extent of additional problems from Miss E. As the daily routine when I arrived at the office, the first phone call was from Miss E. In a loud, sharp voice she screamed that our sewn Barbie fashion samples were terrible and unacceptable. The worst samples she'd ever seen and we were incompetent. The critique was all about minor details with millimeters of variance, visible only on the fashions' insides, and only noticeable after meticulous inspection. I took all the harsh criticism because I'd never made samples for Mattel and deferred to what I thought was Miss E's helpful expertise.

Jessica and I would stressfully review all the comments together. Generally speaking, the majority of samples had to be remade to meet Miss E's critical demands. This was a learning process taken to the extreme. Jessica cried almost every day because Miss E's criticism was so very intense and cruel. She asked me multiple times to accept her resignation. I refused Jessica's request and encouraged her by telling her that my poor teaching had caused the problems.

Miss E's comments were doled out in a vicious manner, void of any mentoring or humanity. Miss E told the California team how badly the HK samples were executed and that the HK team was useless. From Miss E's perspective, the need for corrections seemed to validate that HKSG was a failure. This was sabotage from Miss E, who didn't want to transfer products to HK, which might result in her team being less significant.

Although no other colleagues in California were as critical, many staff made no effort to give me proper information. Whether the omission of design details was consciously withheld is unclear. I speculate that it was deliberate, since the omissions were obvious. The consequences of HK not being told the complete story caused mistakes. Therefore, when HK failed it was a confirmation for the California office that HKSG couldn't do the job. This political game, of the California team trying to look more competent than HK, became the norm.

I wasn't going to let the negative cooperation ruin HKSG's reputation or derail my **Proposal**. I focused on pursuing credibility from Mattel California design and marketing customers that could make a difference in how my team was perceived. If these two groups saw positive results from HKSG, then the negative comments from the SGE in California would be considered inconsequential. My target, as always, was to accentuate the positive, show off, and promote what we did well. The areas that needed improvement I would definitely correct, but in the meantime downplay by being extraordinary in other areas. Just as I'd done with all my previous jobs that were beyond my capabilities.

We feverishly improved the Barbie fashions' quality, even though the time-consuming aim to be over the top with perfection delayed the production schedule. Even with our improvements Miss E continued her campaign of negative and insulting comments about HKSG capabilities. When she finally decided to admit the samples were good, of course she took the credit for being a "great teacher."

The balancing act began with focusing on customer service to our design and marketing partners and making sure every detail of aesthetic concern or suggestions surpassed the requirements. The teams in California were overwhelmed with our positive information and caring about aesthetics. Mattel never had this service before. Miss E complaining about a few threads hanging off a fashion sample became insignificant compared to the service and feedback HKSG was providing.

The lines of staff waiting outside of my office to be coached never stopped. I was constantly on the phone giving updates, as well as letting the design team know about limitations, so they heard it from me first, before any problems arose. This was a huge **change** and the effort was worth it. California was getting the results they'd never seen before and my staff was gaining confidence.

I protected Jessica from Miss E's many insulting phone calls, taking the verbal abuse myself. I was in a better emotional position to handle the criticism. I didn't want Jessica to quit. She was too valuable and Miss E's daily abuse certainly would have sent Jessica out the door.

Personal Brand Image:

One of the most important things to do as a manager is protect your staff because they see you will take care of them. When you go that "extra mile," this builds your team's trust in you.

(An investment for the future that no one ever taught Miss E.)

The Miss E episode had an interesting end:

A few years later Miss E was suddenly dismissed from her job, due to the discovery that she was—I'll put it politely—"not totally honest" in her Mattel accounting records. Most people avoided her because of her attitude, but the reality was that she hid behind her difficult personality to avoid confrontation about her own ethics. This confirmed my feelings that all the negative noise she made about countless colleagues in California and HK, and her tight control of her staff, were all a diversion so she could continue to follow a less-than-reputable road. The truth usually comes out, and finally her suppressed staff and colleagues could sing, "Ding Dong the Wicked Witch is Dead."

Yes, she just melted away and was never heard from again.

Mattel HK Executive Partners

To make sure I had support in my decisions I had to connect with the Barbie manufacturing plants. The Barbie fashions HKSG developed were released for production to the China factory, Mattel HK Ltd. (MHK). This factory was in China and the executives were based out of HK, routinely traveled to China as opposed to being stationed on the mainland. John McMullen, still sucking on a lead pipe because he was working with me, had TC Li, Director of Engineering, as his second in command. TC was a HK native, who could be thorny to deal with. John and TC had worked together for years and earned well-deserved admiration for their great accomplishments of building MHK and training the staff to have a reputation as Mattel's flagship Barbie plant.

My team's responsibility would eventually **change** the way products were released to MHK and give HK local approval authority, to improve the quality and schedule. That meant my team was onsite and could give immediate feedback and expedite the process. However, John and TC thought I could be a problem, by adding more complexity to the production cycle. They perceived me as having a "designer's attitude," with a potential to constantly reject product while chasing perfection. Not to mention that I was female in a male-engineering majority and new to the doll-manufacturing business. I had no credentials as far as they were concerned and they didn't have any confidence in my abilities.

I knew where I stood with John, so I made a conscious effort not to confront him. As for TC Li, his reputation was that of a brilliant engineer who'd been essential to MHK's success. The talk at Mattel was that with his extreme intelligence came a very harsh, in-your-face-type of personality. Not long after I arrived in HK I learned TC Li's reputation was fact not fiction.

I was searching to hire a qualified pattern engineer. Someone with the skills to engineer doll fashion patterns that would be used as a standard to cut the fabric in specific pieces and then sewn for production at MHK. The sewing manufacturing operations had to be precise to deliver a perfectly dressed Barbie doll in the package.

The Mattel HR team had given me the résumé of a young lady who was working for MHK. I was told she wanted to leave MHK and was looking for a good opportunity at Mattel in another department. Her skills fit perfectly with my requirements and HR arranged a meeting for me to interview her. Within a few hours of this arrangement my phone rang and a gentleman I'd never met said in a loud voice, in perfect English, without any common-courtesy-hello-how-are-you,

"This is TC Li. Did you know that you broke The Code?"

"What code?" I replied.

"The Code about hiring someone from another Mattel department can only be done with their management's permission."

"I had no idea about this code. I am new to Mattel and HR was the one to give me her résumé. I assume this was discussed with MHK."

"No it wasn't and I will not let her interview with you. You broke The Code"

"But, TC, I was informed that she will leave MHK eventually."

"No matter. I will not permit her to attend the interview."

"I am sorry for the problem. This issue doesn't seem fair to the young lady. Anything I can do to change your mind?"

"No."

He hung up.

I really didn't think this situation was so big to warrant such anger. I decided to call his boss John McMullen to see if this decision from TC Li could be changed. John wasn't in a friendly mood when I called. He told me he knew of the interview request and agreed that I'd broken The Code. John confirmed that he and TC Li wouldn't permit their staff to interview with me. I mentioned to him that the young lady was going to leave her MHK job. After all the training from MHK wouldn't it be better to have her still work for me at Mattel than to leave? John replied that The Code was broken and he would rather that she resigns than work for me. John hung up the phone.

I was stunned and was going to talk with HR when I received a phone call from my colleague, Mr. Ron Montalto. He told me that John had spoken to him about me "breaking The Code," and his advice was to be quiet and do nothing more. I felt this was a good-old-boy, unwritten Code and if I didn't obey I might be tied to a huge piece of concrete, given my last meal of a bowl of steamed rice, and dropped into Victoria Harbour at midnight! I decided to follow Ron's advice and do nothing. No interview followed and the potential interviewee resigned from MHK in the next few days. That was the end of the drama and my introduction to TC Li and "The Code."

I finally met TC after this phone exchange. TC was about forty years old, a very handsome Chinese man, extremely articulate and spoke English without a trace of any accent. I decided when we met that I would never mention the incident on the phone or my inadvertent "Code-Breaking" disaster.

I needed to be able to work with TC. Friendship wasn't even an expectation. He was courteous, but speaking with him was always a challenge. He always seemed to be looking for fault with my department and most of all for ways to minimize my authority. Our cold business relationship was on an even keel until I received another famous phone call from Mr. Li. He started off in his usual manner, with no hello and screaming into the phone.

"Did you know I have to stop production because one of your staff approved a small, artificial sunflower decoration that is to be sewn on Barbie's dress and on her hat? One problem—the flower has a plastic center and we cannot sew it on the doll! What is wrong with your staff? Our production is stopped! How could your staff do this? What are you going to do to fix this?"

"TC, please stop yelling at me! I have no idea how this happened. If we approved something like this, it's definitely a mistake. Let me review the situation and I will get back to you on how to resolve the problem."

He hung up.

I quickly reviewed the product and TC was correct. One of my staff had mistakenly approved this unsewable flower with a plastic center. We immediately contacted the vendor to send us a sunflower with a soft center, which would allow a sewing machine needle to tack this decoration on Barbie's fashion. The replacement would be available in a week. Barbie production would still be delayed but it wasn't hopeless.

I was ready not to make any excuses. It was a human error and my department's mistake. However, I was furious about TC's rude manner and determined that I would reply to him with my good-old New York Attitude and rip him to shreds for his uncivilized style!

Just as I was getting ready to call him and match his loud-voiced approach, I thought, this is what he wants. TC wants a reason to fight, prove me incompetent and ridicule me. I could never win with TC. He was far more crucial to Mattel's organization than I was and he would never admit he was wrong. If he wanted a fight, I needed to do the exact opposite. I wasn't going to give him what he wanted. I must give him something he would never expect as a response to his screaming.

It didn't take me long to get Norma to help me order an arrangement of fresh sunflowers from a florist that could deliver to TC Li at his office in China. I'd written a note to be attached to the stunning floral arrangement:

Dear TC Li,

I am so very sorry the wrong construction for Barbie's accessory was approved by my staff. It was our mistake. The correct flower replacement will be there next week. Please accept these beautiful fresh sunflowers in the meantime ... even though they have the same problem and cannot be sewn on Barbie's fashion!

Sincerely,

Paulette

Everyone at the factory was in shock that flowers from Paulette Bazerman were sent to TC. The gossip was nonstop. The next day I received a small envelope from MHK. It was a notecard from TC Li. The picture on the cover was a painting of a sunflower. Inside was a handwritten note expressing his thanks for the flowers I'd sent. I couldn't believe that he'd actually looked for and found a card with a sunflower to send me. I was impressed that I could get him to show me his softer side.

I finally brought about **change** and TC Li never yelled at me again.

I wouldn't call this a victory, but rather an enlightened experience of ways to accomplish success. Instinct is an impulsive reaction that may not get you the best result. Once again I took a page from Dr. D's lesson book: I thought before I acted and did what was appropriate. I felt like yelling and screaming, telling TC that he was an idiot. That instinctive response would've been the opening bell for a boxing match I couldn't win.

Personal Brand Image:

See things from the other person's viewpoint. Think before you act. Being appropriate for the situation may be the opposite of what you feel like doing.

Asian Vendors

Outside of the Mattel circle, I worked with the Asian vendors to develop customized fabrics and soft good accessories. These vendors were mainly from HK, China, Taiwan, Korea, and Japan. All the representatives of these companies were men and most didn't speak English, so I needed an interpreter. I was cautious about working with these gentlemen, based on my experience with the Mattel executives and my preconceived opinion that the working force of Asian men were all anti-women in business.

I was prepared to expect the worst and hoped that my textile manufacturing knowledge would be the focus, not my gender or Western origins. To my amazement the Asian vendors' reaction to me wasn't what I'd anticipated. The fact that I was a female expatriate was an advantage, not a disadvantage. Their work ethos was the opposite of what I'd experienced with the majority of my Mattel executive partners. I didn't have to do much to prove myself. To them, the fact that I was an American woman, in an executive position for Mattel in HK, meant I was either very wealthy or very talented—or possibly both! In Asia, wealth and knowledge are highly respected no matter your gender. I think this is far more fair than acceptance based on being one of the "good old boys."

The respect I received resulted in a **change** in my perception of Asian vendors. The relationships that followed were of mutual admiration and the best professional service. These vendors never questioned my competence and honored my assignment in HK by going out of their way to meet Mattel's soft goods requirements. What a fabulous surprise to see that the reality wasn't the expected stereotype that business in Asia is only for men.

Personal Brand Image:

Observe and decide for yourself. Preconceptions are not reality.

Chapter 16

On the Road to China ... Really?

We'd been living in HK for about one year and I made a conscious effort not to travel to China. I was afraid. Being from the US, I was fed the news media's propaganda that China was the enemy. It was "Red China" and not to be trusted. They were the bad guys and we were the good guys. Mattel had their factories and vendors in China, and I pictured those factories under lock and key with high security to prevent an imminent attack. The US government and the media would never exaggerate or lie, right?

Even my HK staff didn't want to travel to China because of the "threat" of the communist government, personal safety, and the lack of modern conveniences. This was double confirmation to me that China wasn't safe. I made every excuse to delay making the short trip across the border.

Because of my strategy to provide exceptional customer service and quality, HKSG was gaining a positive reputation from the California design and marketing teams. My boss, Don Hartling, was pleased with what we were accomplishing and he kept encouraging more work to be sent to HK, which I never turned down. My philosophy was to have a positive attitude up front, then later figure out how to get the work done. I was still supervising every detail of the projects and for those staff who'd started to understand the concepts, I gave authority to take the risk alone. Baby steps.

Thanks to our job well done, as Don Hartling had promised, we were rewarded with new and more complex Barbie projects.

All the efforts to coach, mentor, and communicate were paying off. There was no turning back or stopping this progress because of any of my own insecurities. It became necessary to personally understand Barbie production methods and meet the people I'd been interacting with at MHK China for over a year. I had to forget about my comfort level and plan a visit to the Mattel China factories immediately.

Norma, fearing for my safety, made the arrangements for my China trip, including having someone from MHK accompany me. In 1993 it was considered unsafe for an American woman to travel alone to China. To be honest, I was grateful for the precaution. I needed to have a China visa to cross the border from HK, and receiving that item would take a couple of days. The plan was for me to visit the two Mattel China factories, at different locations. First I would make the shorter trip to Chang An, China, the smaller MHK facility located near the city of Shenzhen, only about a forty-five minute drive north of HK's Mattel office. A week later I'd visit the larger MHK plant in Guanyao, China. Traveling to Guanyao involved a three-hour nonstop commuter train ride, plus another hourlong car ride from the train station to the MHK factory.

Melvin was very anxious about me going to China. He too had been exposed to the same US propaganda of anti-China brainwashing, before I was even born. I admit I was frightened, but I also knew Mattel had many staff traveling to the mainland on a daily basis for many years. If anything happened to me, Melvin wouldn't hesitate to hire the best lawyer in the universe and make international news with a major lawsuit against Mattel for any injury or loss of life incurred while I traveled in China. Not sure how reassuring this was, but it was all I had to help with my anxiety. We still didn't have mobile phones and that would mean a communication blackout for most of my trip. Melvin understood I had no choice but to go and he had to stay home with Haris, since we would never allow a little five-year-old American kid to visit China. I had visions of Kidnap ... Ransom ... Torture!

I went to Mattel Chang An with another expatriate colleague, the director of manufacturing at MHK, Mr. Bill Browne. Bill was transferred to HK from the US a few months before I'd arrived, which put us on a level playing field of camaraderie as new HK residents. I was so happy to have Bill as my tour guide, not because he was American, but because his physical presence gave me an edge. I admit it boosted my safety level because he was male and most certainly due to the fact that Bill was over six feet six inches tall! Compared to my slight frame and short height, I was in "bodyguard heaven" and felt the Chinese didn't have a chance against Mr. Browne.

Stopping at China immigration, my passport was examined and my photo was meticulously compared to my face numerous times. Was this it? Was the officer going to hold me for questioning because I was an American? I was back to the kidnap, ransom, and torture thoughts! Nothing was further from the truth, as I got the nod and hand-stamped passport page allowing me to enter China. There was no danger, just lots of Chinese folks staring at me because I was the only Caucasian in the immigration hall, but that wasn't the only obvious identifier. I looked different with my colorful clothes and accessories, compared to the local Chinese people, who all wore black and dark gray attire.

Bill exited immigration first I met him in the car and the journey continued through the city of Chang An, with rows and rows of small stores selling mops, brooms, plastic buckets, food, or simply cutting and shampooing hair on the street in the open air. As I approached Mattel's location, the area was noticeably run down, without any contemporary architecture. It was more rural, with huge amounts of dust and dirt everywhere. The buildings were all concrete, with mold accumulating on the outside from the high humidity. I would say that China was anything but red—it was gray! Once inside the hot non-air-conditioned factory, the noise of sewing machines was deafening, the heat from plastic molding machines was suffocating. It looked like a war zone, with Barbie body parts on the production assembly lines as far as the eye could see.

Within all this organized chaos I received a warm welcome from the local Mattel China staff. They truly were happy to see me and graciously offered me refreshments. Tea in a beautiful, delicate porcelain pot, fresh fruits, and cookies were waiting on elegant serving plates. We introduced ourselves with hand-shakes and a slight head bows. After tea the tour began, introducing me to how the famous Barbie dolls are made. Hundreds of ladies were lined up at long tables with sewing machines, each creating parts of the fashions. More operators were located at other tables, inspecting and dressing dolls with lightning speed and accuracy. If you've ever dressed a Barbie doll, you know how difficult it is to quickly slip the clothes on her body. It brought back memories of my first day at Mattel, when I failed to properly shove Barbie's legs into those tiny pantyhose. These skillful ladies were Olympic champs at doll dressing.

I was amazed at the effort put into the small details. Never expected the immense scale and complex engineering that went into the production of just a doll! I was only familiar with making Barbie fashion prototype samples. Touring the factory educated me about how design and development affected production execution. Creating a doll design in the studio didn't mean you could reproduce it exactly in mass quantities or maintain cost and quality.

The huge amount of workers were like bees swarming over sweet pollen in a fragrant garden. One advantage of manufactur-ing in China is that the labor force was very large and inexpensive; therefore, mechanical automation wasn't a priority. It was more cost effective to employ people to do the labor than to install machines to execute a process. Much of what was done in the factory was by hand. Barbie's hair was rooted on her plastic, molded head. An operator held the small head under a sewing machine as hair fibers thread through the needles, riveting in and out like a machine gun to attach the specific hairstyle, rather than gluing on a wig.

Barbie's face paint was hand sprayed using a mask/stencil for each color in her eyes, lips, cheeks, and brows. Sewing machines were used for Barbie's fashions, but the techniques to sew the fashions were all human hand operated, carefully creating these tiny dresses with skillful speed.

It was a humbling experience to see these workers so diligent at their duties. They never even looked up at me, no nods, no eye contact, due to a combination of their shyness and shock of seeing, perhaps for the first time, a Western woman. The vast majority of staff were from northern China, which was mostly farmland and didn't offer many opportunities for industrial jobs or increased income. The trend was to find work in southern China, particularly the Guangdong Province area, making the famous Mattel an attractive choice.

Working for an American company in China was prestigious. Mattel had a good reputation, providing dormitory living for staff and three meals a day at the canteen to encourage the workers to stay after the long training process. These young Chinese bravely left their families to travel thousands of miles to earn a living and send their wages back home.

I was personally touched by the Chinese diligence at work, which would support their families. After hearing about their long journeys from home and the sacrifices they were making to earn a living wage, I was brought to tears and embarrassed that I'd been an American critical of the Chinese before I'd even set foot in Asia. Being uninformed isn't an excuse for developing the wrong perception. I'd certainly gotten sucked into the political propaganda I'd been exposed to all of my life in the US. I'd never heard one positive comment about China. Even when working at Mattel in California, there was the naive attitude of "them and us."

The realization from my first experience in China was that different is not necessarily bad—it's only different. I felt honored to see for myself the work ethic and the standards that Mattel provided for the Chinese. Most Americans wouldn't want to live in a dormitory without modern Western conveniences. But for these migrants, the circumstances at Mattel were better than the lives they'd had back home, combating poverty and starvation. Now they had a job and income to help their families.

After my tour of the MHK production area I was escorted to the second floor to see how the factory prepared the sewn samples that were sent to my HK team for review before production. The configuration of the sewing tables and process was completely different than the production floor. Actually, it was very similar to the layout and methodology of my HKSG sample sewing department. The sample making was slower and the operators focused on getting the aesthetics to match what HKSG set as a standard. In addition, these skillful operators knew the production capability firsthand, then made adjustments and recommendations accordingly.

My excitement was high on this tour. I had a vision for the future of Barbie sample making. A similar feeling of enlightenment as when I'd first visited Mattel HK in 1986. After that visit I'd written my **Proposal** for the very job I was currently doing in HK. Now I saw the next step in the evolution of product development in Asia. Because of my HK staff's efforts and success, we were getting increased work and more complex assignments. We were on the verge of overload and I could see that if HKSG kept its high standard and continued succeeding, we'd have to increase staff to meet demand and avoid delays. This would add labor cost to the products.

The sight of the MHK China sample makers' process gave me the idea that HKSG could have a team in China devoted to sewing premium samples, supervised by HKSG staff. The department's growth would be less costly at the China location. This seemed obvious and would be an efficient way to support Mattel California and the next step in expanding Design and Development in Asia.

Before beginning my written **China Proposal** I wanted to complete the experience and gather knowledge from my second trip to the mainland, planned for the following week at the larger MHK manufacturing facility in Guanyao. I would have to stay overnight at the only hotel considered safe for "tourists." The **White Swan Hotel** was located about twenty-five minutes from the Guangzhou train station, with easy access for my return trip to HK the next morning.

Now that I felt like a veteran of China travel, I didn't have my bodyguard, Mr. Bill Browne, accompany me. Instead I had one of the HK staff, from MHK, take me on the train ride and through China immigration. I departed HK in the early morning on a nonstop express train to Guangzhou. This train was more like a freight car hauling cargo, not what I expected from a commuter train. It was dark, dirty, and had an odor of day-old food rotting in the sun. I was one of two Westerners, and everyone else on the train was local HK or mainland Chinese commuters.

Some of the passengers were in business attire, but the majority were local residents, very casually dressed and carrying supply or food packages. The most noticeable item they carried were large red, white, and blue plaid or striped, polyurethane-coated, heavy-duty shopping bags filled to overflow with poultry (yes, chickens), complete with feathers, being brought to China. The chickens weren't clucking so I had to assume they were already dead. I know the Chinese like fresh food. The chickens were probably being transported after the morning's fresh kill at a HK slaughterhouse and were now in the process of dying in the bright, patterned bags as the train pulled out from the station. I was extremely uncomfortable with the unexpected, although novel, atmosphere. The train ride was three hours long and I thought it moved slightly faster than those dead chickens.

The accommodations were definitely basic, including the restrooms, which were at the end of each train car. They were enclosed cubicles with a sink and the traditional Chinese squatting-type toilet, which had a direct exit route for the waste matter onto the railroad tracks below. Interesting sight beneath your feet, of the train rails on the ground as you relieved yourself.

Oh yes, food also was for purchase on the journey. Around 9 a.m. a lady dressed in a railway uniform came down the aisle, pushing a cart with large, hot steaming bowls of fresh-cooked chicken legs in a thick brown sauce, another bowl of steaming pieces of corn on the cob. If you purchased the chicken special brunch item, the leg was scooped up and put in dish for you, with a napkin to use as you held the leg and took those delicious bites, to avoid brown sauce dripping down your arm. Glad to have the opportunity to learn the etiquette of how to eat the hot chicken leg on a moving train. The pungent aroma was almost welcome since it was more pleasant than the bags of fresh-killed chickens on board. No surprise, I graciously passed on purchasing the brunch selection.

I admit the view from the window was a stimulating grand tour of the South China countryside. After the first hour the cityscape scenery turned into farmland mixed with old factory buildings. My eyes focused on the rice fields, with farmers wading knee deep in water, tending to the crops, intermingled with pigs grazing on hills. Then the pigs wandered into the covered broken-down shacks, in the middle of the fields, to defecate.

Row after row of vegetables were growing next to factories releasing fumes from their chimney stacks directly onto the produce and the irrigation water. There were obviously no controls or government regulations on the pollutant emissions. That day I consciously made up my mind that I would never purchase locally grown, poisoned vegetables that were available in HK from a China source. It was bad enough I would eat imported China vegetables in HK restaurants, but I didn't have to make it worse by adding them to my grocery list for home cooking.

The train ride was painfully long, even with all the passenger entertainment and the views out the window. I was squirming to escape. After two hours I was ready to move on, but braced myself for another hour with the gray atmosphere and toilet fragrance emissions. Finally we arrived in Guangzhou, the capital of Guangdong Province in South China, located on the Pearl River, seventy-five miles northwest of Hong Kong. Population over twelve million, making it the third-largest city in China, after Beijing and Shanghai. This area was formerly known as Canton, which influenced all that great Cantonese Chinese food I ate growing up in New York City. (However, I never saw any of those brown chicken legs in Brooklyn.)

My expectations were high on this visit to a prominent Chinese city. Guangzhou was now my "real deal," to see if all my inhibitions about visiting "Red China" were valid. I departed the train and walked down the steps, or more accurately was pushed with the crowds of people trying to rush through customs. The China immigration hall was no more than a cement-covered room with metal tables that had immigration officers sitting on small metal chairs, wearing wrinkled uniforms too big for their slender physiques. They looked like little boys wearing their fathers' old clothing. My passport was quickly stamped and no word was spoken or eye contact was exchanged. I was directed to the door that opened to the East Guangzhou Welcome Area.

One step out the train station door I was swamped by small, tattered-looking children, holding out their hands, begging for money, pulling on my clothes. My escort advised me to ignore them and walk quickly to the car. My heart was broken to see this poverty and little children's sad eyes, but I was told if you give one child money they won't leave you alone. It was a begging-business, so best to be stone-faced and keep walking. My goodness, this is what America feared as the Big Red Monster that was going annihilate all Westerners? Once again I was ashamed that I'd believed the American propaganda about China being an evil empire.

We exited the parking lot, the screaming children following us until we gained enough speed to reach the main highway. This was downtown Guangzhou, which looked old, ugly, and impoverished. No thought to building design. It had no Asian-style construction and the architecture was either dilapidated or just unimpressive. The buildings seemed only functional, meant to hold offices and employees, nothing more. There wasn't much vehicle traffic either, mostly pedestrians and folks on bicycles, dressed in the Chinese black and gray attire, quickly moving in every direction to reach their destinations and avoid getting hit by a bus.

I felt no fear, I just felt really depressed. The people were expressionless and poor, yet they were orderly and calm as they went about their business to survive. Whether it was sweeping the sidewalks with a straw broom, selling hot tea, or giving shampoos to customers on the streets, they chose work instead of begging.

The one-hour ride to the MHK factory in the small town of Guanyao was slow and steady. As soon as we left the downtown Guangzhou area, the rice fields, farmlands, and factories repeated throughout the balance of the trip and were no longer interesting, they were just the norm. We arrived at MHK and the staff was warm and welcoming. This Mattel facility was similar to the operations I'd explored at Chang An, except the scale was more than double in size, and the majority of product being manufactured was Barbie. This was indeed the flagship Mattel factory.

After the tour in the hot, humid factory, we drove forty minutes in the company van to the White Swan Hotel. I welcomed not going back on the train to HK that evening. I was exhausted physically and emotionally. I didn't dwell on the fact that I had low expectations about the White Swan Hotel after what I'd witnessed in the downtown area that morning. I didn't care about the hotel quality. I just hoped for a clean, safe place, with a bowl of steamed rice and a cup of hot tea, and I would be so very grateful.

The van made a sharp right turn which landed us on a road built like a bridge over the Pearl River, leading to the White Swan Hotel. The formally dressed doorman in red with white gloves and top hat greeted us. I was amazed at the beautiful white hotel building—yes, like a White Swan. The building was only ten years old and had thirty-four floors. This was no small, broken-down, dirty hotel, this was an oasis in the middle of a city covered with industrial mold.

The lobby was impressive, with lush indoor landscapes, a man-made indoor water stream filled with golden koi fish, and a cascading waterfall, whose gentle rushing water sounds filled my heart with tranquility. There was even a giant jade carving of an ancient Chinese junk by the reception area and dozens of examples of Chinese artifacts. The White Swan Hotel had a beauty salon, business center, gym, shopping mall, ten restaurants, and lobby bar. There I was, standing in the middle of the marble floor, surrounded by landscaping of lush vegetation, with sweat covering my entire body, due to the long, hot humid day, stress, and high anxiety.

My room was in sharp contrast to the sights on Guangzhou's streets. I had a fully appointed room with all the amenities you would expect in a luxury hotel. As soon as I entered the room there was knock at the door. A high-pitched voice called out for me to open the door. I hadn't ordered anything and I was fearful about who was outside. I looked through the peephole and there in the dim light was a small young lady holding a tea tray and fresh fruit. I opened the door for her. She bowed, smiled, entered my room, and poured my tea. "Welcome to the White Swan Hotel," she said in perfect English, as she backed out of the room with her head bowed.

I agreed to meet my Mattel colleagues in the lobby bar for a much-needed happy hour drink before dinner. I was the first to arrive, led to my seat by a smiling young lady wearing a traditional red and gold-embroidered Chinese *qipao*, a long, tight-fitting dress with side slits showing her gorgeous legs. The leather chair I sat in, next to the window, had a spectacular view of the Pearl River at sunset. I slowly sipped a glass of red wine, letting the relaxing effect set in while I snacked on the best crispy salted peanuts that were ever harvested. There was no doubt: that day I set in motion the plan to open a Mattel office on Mainland China.

Not bad for a girl from Brooklyn!

Personal Brand Image:

Doing the same gets the same results. Get out of your comfort zone and learn something new.

There were no dead chickens stuffed into shopping bags on the train ride back to HK from Guangzhou the next morning. The bright-colored polyurethane shopping bags were now overflowing with local Chinese food delicacies unavailable in HK, packed in jars, plastic bags, and tin boxes. The lack of visual entertainment of dead chicken heads hanging over the seats, moving to the train tracks' rhythm, was a big letdown from the previous day's train ride.

The experiences in Guangzhou certainly provided me with many lessons not listed in a guidebook to China. The example at Mattel was stunning. In the past these factory workers had been plowing fields and milking cows, and now they were learning the technical skills to make Barbie dolls and sending money to their families. I was impressed with the respect they had for Mattel as an employer, which provided accommodations and benefits previously unattainable in their hometowns. The Chinese people I met and the atmosphere of my visit were opposite to my perception created by a lifetime of ridiculous information spread in schools, books, and the US media. I have more fear walking down an alley in New York City than being the only American on a train traveling in China.

Sitting on the train heading back to HK, I got the idea to write a **Proposal** for a China soft goods development office. I hesitated to make the effort to propose this new project in China to Mattel because this would take immense power of persuasion on my part. I didn't believe that Mattel management in California would agree with my vision of the potential to train the mainland Chinese on the aesthetic side of the fashion doll business.

More important was the issue for me to overcome Melvin's concern for my safety in China. He too was conditioned by US propaganda. After I described my introduction to Guangzhou, Melvin insisted on taking a trip with me to see the reality for himself. We arranged to travel there in the next few weeks, on the same colorful train ride with the dying chicken entertainment that I had experienced. I'd refrained from telling Melvin about the children at the train station begging, crying, and pulling on your clothes. Upon our arrival in Guangzhou, my outspoken, aggressive, smooth-talking salesman husband was absolutely silent. Riding in the van to the factory the sight of begging children, the endless sea of people wearing black clothing, old folks sweeping streets with twig brooms, huge crowds riding bicycles and moving in all directions while cars plowed through was totally unexpected.

Melvin started to cry, devastated and deeply touched that in this small space, the masses of people were busily trying to work and survive life. Melvin grew up in the 1940s on the Lower East Side of New York near iconic old Delancey Street. It was a poor neighborhood of Eastern European immigrants and that picture of his childhood seemed luxurious compared to what he was seeing fifty years later in China!

Wiping away tears and forcing a smile, Melvin turned to me and said, "You have nothing to fear here ... go for it when you're ready."

It took me a few weeks to focus on writing the best business plan for Mattel soft goods development. I overlooked my own discomfort and planned what was best for business. My HK assignment was still temporary, so it might not be me who would need to venture to China and build this department. I decided to propose my vision to Don Hartling. My persuasive discussion and written plan were admired for progressive thinking, but declined by Don. He felt China was too unknown and risky to start a new department, especially with a female expatriate in charge.

On one hand I was disappointed, on the other hand, relieved that I didn't have this major task to implement.

Personal Brand Image:

Pursue what would make business better. Be a visionary and eventually you'll figure out how to achieve the goal.

Chapter 17

Barbie

My temporary two-year assignment in HK continuously extended with each achievement. The more competent my team became, the more difficult the degree of projects we received and the more onsite approval responsibility was given to my group. The more I lived in HK and traveled in Asia the more I loved this part of the world, the people, and my staff. This was now home.

After many years working at Mattel, I still had no emotional connection with Barbie. I was only concerned with the doll's fashions, which for me were just miniature versions of adult clothes that needed to fit an eleven-and-a-half-inch plastic body. That was all the doll meant to me, a small plastic mannequin to dress for my job. I was embarrassed to even hold her. This was my painful secret. All the products my team developed were Barbie fashions yet I was basically ambivalent about the doll. I continued to feel she was just a stupid piece of plastic, even though I was in HK for many years overseeing Barbie's fashions and directing the soft goods aesthetics.

When Haris was four years old I gave him a Barbie doll just to see his reaction and play-pattern. He instinctively took Barbie, turned her so her feet were pointed at me, held her head, used her hand as a trigger, then pretended this doll was a machine gun and started to shoot at imaginary enemies in the room! We never had a toy gun in the house so I'm unsure where the role-play came from, but this surely didn't endear me to Barbie's iconic appeal. What on earth did girls see in her that was special?

I recall one hot, humid weekend in HK, walking with Melvin and Haris in the Central shopping district. Out of a dirty alleyway overflowing with garbage, hidden between two modern high-rise skyscrapers, emerged a very elderly Chinese lady who was collecting corrugated cardboard boxes being disposed from the shops located in these buildings. It appeared that she was recycling them to earn a living. She looked to be in her late sixties with long, gray, disheveled hair. She was so extremely thin that her arm bones were visible, and her blue veins showed through her translucent skin. She was dressed simply in very worn, shabby black pants, with a black and brown printed sleeveless shirt. On her tiny feet were the traditional black slippers strapped tightly over her instep to keep them from falling off as she shuffled down the street.

She had dozens of used boxes neatly folded and stacked on a metal handcart. With her frail, thin arms she struggled to pull the cart down the crowded, uneven sidewalk.

Sitting on top of this high box pile was an adorable little girl, maybe five years old, with her long black hair neatly tied behind her head with a pink ribbon to match her sweet, pink, immaculately clean dress. The child looked to be the granddaughter of this elderly lady. The child's parents were probably at work and grandma was the caregiver while she made her rounds to pick up the refuse. As the elderly lady struggled to move the handcart, the little girl was all smiles as she bobbed up and down on top of the boxes, giggling as if she were a Queen on a magnificent throne. Then my eyes were drawn to her small hand, in which she lovingly clutched her seemingly only prized possession: a beautiful blonde, blue-eyed, pink, glittering Barbie doll, which she waved high overhead as if it were her royal scepter.

My eyes swelled with tears, my heart raced and I stared long and hard at this sight, which obviously was so impressive that it remains in my memory more than twenty years later. With all her poverty and hard living conditions, this little Chinese girl had Barbie in her hand, in her mind, and in her heart, which made her feel like a Queen, even though she was sitting on top of a pile of dirty cardboard. For the first time I realized that Barbie wasn't just a stupid piece of plastic—she was a vehicle for a dream. This "Barbie Magic" could inspire joy for a little girl sitting on a pile of garbage. This was powerful. This was **more than a doll**!

I couldn't contain my emotions. I stopped walking, bent my head down, began to gush tears and make whimpering noises. Haris was embarrassed to be near me. Melvin and Haris were shocked with my exhibition in the middle of a crowded street and they rushed me into the nearest restaurant for lunch so I could calm down. This was also the first time I knew what I had to add to my repertoire of being a Mattel Director: not just to direct the work, but to inspire the staff about Barbie. Not because it would sell more toys, but because the truth had to be shared with the staff, since they had less of a connection to Barbie than I did. I'd been negligent due to my ignorance of Barbie's history. I had to change my attitude and share what I'd just felt, because Barbie and all those who created, designed, and gave her to millions of little girls deserved this respect.

By this time, Mattel finally provided personal computers on our desks. We were out of the dark ages into the world of information and global communication. The Mattel network installed was slow and could barely download a file, but at least I had a tool that not only could connect me with Mattel's internal network, but also could be used for research. I decided to take on my own challenge and find out about Barbie's origins and fulfill my duty to inspire my staff. I read everything I could find about Mattel's history and Barbie's creation. I was fascinated by how the idea of an adult-like fashion doll was designed and how much information was available as to why a small piece of plastic became so famous.

When Mattel hired me, first in 1985 and again in 1989, and I went through two official Mattel orientation meetings, why didn't anyone ever give a presentation on Barbie's history? Barbie has a lusciously rich past, a fabulous example of product development evolution, the stuff movies are made of. It seemed obvious to me that a new employee should start with some understanding about the iconic Brand before they're seated at desks to learn corporate rules and regulations. Our job, no our goal was to make a child happy. How could that be accomplished with the staff's full engagement if they weren't passionate about Barbie?

Many books and articles have been written about Barbie. I'll just give a brief overview of what I know from my own research and talking with my Mattel colleagues. I knew nothing about Mattel and started at the beginning, to find out about the company name's origin. To my surprise there was no Mr. Mattel who had founded the company. It was actually a married couple, Ruth and Elliot Handler, and their friend Harold Matson, who created a doll furniture company in 1944, in the Handlers' Los Angeles garage. Okay, we now take Mr. Matson's nickname, Matt, and add the El from Elliott, and you have the maybe not so exciting, but very famous name **Mattel**. Matson eventually departed the company, which left Ruth as the marketing genius and Elliot as the creative designer.

Further into the story, we have Ruth Handler thinking about creating a more adult-looking doll for girls. Most dolls at this time were either baby dolls or childlike female bodies wearing adult fashions. Mattel's engineering men and even Ruth's husband Elliot thought Ruth was crazy and shot down her "adult doll with breasts" idea for years!

The Handler family visited Europe in 1956, and the stop they made in Lucerne, Switzerland, with their children—yep, their daughter Barbara/Barbie and son Ken—changed everything. The short version is that they visited at a toy store with a display of an adult female doll called **Lilli** wearing fashionable adult clothes. This doll was modeled after an adult cartoon character in the German newspaper *Bildzeitung* in Hamburg. Lilli was a rather risqué character and not afraid to talk about sex. The doll was mainly sold to adult males to give to their girlfriends or wives, to be suggestive of the men's sexual desires.

When Ruth saw Lilli in the store window, as well as Barbara's reaction to seeing Lilli, she knew this must be the prototype for the adult doll she'd envisioned. Ruth was always fascinated when she watched her daughter Barbara play with paper fashion dolls, dressing them with paper clothes and imagining to actually take on the doll role she was dreaming. Ruth bought one Lilli doll and an additional doll when they visited Germany. She brought them back to California to have the Mattel engineers create a doll that was softer looking, more for the American market, and engineered to be mass produced. In my opinion Lilli and the original Barbie look like sisters.

Who would have thought that darling Barbie, suitable for a three-year-old girl's playtime, was inspired by a European, ambitiously sexy female character. The journey from "sexy toy" to Barbie's introduction at the American International Toy Fair in New York on March 9, 1959, was a hard sell, with most critics expecting the doll to flop. What child, or for that matter what mom, would want a doll with breasts?

Mrs. Handler decided to insure the doll's success with effective marketing research and execution. In 1959 there was the popular TV show, **The Mickey Mouse Club**. (Yes, I was eleven years old and I watched the show as well.) The Handlers approached Walt Disney and bought advertising time on the most popular children's TV show for a strategically planned Barbie commercial. This black-and-white Barbie commercial included a song sung by a lovely, sweet, female voice—"Barbie, beautiful Barbie, I'll make believe that I am you"—in the background, as the camera focused on many fashionably dressed Barbies, including one in a bridal gown.

It was amazing how this commercial subtly targeted young girls' imaginations to think about being anything that they aspired to. What a sales pitch to the mothers and girls. A wholesome adult doll that would allow your daughter to be anything she could imagine, including being married. The commercial hit the target mother and daughter audience and was a surefire winner. Barbie was a vehicle for *the dream*!

Now I had a story to tell about Barbie and needed to convey it in an exciting manner to an audience whose first language wasn't

English or who didn't understand any English. I realized I had to depend on a visual performance to make a point, just as I had done before with whipped cream pies, rhinestone jewelry, and glittering tiaras. No costumes or props—this time I had the tool of the computer to show the story. However, my technical ability on the computer was limited to emails and research. I wanted to create spectacular visuals to tell the Handler story and to show how Barbie was created and marketed. If I couldn't show the first Barbie TV commercial current TV ads and photos to make my point, I would never be able to inspire passion in my staff.

I wanted them to love Barbie and what she represented to every little girl who played with her. They should all feel like the small Chinese girl in Central HK, sitting on the pile of boxes, who was transformed into being a princess, ballerina, teacher, astronaut, or doctor just because Barbie was in her hand. Now her dream seemed real. I didn't want any of my staff to have a dry eye after I shared Barbie's glorious history.

Even my capable secretary Norma was limited in her computer skills. This technology was new to us all, but I had backup technical support at home. Melvin and Haris were extremely computer capable. It was Melvin who'd convinced me years before that we needed to have a PC to handle our personal communication back to the US and for Haris's education. Haris was only 5 years old when we bought our first computer so Melvin focused on gaining technical skills and teaching Haris how to be computer literate. Of course the student Haris surpassed the teacher Melvin at a rapid rate. I hadn't asked Haris for any Mattel support since the **My Size Barbie** fit model episode in 1992. Haris was nearly eight years old now and I asked him to help create my complex multimedia presentation. I know this sounds crazy, but we had no one in HK at the time to help me. Haris was more than happy to assist. A much more professional project for him than dressing up in pink like a princess ballerina Barbie.

I had music, photos, and videos of commercials past and current. The file was huge. Haris came to the office with me to make sure all went technically smooth. We barely got through the presentation since Mattel had minimum bandwidth. It was like putting three pounds of glitter into a two-pound bag! Haris made it work and the result was magnificent. The staff was emotionally touched with every detail. The company's history was a revelation and they felt proud to work on a product that had this warm iconic identity. I pleaded to everyone's softer side: we were in the business to make children happy and the staff had a role to play in helping girls aspire to their dreams. I couldn't control myself. I was emotional and turned on my faucet of tears in front of everyone.

My newly discovered devotion to Barbie came from witnessing the joy she brought to little girls, and for that matter, adults. Love Barbie or hate Barbie isn't up for debate in my discussion. My goal at Mattel was now transformed from just teaching the Asian staff about Barbie aesthetics to also having them recognize that she's a work of art.

This new perspective made a huge difference in how my team approached protecting the Barbie Brand. It all made sense now. Reason for rejecting and reasons for approving products were based on Brand Image, not just matching a standard. I felt the Barbie Brand Image in my heart and soul and this is what my mentoring for Asia focused on. If you knew the melody you could sing the song, and I was out to record a platinum record.

After this presentation I never felt or conveyed to anyone that Barbie was a stupid piece of plastic again, because that point of view came from my ignorance. I was now enlightened and wanted to open hearts and minds to all, that Barbie was **more than a doll**!

Barbie isn't a toy gun or some destructive, dangerous object. I owed it to Mattel, her creators, and forty years of designs to maintain and improve her appearance. In other words, keep **Barbie's Personal Brand Image**. SHE was a personality, not cold hard plastic. When my staff suggested certain fabrics for Barbie's fashions I replied with either, "She would never wear that!" or "Barbie would look fabulous!"

I had a good sense of Barbie's personality, which brought my own **Brand Image** at Mattel to extraordinary status and built my reputation as a trusted executive who was leading a passionate team in Asia. My temporary job continued.

Personal Brand Image:

Make it personal and be an advocate for your product. To inspire, empathize with your customers to magnify the degree of passion that you share.

Chapter 18

The Fishing Village

A sure way to fail at work is to become a nonentity and fall into the "black hole" of an overseas assignment. I had no onsite boss to be my mentor or campaign to support my staff. I was the one who had to reinforce HKSG accomplishments and bring attention to our team's efforts. I learned to direct my secretary to make colorful charts, elaborate graphs, and eye-catching photos that explained our team's success and constantly expanding role.

This visual methodology started with reports and then escalated into presentations for the California team executives and visitors to the HK office. Of course I refused to sit relaxed at a desk and just share slides with numbers and charts. Instead I used contemporary music juxtaposed with vivid images and gave small souvenirs to all guests, reinforcing my points with showtime style. It was my passion to perform and put on a show emphasizing our creative Brand.

I ran my department like an entrepreneurial business owner, following my instinct and not necessarily corporate procedures if they didn't make any sense. The drive to add spectacular visual color and performance energy was necessary to help overcome others' perceptions that we were an insignificant team occupying small office space. Little did I realize this practice was only a rehearsal for the next office location.

Early in 1997 I was called into Ron Montalto's office and he said, "Bazerman, you have to move—there's no space for your team in this building any longer." That was it, we had to move.

We relocated to the Eastern District of HK Island, a remote area called Shau Kei Wan (SKW), literally translated as Colander Bay. The first time I went to see this location was with one of my most trusted staff, Jessica Choi. I respected her input and the strong influence she had on the rest of our team. Although Jessica was born in HK, she was unfamiliar with this remote Eastern District area. We took the MTR (Metro Transit Railway) about a thirty-minute train ride from our current office. The SKW location was so offbeat that we had asked Barry Fichter, VP of the Mattel Overseas Design & Development (MODD) engineering team, whose office was in that building, to meet us at the MTR exit and guide us to the building.

Barry Fichter was an American engineer who had over thirty years' experience in the toy business. He'd recently been assigned to head the engineering team in HK and China. Mr. Fichter was a soft-spoken, courteous gentleman, who was patiently waiting for me and Jessica at the MTR station exit. Once out of the station we found ourselves on Shau Kei Wan Main Street.

The first thing I noticed was the quiet village neighborhood so opposite the busy tourist atmosphere at Harbour City, Tsim Sha Tsui. Shau Kei Wan used to be a small fishing village and now it was a residential community with old-style buildings and small deteriorating storefronts that had a great view of Victoria Harbour. We walked the few blocks with Barry to the Mattel office, passing the many tiny businesses of fragrant noodle shops, grocery stores, and multiple fresh fish markets. These fish markets were all crowded with local residents huddled over ice-covered tables accommodating wiggling fish that customers were purchasing for dinner. The distinctive fresh fish and stagnant water smell wafted out of the markets' doors and the stench made it difficult to breathe deeply in the summer heat.

I was dressed to impress in my business attire with state-ment jewelry, coordinating accessories, and matching high-heeled purple shoes, which made it difficult to quickly tiptoe over the path of seafood entrails, discarded fish scales, and fish blood running out from the markets. I did my best not to stain my shoes or get the unavoidable blood spattered on my ankles!

Overwhelmed with emotion at this experience, bordering on depression, I remember thinking to myself, **"What the fucking hell am I doing here?"**

After walking a couple of blocks we turned the corner to A Kung Ngam Village Road, where Mattel had their offices. It was a dark green, five-story warehouse with a huge sign on top of the building that said Mattel HK (LTD). Many years earlier this facility had been used to manufacture Mattel toys before production moved to China. There was no lobby, the main entrance was a dark, dirty, disgusting, mold-ridden parking garage, with an old freight elevator emitting fumes from the accumulated garbage debris. We took this elevator to the upper floors.

HKSG was to occupy the third floor and the plan was to share this area with two other groups, one team that did the fabric sourcing and another that developed package graphics. There was no room any longer for either of these Mattel staffs at Harbour City and it made sense that we would be located together at SKW. The other half of the floor was occupied by a non-Mattel company that made display mannequins for department stores. The hallway was strewn with plastic arms, legs, torsos, and heads of adult- and child-size mannequins. It looked like an ancient mortuary, which was almost refreshing to see after walking through the fish blood-covered streets, until I passed by the public bathroom located next to the elevator. Now I found the streets filled with fish blood multiple levels above the hygiene standard of our new office location.

As we entered the existing abandoned third-floor office space, the filth and decrepit environment repulsed me. How could a Barbie Design and Development team work out of this dreary dungeon that was basically in a slum building? Never mind my team or Barbie's image, now it was getting personal— what about my **Personal Brand Image**?

After the facility tour we took the freight elevator back down to the garage entrance and walked to the MTR station. We were careful not to trip over the empty discarded produce boxes or slip on the still-moist fish blood and animal body parts pouring out from the markets, covering the sidewalk. Stray dogs now lined the street, targeting the blood residue or a morsel of fish head floating over the concrete.

Jessica and I were silent and stared at each other until I cheerfully declared we could make this move beneficial for us and design an office that would be a like a diamond at the bottom of a coal mine. I told Jessica not to worry, that I would make sure the staff would be happy to move to this quiet fishing village in Shau Kei Wan. The office would be a palace, Barbie's Dreamhouse!

Actually, I had no idea what I would do, but as Director I had to present a positive, optimistic attitude to overcome my personal shock at the thought of moving to this hideous hell on planet earth. I wanted to make Jessica feel I could handle whatever obstacles came our way. I would create a beautiful office and design a great working environment to insure a good transition for the HKSG team. I gathered all my strength to cover my real feeling of "get me out of here" and proceeded to think of an economical way to make this office into the dream I'd promised. Cosmopolitan life near this new office would only be a memory for our team at SKW.

Personal Brand Image:

Even if it looks impossible, but you know it's right, support it—you will find a way

It was outside my realm of knowledge how to create a new office from the bottom up, or even from the top down. There was nothing in this warehouse to build on, even the toilets didn't meet any twentieth-century sanitation standards. Mr. Ron Drwinga helped me get a contractor that would handle the construction and provide the drawings of the interior for my approval. I was given the responsibility of creating the office design the contractor would execute.

I thought giving me this assignment was ridiculous. On the other hand this was an opportunity to expand my creativity and have on-the-job training for how to select air-conditioning units, doors, desks, toilets, and urinals! I decided to make this fun. My boss, Don Hartling, gave me a free hand in the design as long as I was within budget. There were no corporate standards or office specifications to follow, and anything would be an upgrade from the mold, dirt, and fish-blood stains of the current decor.

I told Melvin about Shau Kei Wan and the building that needed major renovation. With a worried look on his face, he insisted on seeing the area and building for himself. We went on a weekend via taxi since there was no public transportation from our flat. The taxi left us at the MTR station and I took Melvin for a walk on the same path from Main Street to the office. The first thing he wanted to know was whether this location safe to work in.

It was a long walk to the MTR station, and my staff was mostly women who worked late in the evening. I'd never thought about the safety aspect. I'd been focused on the inside environment, not the outside. I had an obligation to my staff to make sure this new neighborhood was safe. Our Harbour City office location was filled with offices, shops, lots of tourists, and bright lights. Shau Kei Wan was desolate by comparison. The Mattel admin staff was noncommittal about Shau Kei Wan's security. Melvin wasn't satisfied and asked me to get him a contact at the police department. One of my colleagues was married to a lovely young lady who worked for the HK government. She gave me the English-speaking police officer's contact information and Melvin arranged a meeting with him.

This was unbelievable. In a couple of weeks we met with the police officers, who reassured us that the neighborhood was very safe and had one of the lowest crime rates in HK. If any of our staff was working late and afraid to walk to the MTR, we could call the police for an escort. In addition, when we opened the office, they proposed to visit us at our location to answer any staff questions. This was an amazing response and very caring. With all of New York City's sophisticated sparkle, cosmopolitan atmosphere, and modern conveniences, if I'd asked the police about safety they would've said, "Be careful and call us when you have a problem."

One of the most prestigious HK locations is the Central District. In the 1990s this was my favorite pick for upscale shopping as well as open vendor stalls for bargains. Loved walking through the streets and alleys, browsing new and old HK culture. Among this festival of shopping were hotels, restaurants, banks, and a never-ending supply of gold jewelry stores. Central was the best example of HK capitalism at work. Everyone had one objective: to make money. In the heart of Central, mixed with all these contrasting sights, is a historic commercial building, **The Pedder Building** (circa 1923), filled with shops and doctors' offices. In 1994 a prominent HK businessman, David Tang, opened a breakthrough flagship store in The Pedder Building that occupied the first and second floors, called **Shanghai Tang**.

This was a store with unique clothing for men and women, but more impressive than the merchandise was the interior design. The clothing designs combined the nostalgia of the 1920s and 1930s with a twentieth-century attitude. When the store opened I was amazed at every detail. The facade, window displays, clothing, and home goods created a contemporary Chinese eye-candy environment. Now, seventy years later, Mr. Tang designed the store as if it were still 1920s Shanghai, but with touches of vivid contemporary colors and modern design.

WOW! The dark wood reception counter as you opened the glass doors, the wood columns, the multicolored tiled floors, the velvet-covered chairs, the lighting, spiral staircase, tea sets, and at every turn there was another amazing artifact. Everything was perfect to take you back into history with an exquisite journey in style. I loved this place. I could have moved in and stayed forever. All details were matching and color coordinated with the clothing that matched the shopping bags, gift wrapping, packages, and note cards. All saturated in turquoise, purple, orange, lime green, and fuchsia with Chinese styling melting together like hot fudge over ice cream. This atmosphere was invigorating and at the same time calming. It had a definite **Brand Image** that became identified as **Shanghai Tang Style**.

I pondered my new office space in Shau Kei Wan. Why couldn't I make a similar statement and transform the old, run-down, filthy warehouse into a design haven on the third floor, with inspiring style and creativity? It would be a surprise, a showplace for staff and visitors after walking through the village, passing the smelly fish market, jumping over blood, and entering through the parking garage entrance. I could take inspiration from the transformation David Tang accomplished with Shanghai Tang and do it on a budget, with interesting artwork and bright colors. The gray, green, and beiges were out, making way for purple and turquoise. I asked the building contractor to visit the Shanghai Tang store for interior design ideas and to come back with sketches for the reception area at Shau Kei Wan.

With my lessons learned from the Harbour City office, I wasn't about to design a space with bad feng shui. Norma called on Master Au to visit SKW and help us design our new office with a good balance between man and nature. There was nothing left in the warehouse space after gutting the debris. It was like a blank canvas. Master Au was able to recommend the location of our entrance, my office, staff desk positions, the sewing room, the engineering area, and even the badly needed toilets, all to make use of the good energy and improve our luck. Once these key points were identified it was easy to plan the layout.

This would be my own facility, designed as I wanted it, very different from being assigned to an existing small office space in which we just threw some desks together. HKSG would now have a customized atmosphere to meet our needs and inspire creativity. The staff would know I felt they deserved the best environment inside even though the outside neighborhood was old and run down. The inside would be First Class with a mix of East Meets West and Feng Shui Friendly. Creating a unique artistic environment could only reinforce the expectations that HKSG was responsible for the fashion aesthetics of iconic Barbie.

The environment would be a reflection of the staff and vice versa. In other words, it's similar to how someone would answer questions like, "Would you have your hair styled by someone who had a bad haircut?" or "Would you buy flowers from a shop that only had dead plants?"

Looks aren't everything, but they do start the romance. The love story with Shau Kei Wan began with our relocation in early 1997. I selected textiles as a theme for Chinese folk paintings as wall decorations. The conference room had red lacquer antique replica cabinets with paintings of dragons. I found this was cheaper than building storage cabinets and conveyed the style to give HKSG its own Brand Image. The office's main feature was the reception area. As you exited the old freight elevator to our office entrance, there was the surprise "Shanghai Tang" experience. The reception desk was dark wood in a good curved feng shui design. Behind the desk was floor-to-ceiling glass set in a wooden circle design. In one of the giant circles was the famous round red Mattel logo to complete the feel of continuous harmony. The tiled floor, the Chinese antique replica benches, and the display cases filled with stunning high-end collector Barbies set the mood for what was inside the office.

The reception area's highlight was a custom-made Chinese Barbie sculpture. I wanted a strong Brand Image of an art studio to greet all who entered after the dismal journey to the office. I had read in the local HK newspaper about a British artist, Louise Soloway, who was now a HK resident. There was a full-page article about her and photos of her work. Louise specialized in creating "Life Casts." The photo examples in the newspaper were of life-size female human torsos or buttocks, cast in a substrate and painted with Chinese dragons or Asian landscape scenes. Louise actually created plaster casts with real human body parts to craft the three-dimensional models. This was inspirational and the perfect blend of art + humor + visual statement.

This clever interpretation of the human body with an Asian accent had all the elements of playful fun and was perfect for the HKSG office entrance. Louise was commissioned to cast, sculpt, and paint a Barbie image in her unique style. I requested Louise use the three-foot-tall **My Size Barbie** (the same doll that had Haris as a fit model) to be cast in the style of the iconic 1960 Barbie Solo In the Spotlight. On top of the casting, Louise painted a pattern in a style reminiscent of Ming Dynasty blue and white floral porcelain. This was the welcoming Brand Image of Barbie, featured in a high-energy location, as directed by Master Au. There she was, Barbie with a Chinese attitude.

The warehouse, or at least the third floor, was now transformed into a Mattel design studio. Between the feng shui, creative interior design, and police community discussions for our staff, I felt immensely proud of this accomplishment. And I was now qualified to do office renovations!

Personal Brand Image:

Keep the trusted brand, deliver what you promise.

Chapter 19

The Handovers

We successfully relocated to our beautiful new Shau Kei Wan office in early 1997. Later that year, on July 1, Hong Kong would be handed over to the People's Republic of China. Would Hong Kong, this "Pearl of the Orient," implode and the forces of communism rule everyone's lives? Or even worse, would the Chinese government confiscate the residents' enormous wealth, which had been accumulated in this tiny colony under British leadership? These speculations had been the news headlines for years.

By the time July 1, 1997, arrived it was like any day except for the royal handover ceremony attended by Charles, Prince of Wales. The distinguished, peaceful manner in which the British, after occupying Hong Kong for 150 years, handed this territory back to China seemed normal as having late-afternoon tea.

The mystery of what would happen next was in the minds of the HK people and the world was watching. I was watching. Would Mattel still keep its office in HK? Would the Mattel factories in China still exist? Would I still live in HK after the Chinese ruled this city? Would I have a job? The future was unknown. One thing was certain, that China wouldn't want to lose the money-making machine of HK. China agreed that the rule of law in HK would remain for fifty years after the handover, which would take us to 2047. I decided not to focus on the "what ifs" but move in the direction of how to do my best, add to Mattel's success, and keep my job.

My focus was on the Barbie product line, hiring staff, and building a rapport with all my American male engineering colleagues and the local Chinese. In addition, I had to continue to keep the Mattel California design office happy with great product results from my new staff. After all, we were developing the glamorous fashions for the iconic **Barbie** doll. Her detailed clothing, with tiny buttons, sequins, and intricate details echo human clothing on an eleven-and-a-half-inch plastic body, would have to be closely monitored, like a newborn baby on life support. Any poor workmanship or defect in fit, design, or color is very noticeable on Barbie's small figure and a wrong decision would mean failure. Her whole fashion ensemble needs to make a perfect impression with only a few inches showing in a package. A small defect on human-size clothing would virtually go unnoticed, but for Barbie, a tiny wrinkle, hanging thread, or color mismatch in clothing on her doll-size body would look like a huge error and would be rejected by a customer.

It took a trained design eye and a passion for perfection to ensure the fashions were produced as if they were haute couture, a collection for a high-end apparel company. I averaged a twelve-hour work day, so I was almost relieved that my China office proposal was on hold, even though I thought it would be a great business opportunity for Mattel. My focus was on making the HK team more integral to the creative aspect of product development.

Months after the handover of HK to China, there was no communist infiltration as anticipated. Mattel California finally realized that the China risk was worth taking. As I predicted, the cost of doing business in HK was increasing and my department was expanding. It was all about the money. Capitalism was alive and well. Late in 1997 I received the go-ahead for my **China Proposal**, to establish a soft good design and development team in South China, near one of the Mattel doll factories.

My vision would become reality. What have I gotten myself into? Would being a woman in a leadership role in China be the end of my career? Would the Chinese respect me? I had to make this work. I not only had to prove I was right, but also change how Mattel executed the design and development business. I was ready to jump into battle.

Personal Brand Image:

It may take a while, but good ideas will not go unnoticed.

We needed a location in Guangzhou, China. I imagined a design studio, not a factory atmosphere. My feeling was that if you wanted to eventually design in China, you had to have an environment that reflects and influences that objective. I had two options. One was the Mattel factory that manufactured millions of Barbie dolls, and the other was a facility few miles away, a Mattel tooling factory for plastic parts, which had an empty third level fitted with a roof, dirt floors, and concrete walls. This empty "dirt room" appealed to me, an artist's dream of a giant marble block ready to be chiseled into a masterpiece.

The building's two lower floors were occupied by machines that produced the dolls' plastic parts. It was like a bakery with different-shaped cookie molds. Only instead of assorted cookie-cutter shapes like hearts or cute animal silhouettes popping out of the molds, they were Barbie legs, arms, heads, torsos, shoes, and various fashion accessories. After the liquid plastic was poured and solidified into the molds, the parts were ready to be taken to the manufacturing plant to be assembled into recognizable Barbie dolls.

The color palette of the furnishings in the dark, dusty building, other than Barbie's many skin tones, was gray accented with gray concrete floors. Some offices were "avant-garde" and contained light beige fabric on the chairs. I commented to the factory director that this location was very dull looking and depressing. The director replied, "Well this is the standard in China and you can do the same on the upper floor with your new offices. Nothing else is expected!" I humbly thought to myself, "Maybe China standards but it is not my standard."

I was no architect or interior designer, but as I'd learned with the Shau Kei Wan office, the environment would be a big influence on the staff's creativity. The building location was in a remote area surrounded by large, swampy rice fields and the shocking sight of dogs being sold on the corner to be slaughtered for the local residents' dinners! In this atmosphere, how would we find staff to think about pink glitter and sparkle to fashionably dress a blue-eyed, blonde Barbie doll?

It was important to make sure our working environment looked like a design studio and attracted good fortune. The Chinese staff would expect a harmonious atmosphere to bring good luck. Feng shui was necessary to create a positive energy design space. Now I'm not superstitious. However, I'd learned over the years with the HK office's success that a harmonious environment can produce positive feelings and this feeling can attract good luck.

I went with a winning formula and asked feng shui Master Au to accompany me to China. Once he walked around with his giant compass in hand, he advised me on placement of all the offices, the best entrance site, and furniture positions. No need to have an interior designer—Master Au did it all, to keep humans in balance with nature. He even recommended the specific color palette that would bring good fortune and calm.

The result was a large, open studio with turquoise tile floors, bright multicolored upholstered chairs, purple tile bathrooms, and a lime-green colored tea pantry. I made sure the dishes for dining were color coordinated, and the wall décor was Chinese folk art that reflected the bright colors and positive energy. Symbolic paintings of waterfalls were displayed at the entrance, to carry in good fortune. A large tank with eight plump, healthy goldfish was placed outside the managers' offices to insure good luck and attract fortune, which equals success.

This was an amazing office located in a colorless environment. Any visitor or staff that made the long journey to get to this remote location would enter this world of bright colors after the long, gray, dusty concrete journey and would find an emotional ease and welcoming environment at the **Mattel China Soft Goods (MCSG)** office. The smiling faces and expressions of joy from staff and visitors were a welcome sight for the new challenges ahead and a great way to start business.

When the office was complete, Mr. Ray Faulkner, the factory's vice president, told me, "Paulette, you brought first-rate class to Mattel in China." Ray was so impressed that in the next year he redecorated the factory offices to coordinate with what I had colorfully designed for MCSG. Gray and beige were finally history.

Personal Brand Image:

If you want to be treated as creative, show creativity in your personal style as well as in your workplace.

As a child in Brooklyn, New York, I never could have imagined that on the other side of the world, in a place I couldn't find on a map, I would create an organization, design an office with a feng shui master, and train staff to develop fashions for the most famous doll in the world.

Master Au picked the numerically auspicious day of January 8, 1999 (1-8-1999) to formally open our new office in Guangzhou. This would be a traditional Chinese festive ceremony with staff, friends, and family invited. This Grand Opening, in a very small way, could be compared to what happened in HK, another handover, only reversed. My office had been a location governed by communism, ruled by men, and focused on pumping out massive amounts of product. Now this same location was being handed over to an American female desiring to bring color, creativity, and local jobs to a rural, dirt-filled, rice-field dominated neighborhood.

Keeping with Chinese tradition, I wore red and gold. I made sure to add my style of embroidered jacket over a red dress and matching red high-heeled shoes decorated with large, gold metallic beads. The good energy existing around my office needed to be brought in and any bad energy needed to be removed for the staff to safely enter the building and start business. This was the purpose of the Grand Opening ceremony.

I anxiously approached two large reclining Chinese lion replicas in front of the new office building. My staff instructed me to paint their vicious eyes with a large brush they handed me. This symbolic action would bring the lions to life, so they would dance and jump to the loud beating of drums, which would scare away all the bad spirits. As soon as the brush touched the lions' eyes, the creatures came to life, standing high over my head. A rush of excitement filled my heart and the crowd. The men inside the lion disguises became animated and made these ostentatious, gigantic puppets seem fiercely alive. They were frantically dancing to loud drumbeats from the three drummers behind me, to scare off bad spirits. The lions and drummers entered my office building to remove negative energy from the new Mattel China Soft Goods office.

Inside the office two large roasted pigs, a symbolic offering to the gods, were placed on a colorfully decorated table. I cut into the crisp, cooked pork skin with a huge knife, followed by another offering to the gods, when I poured three cups of wine on the floor.

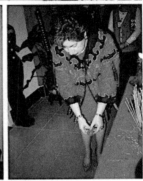

Thousands of firecrackers were ignited outside, and the explosive blasts were intentionally deafening in order to eliminate any more bad spirits. Long sticks of incense were dipped into an oil lamp flame, and when ignited released fragrant smoke to add calmness to the air. I ceremoniously bowed my head three times and meditated about this glorious day and how my unpredictable journey led me to experience this Chinese tradition of a Grand Opening. A start of opportunities not just for me or Mattel, but for all the Chinese staff who would soon be hired.

I found that with focusing on my personal strengths and not following the norm, I could be colorfully brilliant in a sea of gray and concrete. I learned my lessons of how to survive by being great at the small things, which my bosses recognized. Small stuff added up to big accomplishments and my temporary job kept being extended. My life experiences enabled me to lead the breakthrough "China Vision" long before working in China was fashionable.

Melvin and 12 year old Haris joined me to witness this milestone that was not part of our family plan but occurred as the next step to strengthen Mattel's business. The 1999 Grand Opening was a Handover to me of my new office and responsibilities in China.

Chapter 20

Tone It Down

I received a phone call from Don Hartling. He hardly ever called me and when he did it was always a calm business update, no casual chatting. This day was different. He was happy and his voice was relaxed. Don informed me that after thirty-three years working at Mattel and achieving a position of Senior VP, he was taking early retirement at the age of fifty-five. At first this was no big deal for me. Don had been instrumental in supporting my **Proposals** for the HK and China soft goods development teams. He had always been my advocate and trusted me so much that he left me on my own. Because of Don's hands-off leadership style I had an amazing entrepreneurial opportunity in creating an organization, training staff, and learning office interior design. It takes intelligence to know when to back off and I was grateful for his conservative attitude, which let me sink or swim! This experience was more rewarding than going to graduate school and obtaining a master's degree.

I felt if I continued to focus on job excellence, my HK and soon-to-be China office successes would validate me no matter who became my boss. Shortly after Don Hartling left Mattel, I received a phone call.

"Good morning, Paulette—I am your new boss, Gene Insley."

I had no idea who this was. Gene's voice was warm, friendly, and upbeat. He told me we had met when I'd visited California the previous year. Embarrassed, I couldn't recall us meeting, not a reflection on Gene. It was always a whirlwind to go to the California office and I met dozens of people each visit. Gene was

VP of the Fisher-Price Preschool Engineering group, which had recently moved from New York to California after Fisher-Price merged with Mattel. I'd never worked with the Fisher-Price team, so I probably hadn't focused on meeting Gene. Lesson learned—engage with everyone you meet at your company since you never know who will eventually become a vital colleague, or your boss!

I was reintroduced to Gene when he came to HK to meet his new direct reports: me, Barry Fichter, and our teams. Gene walked into my office with a warm smile and casual attitude. It was like getting a visit from a long-lost relative you'd met years ago and felt comfortable the minute you saw him. Gene was a tall gentleman, about my age, with a round face, wavy brown hair, dressed in typical engineer-style attire of a long-sleeve shirt and brown pants, holding a traditional notebook in his hand. He was an impressive man with a noticeably friendly style. As an experienced engineering executive with over twenty years in the toy business, specializing in product development and operations, Gene seemed to be a great choice to lead our teams.

Quite different from Don's formal business personality, Gene scheduled a weekly phone call for our updates, including a weekly "significant event" report to highlight both problems and successes. I now had a boss engaged in the details of what I was doing. The attention was unsettling. After six years of basically being on my own to run my department, I now had to explain everything to my new boss, who was learning about what I did from seven thousand miles away. On the positive side, I believe I impressed Gene, who recognized all my contributions to Mattel. He also became aware of how important soft goods development was to the Barbie Brand. After all, Barbie is a Fashion Doll that needs fashion to wear.

I made sure Gene knew everything I was doing and the struggles I had to overcome. If I had a problem I would always update him and advise him of an intended solution. I made sure Gene knew I had a brain and I wasn't just pink fluff relaxing in an overseas assignment.

Soon after the Grand Opening of my China office, Gene Insley was promoted to Senior VP, Engineering of Worldwide Girls Products. My big boss was now even bigger. During one of our weekly phone conversations, Gene wanted me to know how much he appreciated all my efforts and successes at Mattel. He continued to tell me how happy he was with what I was doing and the giant effort to expand into China. He thanked me. This compliment from Gene was more verbal communication and outward appreciation than I'd received from any boss in all my careers.

In that phone call Gene also talked to me about the many promotions recently implemented in other HK departments. He was wondering if I felt left out because my Asian counterparts were being recognized and rewarded. He wanted me to know he was aware I'd been overlooked for a promotion. Gene promised to work with me and help me reach the next level, to become a vice president. In the meantime, after reviewing my salary compared to others with similar responsibility, he found an inequity that he would correct. I won't even get into the fact that I was the only female, yet he compared me to the male directors who had been promoted to VP. I was unaware of this discrepancy and was amazed that Gene brought up the issue.

In my nearly thirty years of working experience, I'd never had a boss who wanted not only to help me get to the next level, but actually initiated the subject of a promotion. I'd been a director at Mattel for more than seven years and I hadn't been promoted. My HK team had expanded from the small nine-person group to over thirty staff, in addition to another twenty-five staff in China. A few years earlier I'd asked Don Hartling, in a politically appropriate dialogue, about the outlook for my career path. Don simply said that my scope was small and I'd reached the highest level for soft goods engineering. After a moment of confusion and disbelief, I accepted this corporate policy, since moving up the corporate ladder wasn't a priority for me. If Don felt my scope was small it was most likely because I didn't emphasize my own importance and just assumed Don would watch out for me. I decided to move on, knowing that my director title didn't define my accomplishments. It seems I still had the mentality that this was only a temporary job.

Gene had visited HK many times over the years and by 2001 he wrote his own Proposal for what he saw as the future of Design and Development in Asia. He believed that the example of my departments' success, combined with the engineering skills of Barry Fichter's team, were the foundation and precedent for major change in the product development process. The soft goods and hard plastic parts were done in Asia; however, the design, costing, and project management were all executed in California. This disconnect caused repetition and delays. Simply put, Gene proposed adding to Asia all the missing disciplines, to fully complete and approve products in HK.

Revolutionary and brilliant ideology. The surprise was that Gene would relocate the additional skilled staff needed from California to HK, included him to head the division. He named his new team **Asia Design and Development (AD&D)**. Gene Insley was moving to HK!

Personal Brand Image:

No matter your career status, either get used to change and adapt or become a dinosaur.

My boss was now going to be located one floor beneath my office in Shau Kei Wan. When Gene arrived for his expatriate assignment, he asked me how I felt having him in HK after more than two years of our long-distance telephone relationship across the Pacific Ocean. My reply was "It felt that after years of dating we were about to start living together. A new relationship that had no guarantees of happiness!" We laughed since we knew it was the reality.

To complete the AD&D team in HK, a designer was needed who had the trust of Mattel designers in California. That person would join my staff, reporting to me. Gene respected my talent and was expanding my role to have design capabilities. I immediately knew who I wanted, a designer who would be perfect for this assignment.

After HKSG was established, it was routine that California designers would come to HK for onsite approvals of doll components—i.e., hair, face paint, plastic parts, or a complex electronic function. It was more efficient to have a designer fly to HK and stay a week or longer to work with the factory and vendors. Knowing that HKSG was there, Mattel's California staff's comfort level in traveling to China increased. My presence proved that a foreigner could survive in Asia.

After years of China train travel, I had a reputation as a professional escort, accompanying visiting designers on the famous train ride. The common denominator and great equalizer for all Mattel visitors, no matter if they were high-ranking executives or entry-level staff, was this long locomotive experience to Guangzhou. There was no escape from the person you were traveling with because you were on an express train, with no stops and no dining car. You were a prisoner in a moving cell for the entire journey. On the bright side, this was a great opportunity to get to know colleagues and for them to get to know you. Even if you had an obnoxious, opinionated guest you had no choice but to spend a few hours with him or her and either have your perception confirmed or your attitude changed.

The day arrived when I was the train escort for Miss Vonni Yung. Vonni was of Chinese heritage; her parents were from Canton (now Guangzhou), China, and had moved to HK and then the US. Vonni was born in Boston, Massachusetts. She was traveling to a China vendor overseeing a complex package structure's aesthetics. We'd never met before, since Mattel hired Vonni in 1998, while I was working in HK. Our paths never crossed before boarding the early-morning train to Guangzhou.

The first thing you noticed about Vonni was her outstanding classic beauty. She was in her late twenties, about five foot four, and weighed less than ninety-five pounds, but with a muscular, at-the-gym-every-day body. Her hair was an impressive statement. Short, thick black hair with a geometric cut that parted down the middle, and each tendril hanging at the sides of her head trailed down to her chin and was held tight away from her eyes with large, bright-colored, symmetrically placed plastic clips. A tank top, jeans, and trendy shoes completed the fashion statement. To put it simply, Vonni was uniquely exotic and gorgeous.

As prison cellmates on this train, I learned about Vonni's background. She'd graduated from the prestigious Parsons School of Design in NYC with a bachelor of fine arts degree and she'd previously worked for the famous collectible doll company, **Madame Alexander**, in New York. Vonni also was an accomplished theatrical costume designer. It was no surprise that Mattel discovered Vonni and offered her a fashion doll design position in California.

So here she was on her way to Guangzhou, captively sitting next to me for over two hours. It was a continuous conversation between us about NYC, what my group was doing, my philosophy and vision for business, and some Mattel gossip. The train ride seemed like it had just started, yet it was time to exit. Vonni looked at me with a giant smile and dark brown eyes with long, fluttering lashes. She told me that if I ever had an opening in HKSG she would love to move to HK and work for me. It seemed we had a mutual admiration for each other, and I hoped that future synergy would prevail and we would work together in some capacity. Little did I realize this train journey was Vonni's "interview" with me and a few months later I'd be recommending her to Gene Insley for the designer position in the new AD&D organization.

Early in 2001 Gene and his wife Vickie relocated to HK. Gene began the process of bringing staff from Mattel California to HK for this new organization, which included my recommended designer choice, Vonni Yung. This would be the start of our design staff.

Vonni was perfect for this assignment, not only because we had a good rapport, but because she was already a known and trusted designer at Mattel. There was no need to convince California that Vonni was awesome. They already knew that and were happy to have her transferred to HK to support Barbie projects. Vonni blended right in with my staff. An obvious reason was that she was Chinese. Okay, she was born in the US, but that was secondary. She was of the same heritage and had knowledge of spoken Cantonese. Most importantly, Vonni's creative energy was displayed with every breath she took and when she exhaled this energy, its vapor ignited the flames of ideas and magical visions to everyone. She was absolutely creatively contagious. We all loved Vonni and welcomed her infection because it made us happy. She would become my *muse*.

Personal Brand Image:

Take advantage of all inspiration sources, whether from a teacher or a student.

Through Vonni I now had a connection with creative energy, which I'd missed while stationed in HK. Spontaneous creativity is definitely a rare ingredient in Asian culture. Very difficult to teach and overcome the Chinese fear of thinking differently, which was subdued for decades by the communists, as well as the British colonialists who established stringent rules to keep order and build a strong infrastructure. From many previous generations, HK people inherited the art of keeping quiet. I tried my best to stir the mixture of technical ability with spontaneous ideas. This is why I felt the need to do things dramatically and use visual demonstrations that were better, brighter, louder, and obviously exaggerated to make a statement. If I acted in a quiet manner no one would listen to me, and my direction would have no impact unless I emphasized and presented in a flamboyant style.

I remember putting my "Performance Theory" to the test in 2000 when Mattel hired a new CEO, Mr. Bob Eckert, and a new Executive VP, Mr. Tom Debrowski. Upon hiring they needed to have an overview of Mattel's Asia facilities, to gain an understanding of manufacturing capabilities. One of their first stops was our Shau Kei Wan office. I was on the agenda to make a short presentation about HKSG responsibilities. Their high rank in the organization didn't unnerve me. I had full confidence that no matter who was in the audience, I would give 110% effort and be creatively entertaining.

Well there was no way I was going to throw a pie in Mr. Eckert's face. I do have some sense to pick and choose my "targets." Both these gentlemen were new to Mattel and the toy business. Bob was formerly president and CEO of Kraft Foods and Mr. Debrowski was SVP of the Pillsbury Company, but he knew Bob from when they'd both worked at Kraft Foods. They were the "food guys!" How could I capture their attention in a short discussion about fabric development? I had to make it interesting in my own style, and if they thought I was an idiot I would just have to deal with that. This was my only shot at top management and I wasn't going to run scared. It was to our mutual benefit for them to understand what my team did. My presentation would be a novelty among all the charts and graphs they'd be seeing that day from the other department heads.

The main function of the soft goods department was to support the most profitable Brand, Barbie. Therefore I figured I had to make a "Barbie Statement." The scheduled day arrived for Bob and Tom to be in our office. I knew that after the long journey, the drive through the fish market, then entering the gray parking garage to be transported in the dimly lit freight elevator, the sight of a feng shui-inspired, brightly colored office would be refreshing. Once in the conference room the presentations began, and I was first on the agenda. I stood, looked at Bob and Tom, and told them I was a bit worried about them traveling in Asia and touring Mattel facilities without having a "Barbie Survival Kit." They looked at each other with confused smiles. I proceeded to remove two items from a box and presented them each with a Pink Glitter Vinyl Bag labeled **Barbie Survival Kit** that contained essential Barbie necessities.

I asked Bob and Tom to open the Pink Glitter Bags and announce aloud what was inside:

- a few ounces of iridescent glitter
- a dozen pink ribbon rosettes
- sparkling rhinestones
- pink sequins
- pink high-heeled Barbie shoes
- two Barbie bras

Bob and Tom, not to mention the whole room, were laughing. When the gentlemen reached the final items, the Barbie bras, I told them that the bras were for a textile tutorial. Basically we use two kinds of fabrics: 1) a knit construction that stretched when you pulled on it, and 2) a woven construction that was stable and didn't stretch when pulled.

I instructed them to identify which bra was made from woven fabrics and which was a knitted construction. If they could correctly identify the fabrics they would have passed **Barbie Survival Test** and could proceed to complete their tour in Asia.

I could hardly believe what I was witnessing. Mr. Eckert and Mr. Debrowski had serious expressions as their man-sized hands tugged the tiny Barbie bras to get the correct answer. One by one they correctly identified the knit and then the woven. With Barbie bras wrapped around their fingers, I officially certified them as Barbie Experts. This bra tug exhibit was truly hysterical to watch. They loved it. This was the opener for my brief, but memorable, discussion.

Personal Brand Image:

Humor is a great equalizer and can get you recognition no matter who is in your audience.

I knew when Vonni Yung started to work for me that she not only understood my do-not—be-boring style, but that she would be my accomplice exploring the extraordinary. At last I had a colleague who understood the HK Chinese culture's lack of spontaneity and recognized that the desire for fun at work was nonexistent. Vonni was the exact opposite to the native Hongkongers and she helped bridge this gap just by being herself. She was a prime example that having Chinese heritage in no way limits creative potential. The only difference between her and Mattel's HK staff was that Vonni was born in the US and had lived in many cosmopolitan cities. Vonni's style and attitude was acquired from the culture she lived in. I hoped her mere presence would stimulate a desire for the local staff to break out from being conservative. Vonni was the perfect stimulus for imaginative ways, to loosen up and have some fun at work.

Vonni helped me make my presentations more impactful by adding digital animations and contemporary music to the images of charts and statistics. My refreshed presentations became legendary and my talks always had a full house. I was outrageously funny to get the message across and I became known as the Bette Midler of HK.

Halloween wasn't a tradition in HK. I must say if it weren't for my son wanting to dress up and trick-or-treat, this holiday had no meaning for me either. Vonni made it into a major celebration to get the staff in a creative mood by wearing costumes and treating everyone to candy. Pure theatrical joy with mummies wrapped in gauze, bloody bodies, wigs, makeup, glitter, and hats.

Christmas got the western nostalgia SKW family photo. The Chinese New Year celebration which was usually a formal banquet with lots of red wine, traditional New Year food, and a few speeches. Vonni decided this year the celebration should be a masquerade party with entertainment, a best mask competition, and a photo booth to take fun pictures. It was supernatural to witness the HK and China staff engaged in thinking differently and having fun, drinking up the powerful brew of fantasy.

Vonni's design ability gave us more aesthetic capability. Our creative style increased confidence, our team sucked in more projects. We were overloaded with work and additional designers were eventually hired reporting to Vonni.

Personal Brand Image:

If you continue to be true to your Brand Image you will be trusted, understood, and followed.

My scope was expanding, and the confidence from Gene Insley and Mattel California were evident. During an update with Gene he casually brought up his campaign to get my VP promotion approved. He told me the process was difficult because as VP of a public company, you're an "officer," along with the responsibility that comes with the title. The approval needed to come not just from your boss (in my case, Gene), but from a committee of executives at Mattel California. A promotion was a long-distance run and not in Gene's control. Months went by and Gene never discussed the VP status with me. I trusted him and knew he would do his best to get my promotion approved.

Late in 2001 Gene called me to his office for an update. He had an unusually serious attitude the morning of our meeting. Although pleasant, he was very direct and borderline tactless in his manner. He simply stated that when he sponsored a VP promotion for me, his request was denied. He told me the reason was that certain Mattel California executives felt I didn't have the "proper style" to be a Mattel VP. I had too much "New York Attitude" and this offended some people in California. No names were mentioned, but whoever it was in California didn't see me on a daily basis. Gene was very disappointed, and there was no way to change the minds of those in California who had the power to make my promotion happen. He suggested I watch what I say and **tone down my style**!

Before I could take a breath, Gene offered to send me for a training program at the famous **Center for Creative Leadership** (CCL) in San Diego, California. The aim was to correct any negative aspects of my style by participating in a week-long **Leadership Development Program** at this prestigious school. I sat for a moment, quietly thinking about what was happening to me. Without any hesitation or control over my actions I blurted out in a loud rude voice, "So you want to send me to *finishing school*?" I proceeded to move directly into unprofessional mode and tears rolled down my reddened cheeks.

Gene was obviously uncomfortable with my emotion. He couldn't tell me the details of exactly who, when, or what the problem was, but it didn't matter anyway. Somehow I felt my accomplishments didn't matter as well. The rejection was based on the perception of my style!

Completely devoid of my **Personal Brand Image** at this time, I told Gene I didn't want to work for a company that didn't respect me and I was going to my office to pack my things and go home. Gene advised me to think about the offer and let him know how I felt the next day. I asked if going to CCL meant I would get a promotion. He calmly told me there was no guarantee, but it would be a step in the right direction.

I turned my back on Gene, hiding my blushing, tear-stained face. I immediately went to my office, avoiding looking at anyone. I was in no mood to be cordial. The only thing I wanted to do was go home.

I had a new assistant because amazing Norma had gotten married and was able to stop working. Of course I missed her protective, caring style, but I luckily found a new assistant with different skills. Miss Edith Au started to work for me on February 14, 2000, Valentine's Day, and offered a subdued professional approach to the job. Edith was in her late twenties and recently married. She was an attractive, soft-spoken, smart young lady. What impressed me the most was her warm manner and her excellent command of the English language. Her qualifications offered me more technical support with preparing departmental budgets and she had advanced computers skills. Edith was exactly what I needed to support my expanded role at AD&D.

Edith became indispensable. Her professional capabilities impressed everyone and she looked out for me. Actually she took care of me as if I were her own mother. When I told Edith I had something personal to take care of and wouldn't be back that afternoon, she knew something was wrong because she maintained my calendar and no special commitment was scheduled. I had never taken any sick leave or left the office on short notice. Today was certainly different.

Unfortunately I had regressed to an infantile state after my meeting with Gene. I obsessed about the irony of the situation. If I didn't conduct business in my flamboyant style, I never could have been a success on this assignment or even been offered the expatriate position at Mattel. This was an overwhelmingly sad state of affairs and brought me back to the days when I worked in Lauratex in the 1970s, being told I wasn't getting a promotion because I didn't have the right "style."

It seemed that even after thirty years of work experience I hadn't learned how to play the political game. At Mattel I was only focused on executing the job and mentoring staff. In the corporate world this attitude doesn't place you in an upward direction on the promotion ladder. In some respects I was still in "temporary job assignment" mode. At the beginning of this assignment I didn't intend to remain in HK more than two years, and after that I wasn't planning to work at Mattel in California. Therefore every year I remained in HK was like icing on the cake. However, it was devastation at the rejection of my **Personal Brand Image** that caused me to plummet into the depths of despair, crying nonstop in Melvin's arms.

Chapter 21

Bittersweet

Melvin tried his best to calm me down, but I was too deep into hysteria to be rational or listen to anything reasonable. The best I could do was continue crying, and eventually the flow of tears on my face would relieve the pressure in my heart and on my brain. This Brand Image I certainly didn't want to share with anyone.

After almost ten years of working in HK, this was the first time I'd wanted to resign. With all the inconveniences I'd put up with over the years, the thought never crossed my mind to give up. This day was different. I felt totally unappreciated for this decade of work at Mattel. Although the cultural and financial benefits were immense, I was ready to quit for the insulting rejection of my "style," not for the denial of a promotion.

Melvin agreed with me that I had every right to be upset. Even so he asked me to think it over and if I felt the same way in the morning he'd support my decision. He went on to comment that it wouldn't be so bad to accept the offer to attend the **Center for Creative Leadership** in San Diego. With airfare, tuition, and expenses this would cost Mattel over $15,000. This was a very expensive trip and a costly leadership program for a week. Melvin felt Mattel was willing to invest in me and I had nothing to lose by going to "finishing school." I could always quit my job later and I would still have benefited from the experience.

There were many reasons, other than his awesome good looks, that I was right to marry Melvin, and one reason was his brilliant commonsense approach to life. I couldn't argue with his suggestion and I agreed to go back to work the next day and tell Gene I would accept the offer and attend the program.

Personal Brand Image:

Regardless of feelings take the opportunity for self-improvement. Feelings can change but self-improvement is lasting.

Ice packs on my swollen post-crying eyes and a large cup of strong coffee got me awake and ready to get back to work. I still had mixed emotions about going to "finishing school" versus marching into Gene's office and resigning. Gene was a good guy and tried his best to help me. If it weren't for him, the proposal for my VP promotion would never have been initiated. I wasn't mad at him, just disappointed at his direct style of telling me the news. Then again, he's an *engineer* so I'm sure he thought the direct way was the best way to handle the situation.

I sucked up all my pride and apologized to Gene for my outburst. He looked at me in a fatherly manner and I felt he understood my feelings and didn't take my reaction personally. A rather long pause followed and I told him that I appreciated the offer and agreed to attend the Center for Creative Leadership. Gene was obviously happy with my decision.

The next CCL Leadership Development Program started on January 14, 2002, for five days of classes. I enrolled and put my feelings away for the time being, so I could carry on as usual. I'm not made of steel and the feelings of rejection hung over my head and broke my spirit. Another great performance was needed for me to keep going under pressure at Mattel.

Personal Brand Image:

Hold on to your Brand—you'll need it. Don't break under emotional pressure when you need your Brand Image the most.

I wanted to have a clear direction of where my career was going, not to mention where my home residence would be in 2002. Haris had another three years of high school and I hoped to at least have him complete that part of his education in HK. I was motivated to make this CCL adventure work, but my heart was broken because Mattel wasn't recognizing what I had accomplished for the past decade, instead basing my promotion on someone's personal perception.

The circumstances under which I was attending the CCL program were a bit grim. I felt anger and resentment, while my classmates celebrated the privilege of attending this prestigious program. I decided to have fun because I had nothing to lose. The class was eighteen participants, seven men and eleven women, coming together from different companies. That meant we were all strangers, on a level playing field to mix and participate in the events. I was relieved that I was the only Mattel employee attending, so that I could interact and say whatever I felt without fear of corporate backlash.

The CCL schedule for the week was a combination of talks, lectures, group projects, and role-play scenarios, all run by a facilitator to guide us through the process and keep us focused on leadership development. This week I decided not to "tone it down." I was going to be myself with all my New York Attitude and display my **Personal Brand Image**. If there truly was something wrong with my style, I figured this was the group that would tell me the reality. I spoke my mind, told my story, and didn't hold back any feelings or opinions. I'd been waiting months for this opportunity to ask the following questions:

- What is the perception of my style?
- Why isn't my style perceived as fitting in with the corporate community?
- Do I make remarks that can be interpreted as insulting when the intention may only be humor?
- Do I talk too much?
- Am I condescending?

- Do I overpower by being too passionate?

The last part of the program was with an executive coach. I welcomed some professional input and wanted to tell my story of why I was at CCL. Then I could receive input on how to turn the VP rejection into a VP promotion. I hadn't been Dr. D's patient for ten years and I was looking forward to speaking to someone with a psychological approach to business who could objectively advise me. In other words, another opinion!

The assigned coach was Lynn Rhodes, a woman about my age, who had experience traveling around the world, including Asia, and coaching clients from Fortune 500 companies. Lynn had been a coach, trainer, facilitator, and a mentor for other coaches with CCL for over fifteen years. She explained to me that she had credentials as a Board Certified Coach and Licensed Clinical Social Worker. With a warm smile and soft-spoken voice Lynn asked me how she could help me obtain my career goals. At that point I felt I was in a safe place with Lynn and could tell her the reason I was attending CCL. I was very verbal and emotional when I explained how rejected I was feeling after ten years of devoting myself to Mattel and the creative work I had done in Asia.

Lynn heard my entire story and she also had the results of written feedback from my Mattel peers, boss, and other executives. She shared with me that I had very positive scores from my peers, staff, and my boss Gene. However there was a problem with other executives, who saw a negative style. My leadership scores were very high, indicating that people saw me as a strong, capable leader. The input from my CCL group was also very positive. The conclusion of all this was that I was not crazy! I needed to network, letting my colleagues outside of Hong Kong get to know me. I needed to become more political and manage up to my superiors, especially those who didn't work with me in HK.

From five days' worth of professional evaluations and discussions, I found out that I was healthy but I required some surgery to survive. I was relieved with the diagnosis that I wasn't insane and embraced all the advice to transform the perception of my style into "executive quality." Was I looking forward to changing my **Personal Brand Image**? Absolutely not, but now I wanted the VP title, as the corporate recognition I felt I'd earned. The Mattel promotion rejection and CCL experience was bittersweet. I acknowledge that it was my fault for thinking that in a large corporation you would be rewarded primarily on merit. This isn't the case. Merit opens the door, but you cannot just walk through—you need be invited into the next room after you've obtained A-list ratings. It seems I hadn't seen the sign on the door that said "Members Only."

Personal Brand Image:

You have to be flexible, adjusting your Brand to attract the audience you want applause from.

Immediately upon my return to HK, I thanked Gene for the opportunity to attend CCL. My plans were to change the way the Mattel executives perceived me. I know Gene wanted me to be promoted because he knew what I had accomplished and he cared about me. My political work on my Brand was about to begin.

The first thing I did was painfully watch every word I said or memo I wrote. I put my New York Attitude away in a closet and politely toned down my speech and style. I made presentations that were strictly graphs and charts, without music and flashing lights. I made it a point to focus on the big-picture vision of the soft goods expansion into doing more fashion designs and planning a new soft goods department at our Jakarta, Indonesia, facility (PTMI).

On my next visit to Mattel California I arranged a meeting with key executives to update them on the status of Asia product development, innovation, and new technology. I asked for their input and improvement opportunities. I was soft spoken and professionally serious in demeanor. In my opinion, rather boring.

Personal Brand Image:

Change your Image when needed to get the result you want.

To reinforce my executive style, I planned a major off-site event at a HK hotel to accommodate seventy-five vendors from Asia and key staff. I conservatively named this meeting the **Fabric Vendor Conference**, scheduled in a few months on November 2, 2002. I wanted to inspire all the vendors, as I had with my staff years before, about how special Barbie was and give them an emotional history of the Brand so they could relate to Barbie as being **more than a doll**. I had Vonni Yung design a special "More than a Doll" Barbie, wearing her famous black-and-white striped bathing suit, as she did in 1959, to give as a thank-you souvenir to all conference attendees.

I was really proud to initiate this meeting and hopefully enlighten vendors about the unique Barbie Brand. I remember the morning of the event, I decided to wear something that would subtly capture my **Personal Brand Image**. Even though I wasn't taking center stage with a dynamic performance, I chose a purple custom-made Thai silk pantsuit. The purple was a deep rich shade and the silk literally sparkled in the sunshine. I looked quite stunning in head-to-toe purple, which gave me a special aura and helped impart some of that Wonder Woman Power I desperately need that day.

The vendor conference was held on the Kowloon side, near our office. Therefore I had to take the Star Ferry and across the Harbour. It was late fall and the weather was good. I was looking forward to a quiet, peaceful ferry ride to contemplate the stressful day ahead. Just as I sat down to relax, Gene Insley rushed on the ferry and sat next to me. We had a casual conversation and he commented on how great I looked in my purple business suit. I had previously asked him if he would give a short opening speech at this conference and then introduce me.

I reminded him that he was on stage first and my assistant Edith Au was there if he had questions.

The hotel banquet room was crowded, with our vendors ready for us to roll out the new AD&D process, talk about Mattel's expectations, reinforce Barbie's iconic status, and give the vendors a chance to voice their concerns. I signaled to Gene to go to the podium to kick off the meeting. Gene had a two-minute slot to introduce me. I waited in the back of the room. Edith was with me, overseeing the day's schedule.

Gene started his speech but he seemed to be talking in circles about soft goods. The speech was well into overtime and I looked at Edith with amazement. Gene was improvising, almost rambling and not keeping to his two minutes. I wondered if Gene was having a senior moment and forgot that his speech was supposed to be brief. This was very unlike Mr. Professional Gene Insley. I was worried. He eventually slowed down, paused, and said,

"Finally, I would like to introduce our host for this meeting, the Vice President of Soft Goods Design and Development, Miss Paulette Bazerman."

I really didn't understand what was happening, but everyone in the audience was screaming, shouting, standing, applauding, and turning around to look at me. My staff, who were attending this meeting, got up from their chairs and ran over to me, crying with joy and hugging me. I had no idea that clever, underhanded, plotting Mr. Gene Insley was going to publicly announce my promotion to vice president at this meeting ... or at all. Gene stood on the podium, beaming like a proud parent at his child who did well on a test and received an award. I swear the lights in the room reflected visible tears on his cheek and he was pacing with excitement. My first thought was "How fortunate I wore a purple business suit today!"

Personal Brand Image:

Find a mentor to help grow your Brand.

Chapter 22

Turn It Up

The very public way my VP promotion was announced had to be the biggest surprise of my life, ranking in shock value right next to Melvin proposing marriage after only knowing me for five days. When the applause died down after the promotion announcement, I excused myself and went to the ladies' room to wash my face and quickly phone Melvin to tell him the news.

Back in the conference room I found Gene and ran over to hug, as well as thank him for his confidence in me, helping my career, and the unbelievable surprise. Perfect showmanship, especially from an engineer guy. I then fell into his arms for another hug. Gene was like a big, cuddly teddy bear. In all my past careers I'd made my success with passion and my **Personal Brand Image**. In the case of VP for Mattel that kind of performance didn't bring me recognition. I needed a mentor, a sponsor to walk me through the company's roadblocks and campaign as if I were running for public office. Gene was my campaign manager.

After another round of applause from the vendors, I promptly returned to the planned program agenda, taking deep breaths to calm myself. I couldn't wait for the meeting to end so I could share my excitement with Melvin and Haris. It had been a long road to get to this point. When I'd started this temporary job at Mattel, I never thought (although Dr. D had predicted it) it would lead to relocating to Asia and reaching the level of VP. The title wasn't important, the significance was the recognition of all I'd accomplished in my careers to reach this milestone.

I owed my dear husband and son a great deal of credit for the support they gave me by adjusting to our new life and enjoying HK. This removed the pressure and guilt from me for not being a stay-at-home mom. My family was the most important thing. Working at Mattel was a vehicle to provide financial security for them. I got that and a career as well.

Later that evening I received an unexpected phone call from Edith. She said, "Loban, Mr. Bazerman called me earlier. I know I shouldn't be asking because he wanted to surprise you, but Mr. Bazerman asked me to order **two thousand purple roses** to put in your office tomorrow, celebrating your promotion. The problem is I cannot find enough florists who can supply the total of **two thousand purple roses** and I do not want to disappoint Mr. Bazerman."

I thought about what Edith said. Something seemed wrong. Sure purple roses are my favorite flower and the first flowers Melvin ever gave me, so I could understand why he wanted to surprise me with this selection. However the amount of **two thousand** was not only extremely expensive, but the volume would reach my office ceiling and flow out the windows! I turned to Melvin and in an unemotional voice shared Edith's dilemma. Melvin paled and gently took the phone from me to speak directly with Edith. He said in a voice that was slow, calm, and with clear enunciation, "Edith dear, my request was for **two dozen** purple roses."

Edith asked Melvin to repeat what he said and then she started to laugh because she obviously misunderstood the meaning translated from English into Cantonese! Oh, only **two dozen**! We laughed because her concern wasn't over the amount or the cost, but her ability to fulfill Melvin's request.

Edith replied with great relief, **"Two dozen purple roses is no problem!"**

Then I started to think what my office would have looked like with **TWO THOUSAND Roses!** Honestly, if Edith hadn't followed up with me, I believe that she would have somehow found the huge amount of roses needed, even if she had them shipped from China and arranged to have my office furniture removed to accommodate the floral splendor. That's just the way a great assistant does her job.

The next morning it was business as usual. Brew fresh coffee for Melvin, make Haris's lunch for school (yes, Haris, I did make your lunch every day), and rush around like crazy to leave on time. I was anxious to get to the office this morning, because I had seen only a few of my staff at the vendor conference when my promotion was announced. I wondered what their reaction would be. After ten years working in HK I accepted the staff's reserved nature. Even though they'd upgraded their emotional reactions since I'd been on board, they were never extroverted in their reactions or extremely verbal with expressing their feelings. My expectation was for polite, appropriate, heartfelt congratulations with some hugs. Which was definitely fine with me.

Melvin drove me to the Shau Kei Wan garage-lobby and I took the famous freight elevator to my office. I opened the door and to my amazement, the entire area was filled with floating balloons, making it seem the sky was no longer blue but a lovely shade of purple. My staff, both men and women, were all dressed in purple and wearing purple wigs. Of course I knew that Vonni Yung was the key inspiration and art director for all this attention and creativity. The effect was awesome and the staff was totally engaged in the purple passion.

If that wasn't enough to knock me over, they draped a special purple cape over my shoulders, wrapped a purple feather boa around my neck, handed me a scepter, secured a rhinestone crown on my head, then declared me "Vice President and Queen of HKSG." This meant so much to me, not only the recognition, but the warm love, respect, and most of all their courage to be outrageous, silly, fun loving, and verbal. This was the emotional personality I'd never seen in them. I could hardly believe this was the same team that dressed in black almost every day and had difficulty expressing any opinion. This was an accomplishment I could truly own, knowing it was a direct result of my years of mentoring this staff. I was so proud of this intimate side they finally displayed in public and gave to me as the ultimate gift. This promotion belonged to them as well.

I loved every one on the HK team with all my heart.

Head to toe in purple, laughing and crying, I finally went into my office, and sure enough on my desk were the stunning **two dozen purple roses** from Melvin and Haris. On the floor, on every piece of furniture, everywhere in the room, were baskets of huge purple floral arrangements from many of our vendors, familiar with my Brand. Nothing could have been more gratifying for me in my career than the emotion and outpouring of love I received from the HK celebration. That is, until a few days later when I traveled to my office in China.

The China team was just three years old and my mentoring capabilities for them were limited because I was only in their office a couple of times a week. The China staff's emotional displays were even more reserved than the HK staff's. However, when I entered my office, they too were dressed in head-to-toe purple, with purple wigs, purple flowers, and a purple pot of hot tea with cakes that had purple icing! One by one they hugged me, some crying with joy. Emotions I'd never seen from this team. I guess my style had influenced them as well.

I was truly blessed to have the Chinese—yes, "communist" Chinese—show me such devotion in a totally Western manner. I loved every one on the China team with all my heart.

After weeks of congratulations and celebrations I decided to use the power of my new vice president title to expand my group's responsibility and creative style. I saw it was possible to turn their attitudes around and now I was free from corporate judgment to gradually integrate my **Personal Brand Image** and return it back to full volume.

Yes, **Turn It Up!**

I felt free of politically appropriate bondage, similar to being locked in a prison of executive-style conformity. The doors were now open and I could prove my leadership ability without focusing my energy on trying to *Tone It Down*.

One of the reasons I'd organized the **Fabric Vendor Conference** was to expand our vendors' knowledge about Mattel and Barbie history so they could emotionally connect to the product. I hoped caring about Barbie would lead to improved quality. The pressure was constantly there to improve Barbie's quality without adding cost. I wanted to take the Iconic Barbie message we gave to the vendors and expand it to Mattel's Asia staff.

Gene Insley and I were on our way from a day at the China office, en route in the back of the Mattel van to the famous White Swan Hotel. We started to brainstorm ideas about lifting staff morale and engaging them in improving Barbie's quality at all levels, from the designers to the sewing operators in the factories. Everyone who touched, or was involved with Barbie in any way, should feel the magic she creates. We talked about the souvenir doll we'd given the vendors at the conference as being a symbol. We had called it **More than a doll** to signify that she wasn't just a piece of plastic. The dream that came with her was more than a mere toy.

Gene thought this could be a program of grand scope in Asia. We started to compare our plan to Hollywood's Academy Awards. Instead of receiving an Oscar statue, there would be awards with special Barbie souvenirs for quality achievement. Gene and I created this special program's mission over sipping wine and eating peanuts at the White Swan Hotel. He let me have a free hand to create the **More than a doll** recognition events and introduce the idea at as many Mattel Asia locations as possible.

At that moment I knew Gene had just given me license to *put on a show.*

I wanted the awards to be a statement reflecting the quality AD&D expected for Barbie. We needed to have a professional kickoff and top-quality, meaningful awards. If this couldn't be done with perfection, then what was the purpose of a program recognizing aesthetic accomplishments? You had to give an award for quality that would set the standard for quality. I had one of the designers who worked for me, Catherine Chan, devote time to this special project. I art directed my vision and Catherine designed the awards with a Brand Image theme exemplifying this mission statement:

*Since 1959 **Barbie** has made dreams come true for millions of children and adults. Whether Barbie represents fantasy,* *aspiration, or a role model, one thing is certain: she is **"More than a doll."***

We created metal buttons with iconic Barbie logos, memo pads for everyone, and then the special quality awards. Hundreds of original Barbie 1959 replicas were scaled down to five-inches and made at MHK. She was permanently enclosed in a plastic cylinder, to look more like an award that could be proudly displayed on your desk. This mini Barbie award would be given to those who exceeded their job's quality expectations.

The grand prize for the **More than a doll** program needed to be perceived as equal to the Hollywood Oscar and given to only one person at each Mattel Asia location annually. This award would represent the highest honor bestowed on staff who best exemplified and strived for the high aesthetics of the Barbie Brand. We created an award, a Barbie doll wearing the original style black-and-white striped bathing suit but hugely upgraded. Over the bathing suit, I had my staff hand bead tiny, clear glass beads on the white stripes and tiny, jet-black glass beads on the black stripes. When the handwork was completed, the bathing suit was one, hundred percent covered in glistening beads.

Jewelry and accessories were added, made out of real gold to emphasize the award's special significance. I used a local jeweler, not a toy supplier, to make the tiny doll-size metal hoop earrings, as on the original 1959 Barbie, in eighteen-carat gold. Although the original Barbie didn't have a belt, I had a fine-linked one made out of eighteen-carat gold, as well as a custom eighteen-carat gold medallion, one side with Mattel's logo and the reverse side engraved with **Barbie #1**.This belt would fit around Barbie's waist. The finishing touch was a customized Barbie-size handbag with the **More than a doll** logo. Catherine designed the package, which repeated the iconic black-and-white stripe theme.

A close up of the beautiful award doll. Look at that perfect honey blonde swirl!

more than a doll™

The More than a doll™ Barbie® is a truly unique Silkstone™ doll. Note the 18k gold Mattel medallion around her waist and the beach bag with the More than a doll™ logo.

We rented a small theater in HK to hold the event for over one hundred staff. It was adorned with human-size female torso mannequins placed all over the stage, dressed with replica black-and-white bathing suits as a Barbie Statement. Everyone attending was asked to wear black and white. Videos of the original Barbie commercial and current Barbie TV ads appearing in the US, in addition to music, singing, keynote speeches, and vision statements entertained and explained the Barbie Dream to the audience. Of course, everyone received souvenirs and the Barbie #1 Award was presented.

The show had great reviews. Gene was ecstatic and proud about the philosophy presented. The program's execution was indeed Hollywood worthy and we repeated this "put on a show" at the various Mattel Asia locations. I was now free from being a robotic corporate candidate for VP who had to hold back on my personal style.

This opportunity to perform and creatively find a way to acknowledge all levels of staff was my introduction to regaining my **Personal Brand Image** and now I was back to **Turning It Up.**

Personal Brand Image:

Take every opportunity to exaggerate your Brand and reinforce your image.

Chapter 23

Small Bowl, Big Bowl

If I could have sung like Barbra Streisand or danced like Michael Jackson to inspire creativity and get my viewpoint recognized, I would have done so. My only magical powers were positive thinking, common sense, and that old New York Attitude. Power jackets with rhinestones and heavy metal cuff bracelets were my daily attire. My thought was, if you felt powerful, if you were perceived as powerful, then guess what—you were powerful. Just don't ask me to bend any steel bars.

Vonni Yung was now leading a team of eight designers. Our HK and China soft goods groups were heavy into overtime. I encouraged taking on assignments and then figuring out how to live up to the commitment. To establish my team as first class and globally capable, I felt this was the right strategy. Because my team pioneered the development and onsite approval for Barbie and other girls' products, we were recognized as the champions in Asia. I wanted to keep it that way.

This can-do attitude spread throughout my staff. A great example was Vonni Yung, who wouldn't delay or stop working on any project. I had created my own Design Monster in Vonni and her designers worked late into the evenings, sometimes until 2 a.m. I was unaware of their very late departures. Per my instructions, staff were to take taxis home after 10 p.m. Our office was in a remote village with absolutely no nightlife and dimly lit streets. Vonni would call a taxi and this became so commonplace that every night the same driver would come to the corner of our building and wait for Vonni's call.

When I found out the time the designers actually left the office, I was not happy. My limited influence over Vonni seemed nonexistent when it came to work-life balance. Then one day, Vonni told me her team would no longer be working into the early morning hours. Why the big change? It seemed that the taxi driver had told other taxi drivers that many beautiful young ladies were working in a warehouse in Shau Kei Wan all night long. Vonni said the driver gave her a strange look when he acknowledged other drivers were coming to Shau Kei Wan to take them home after the "party." The driver laughed when Vonni corrected him, saying that there was no party, only designing toys. At that point, Vonni agreed to trim back overtime to 10 p.m.

Our life in Shau Kei Wan, with late nights, noodle shop lunches, and Shanghai Tang décor, ended in 2003, when Gene Insley decided the time was right for AD&D to join our colleagues at the office in Tsim Sha Tsui (TST), the same office building we'd left five years earlier. Gene felt the TST office had more supporting resources than our location in the isolated fishing village. I'd worked with Gene long enough to know he was making this change for the good of Mattel business.

AD&D was a big fish in a small bowl in SKW and now we would become a small fish in a big bowl in TST. It was almost like starting over again. I was in charge of the orientation meeting between my team and the new TST colleagues. The TST team had been together for many years, there was resentment about AD&D joining this location, and they anticipated competition with us. I needed to make our introduction with TST folks comfortable and have a lasting positive impression.

What could be more bonding and safe than a meeting with play focused on a food theme? No encore pie-throwing for this group, but I admit, pies are always motivation. As a friendly reminder of the power-of-the-pie, I bought a few dozen plain cupcakes and displayed them in the conference room, next to containers of colorful sweet frosting, tubes of decorating gel, candy sprinkles, whipped cream, and various fun decorations for cakes. I asked the two teams to write their names on pieces of paper and toss the papers into a jar. Each person selected a folded paper from the jar. Whatever name was identified on their selected paper, they had to design a special cupcake for that person and give it to them as a gift. The recipient would be revealed when the cakes were completed and presented.

Talk about ice breakers. This was a frosted explosion and as close to throwing a pie as I would dare in HK. We were actually having fun and off to a great start in our Big Fish Bowl, with creative cake eating. This team bonding was like a fly landing on sticky frosting.

The one area I was reluctant to be aggressive and increase my "fish size" was establishing another soft goods team at Mattel's Jakarta, Indonesia, location, PTMI (Limited Company Mattel Indonesia). Since the HK and China SG teams were making great progress, it was really in the interest of Mattel business to grant PTMI's general managers the same onsite approval advantages in Jakarta. PTMI was a state-of-the-art facility and started production of Barbie in 1991. Now, more than ten years later, there was still no SG team in Jakarta. I was being pressured to create a team there as soon as possible.

I didn't follow my own philosophy of giving 110% when it came to a Jakarta team. I was probably at only 75% effort, well below my standard. My focus was on HK and China, groups that were faster to reach success. PTMI was so difficult to work with, I was less aggressive in establishing a new team at that location. Geographically speaking, the distance between HK and Jakarta is about two thousand miles, compared to only one hundred miles between the HK and Guangzhou soft goods teams. I couldn't be at PTMI on a weekly basis to mentor them.

In the 1990s the phone connection between HK and Jakarta wasn't good. I could hardly hear or understand the questions they asked. The translation from Bahasa Indonesian to English was crude, and I perceived PTMI staff as having a stubborn attitude. I was so frustrated by the telephone conversations and the PTMI engineers at the other end that I often put them on the speakerphone and let them talk nonstop without interruptions. I'd actually walk out of my office while the speakerphone blasted with monologues from PTMI to an empty room. I paced alone in the hallway to calm myself.

Barbie business was increasing and PTMI was being assigned more product to manufacture. It was obvious that PTMI needed to be more in control of that product. I had to put my personal feelings aside and overcome the cultural differences. Of course, if there were a mature, functioning team at PTMI, it would be great for Mattel to have onsite staff, an extension of AD&D that develops and approves products manufactured in Jakarta. PTMI was only requesting what I'd already created and executed two thousand miles north in 1992. I had to help Mattel do what was best for business.

Before moving to HK, I'd traveled to Jakarta in 1991, on a research investigation for fabric vendors to support PTMI as they were opening their manufacturing doors. My impression of Jakarta was very good. I was surprised at the city's extensive infrastructure, modern buildings, and beautiful tropical foliage. I soon learned that Indonesia's colonial background was under the Dutch in the seventeenth century until 1945, when Indonesia became independent. Over three hundred years of European influence explained the modern buildings and shopping malls, which emerged between the lush foliage and primitive storefront shacks. I thought there was great potential and understood why Mattel had made an investment at this location. I had fun staying at the Hilton Hotel, shopping for local crafts with my PTMI colleagues, walking the streets, and eating fabulous food at special local restaurants. I'd been comfortable and enjoyed myself in the mix of modern and primitive tropical paradise.

It was now 2003, two years after 9/11, and I was traveling to Indonesia, which has the largest Muslim population of any country. It was psychologically intimidating for me, especially following the 2002 bombing in Bali, only seven hundred miles south of Jakarta, which killed 202 people. Then in 2003, a suicide bomb explosion at the iconic Western symbol, the Jakarta JW Marriott hotel, killed twelve and injured 150 people. Traveling to Jakarta wasn't the same this time around. I arrived at airport immigration with a private escort hired by Mattel, so I wouldn't be delayed by immigration officers looking to question or harass me because I was an American. The escort/bodyguard took me to a car with a driver who would transport me directly to PTMI.

Because of the perceived danger to Westerners and the Marriott Hotel bombing, all the Mattel visitors, me included, couldn't stay at any Western hotel in Jakarta. For safety reasons we all were located together at a local boutique hotel, the spectacularly gorgeous **Dharmawangsa Jakarta**. It was designed like a colonial mansion, with dark carved wooden details, glorious Indonesian artifacts everywhere, and magnificent furniture. The service was personal and the staff was focused on making your stay pleasant, in the hopes that you wouldn't remember you were just frisked for weapons at the door.

The basic hotel guest room was fit for royalty and almost made you forget the hotel was occupied everywhere with security guards, an iron gate surrounded the hotel property, car bomb checkpoints and metal detectors were at the entrance. Mattel policy dictated no outside alone times, no walking, no shopping. PTMI staff supervised and chaperoned all events. It basically was a luxury prison environment.

These unfortunate circumstances affected me negatively. I was unable to stop feeling like a prisoner with a target on my back. This made it difficult to feel inspired to return to Jakarta and preach creative freedom, when I was looking over my shoulder for a suicide bomber. Even when entering the PTMI driveway, the company car was checked for bombs and weapons.

Mattel's PTMI staff was warm, concerned, and caring. My Indonesian colleagues appeared even more upset about the terrorist incidents in their own country than the visitors were. Of course they weren't happy about the circumstances of how

Westerners might be treated, bombing scares, and how Indonesian people were generally being perceived.

I was only one person, and I couldn't convince any of my HK staff to transfer to Jakarta to manage and mentor a new team within the tragically cautious environment. It was critical to have a HK staff at PTMI to set up processes and guide the all-important aesthetic training. Fear of the reality of terrorism was what I had to overcome.

The painful planning of this new team resulted in slow implementation, due to my reluctance to expand my personal presence and HK staff in Jakarta. I would have preferred not to have this challenge. It was an uphill battle for me to passionately engage myself and difficult to find the right staff to execute the business plan that had previously succeeded in my other groups.

The saga of Indonesian obstacles to set up AD&D was getting old and I felt limited in what I could accomplish. This race to the finish was lagging and at times I almost gave up. I concealed my reluctance and fears with the "go-to" Wonder Woman facade that fooled everyone. I was really professional at using this camouflage to cover my uncertainty of the fate that loomed over the civilized world with terrorism threats. The concerns I had and the unspoken possible nightmares were on everyone's minds. The situation was so intimidating I didn't know how to overcome my real feelings without seeming anti-Indonesian. This was definitely not the case. I was anti-the-insanity-of-terrorism that just happened to be a threat in Indonesia at the time I was working in Jakarta.

Out of necessity comes big ideas. If the horse has trouble getting to the water, then bring the water to the horse. I decided it would more effective to move forward by training PTMI staff in HK. They would get a taste of AD&D process and values without the stress and constant vigilance about safety. The HK staff would get to know the PTMI folks and hopefully this would be an even better training opportunity than having reluctant HK staff travel to Jakarta. This was the plan for the next year, to have the most talented PTMI staff work in HKSG.

Finally, after cross-training and identifying the most competent staff, we opened the PTMI Soft Goods office in 2004. I convinced one of my key HK engineers, Clarence Sin, to set up the office, train the team, and move to Jakarta for two years as manager. Then, my star of training new teams, Jessica Choi, moved to Jakarta in 2006, following the foundation Clarence established. She remained at PTMI for four years, until the group was competent.

In contrast to the devastating world events during the beginning of this new millennium, the Indonesian people were warm and openly emotional. They were more verbal, gave more hugs and warm greetings. I encountered no prejudice from my PTMI colleagues, only respect for my knowledge, achievements, and mentoring. They only wanted to gain experience and excel at what I was trying to teach. The world could learn by their loving example.

We were now a medium-size fish in a big bowl. My two-year temporary assignment in HK was now approaching thirteen years.

Personal Brand Image:

Stick to your Brand, even if you feel hopeless.

Chapter 24

Blaze of Glory

Melvin and I decided that we wanted to remain in HK. We were in no rush to return to the US. HK was now home. Of course, to remain living in HK, I needed to continue my Mattel expatriate assignment. Without my income, we couldn't afford to live in one of the most expensive cities in the world. I didn't see the end of my job in sight and decided to move at full spend on this highway of working for Mattel, observing how long the road lasted before I had to take a detour.

It was 2005. Haris was seventeen years old, in his senior year at Hong Kong International School. After graduation he would leave HK to continue his education at **Rochester Institute of Technology (RIT)** in Rochester, New York. A four-year university, majoring in computer science and network security. My darling, teenage son would be off to America to study and live eight thousand miles away from our HK home. I'd always expected that when Haris went off to college, his school would be close enough for multiple family visits, as well as phone calls in the same time zone. I never thought I'd still have my temporary job when Haris left home.

Mattel continued to view my contribution as a key function, and in my opinion, moving back to the US later, rather than sooner, would be best for the family. Haris would be busy with his studies and return to HK twice a year. Haris was only four years old when we moved and thirteen years of the HK lifestyle had taught him self-reliance and independence. We quickly learned that HK was one of the safest cities in the world. Low crime, ammunition and guns are illegal. Seems the HK people are more interested in working and making money than committing crimes. The murder rate is less than forty persons a year in HK, versus New York City with an annual homicide rate of five hundred persons.

With HK's world-class public transportation system, parents sent their neatly uniformed, school-age children unaccompanied on public buses, ferries, trains, and even in taxis as young as eight years old. You learn fast about life and maturity when you can take the train to school by yourself before you're a decade old. This would be unheard of and probably considered child abuse in the US.

By the time Haris was a teenager he'd hiked the New Territories in HK, completing an **Outward Bound** survival experience, visited Guangzhou, Xian, Shanghai, and Beijing, China; traveled on Australia's east coast; volunteered at an orphanage in Vietnam; skied in Japan; and toured Singapore; Malaysia; Bali, Indonesia; Bangkok, and Phuket Thailand! Even though we'd never visited RIT in Rochester, New York, it seemed unadventurous by comparison.

If you hold the bird in your hand too tight it will suffocate and die. However, if your hand is open the bird will fly.

Haris was set free to fly with the help of a 747 Cathay Pacific airplane and his parents' good planning. We all traveled to RIT and said goodbye to Haris, who practically pushed us out of his dorm room. Melvin and I were overwhelmed with anxiety and depression realizing we would be returning to HK without our son, who no longer needed us. We drove to the nearest Applebee's restaurant, rushed inside, and ordered food contrary to our usual eating habits—two double cheeseburgers, a giant platter of spicy buffalo chicken wings, a stack of fries, a double portion of onion rings, a couple of ice-cold beers, and two pieces of chocolate cake with ice cream—to comfort ourselves!

The lack of long-term security as an expatriate was a major factor in planning for the future. I didn't have a contract with Mattel; I was an "at-will employee." Meaning that Mattel at "their will" could terminate my position or I could decide "at my will" to resign. I never knew when business circumstances would change and my position would be eliminated, similar to circumstances on any job. However, I was located in Asia and any change in my position would create enormous upheaval in my life, including a relocation.

Asian assignments for Mattel were like a revolving door, with many executives sent to HK. Within two to four years they either left because they were unhappy, were fired, or were relocated back to California. I was one of the long-term expatriates and still the only female Mattel executive expatriate in Asia. My **Brand Image** was strong and Mattel needed me. Nevertheless, we purchased a vacation home in Arizona for family reunions and to serve as our US anchor, in case my Mattel assignment ended.

Personal Brand Image:

Continue to strengthen your Image. The longer you do so, the longer you can hold on to your dream.

Late in 2006, Gene Insley decided to return to Mattel California. Gene was the only colleague I'd ever had in my career that mentored me. He was doing a brilliant job in Asia, and he trusted me 100%. We were great partners in changing the local staff's attitudes, gaining trust from Mattel California, and broadening AD&D's scope. I was devastated about geographically losing my mentor, my boss, my sponsor, and my friend. Gene was basically moving his position to California to integrate Mattel Asia with Mattel California, with the goal of executing a better product development process. After six years in HK, Gene, who had three adult children and a new granddaughter in California, thought it was a good time to return. I respected his decision and understood the rationale, but was heartbroken to see him leave HK.

I would have new boss in HK yet again. Mattel was relocating Mr. R from California. I didn't know him well, since we'd only met a few times in HK and on my visits to Mattel headquarters. Mr. R was younger than me, a youthful forty-seven to my fifty-eight years. He was an engineer guy, nonstop talker, tall, thin, with short light brown hair and youthfully handsome. Mr. R told me the soft goods area was in my capable hands. He would concentrate his efforts on the general overview of product development in Asia. I guess my reputation and Gene's good word gave me the credentials to retain my position, now reporting to Mr. R.

Personal Brand Image:

Reputation can give you the edge with a new boss.

I had been through boss changes and process changes with Mattel many times before. I knew that a new boss would observe, then make his or her own recommendations for what they thought needed improvement. A boss has to improve business to validate his or her existence, so change was guaranteed. I was on a wait-and-see vigil, keeping in mind to continue my pursuance of 110% effort while the dust settled.

During one of my first private updates with Mr. R, he asked me about my retirement plans. The statement was direct, he didn't blink, smile, or hesitate, but noticeably didn't make eye contact with me. I could understand why he asked me this question. Even so, I was rather put off with the age stereotype and his emotionless attitude. I knew then that he wouldn't replace Gene as my mentor. I felt I should reply as directly as he'd inquired. In a low-tone, modulated voice I said, "Sixty-five, that would be about six years down the road."

Mattel had no compulsory retirement age and Mr. R told me that he wanted to get an idea of what my intentions were, since I was considered "critical staff." Translated: he needed me now. Mr. R then told me about a new Mattel corporate policy that would eventually be implemented. This policy would limit the length of current expatriate assignments, as well as limit new expatriate assignments to no more than a total of four years, then localize that position. In other words, this was an attempt to reduce expenses. Of course I was aware of how expensive it was to have a person from the US and their family relocated to Asia. In my case, with a husband and son, my base salary was more than tripled with the expenses incurred.

Mr. R was making it clear, in his emotionless style, that my current expatriate compensation would end in the future. In another triple play, I already was more than three times over the four-year limit for an expatriate assignment. This new policy would affect Mr. R's HK assignment as well, and he advised me that in the next few years, I needed to identify and train my replacement. The handwriting was on the wall: when my position could be localized I would no longer be in Asia. If I'd even remain at Mattel was unclear. This is corporate mentality. The effort I gave, on my own, in a location that Mattel staff from California was reluctant to even visit, or travel to China and Jakarta, wasn't being considered. This was now company policy, a "Here's your hat ... what's your hurry?" ideology.

At this point I had a decision to make. I could either fall into a depression of "how could this happen to me?" or I could go out in a **Blaze of Glory** with a sensational attitude and outstanding performances, using every trick in my little glitter-covered book to make my position of vice president not just relevant but dynamic. This would set the stage for my replacement. It was important to make sure that the foundation I'd built during all these years in Asia was strong and could support my loyal staff and Barbie in the future.

Personal Brand Image:

Use the power of your Brand to strengthen your team.

Two key staff could technically do my job and had experienced my personal training for many years. First there was Winnie Kwok, my Queen of Common Sense in HK, who eventually transferred to my department after her reluctance when I first started HKSG. Another great choice to succeed me was Jessica Choi, my Star HK staff managing the soft goods team at PTMI, Jakarta. I spoke with them about succession planning, when I eventually returned to the US. Neither one of them wanted my job. They were happy with what they were doing and didn't want the responsibility of being a visionary or playing the daily corporate politics game.

All Mattel managers were required to have a succession plan. No matter how hard I tried to convince Winnie and Jessica about the great opportunity for their careers, it was a losing battle. I decided that my departure from HK was years away and it was practical to put the succession plan on hold. Perhaps at the end of the day my replacement would come from outside Mattel rather than be an internal promotion.

A year had gone by without Gene Insley and I was getting used to Mr. R as my boss. I made a conscious effort to get along with him since our personalities were opposite. I was flamboyant, colorful, and design focused, while Mr. R was serious and low key in public. Usually when I entered his office for an update, he'd just start talking about whatever was on his mind while he stared at his computer screen. I'd pretend I didn't hear him and said, "Hi, Mr. R, how are you today and how is your family?" I figured that I'd already received great professional help from Dr. D and Gene Insley, so I gave Mr. R a pass on his management style. He had other attributes of technical know-how, vast experience in the toy industry, and great corporate connections. Mr. R was a smart, technically capable, nice guy, and I respected him for that. Most important he was wise enough to leave me alone to execute my job.

Personal Brand Image:

A strong Brand can overcome corporate politics.

In September 2008 I hired Ivy Leung as my new secretary. I had recommended that my current assistant, Edith Au, apply for an opening in the HK design team, global coordinator for toy samples. Reluctant as Edith was to leave my side, I convinced her that this was an advancement for her career. I didn't want to lose Edith—she was my rock and daily sanity check—but I loved and respected her enough to make sure she had a chance to be recognized for her talent. This transfer was good for her and I wouldn't hold her back for selfish reasons.

Personal Brand Image:

Help subordinates to excel. It will strengthen your own Brand and it is the right thing to do.

Edith had been my assistant for eight years and before her Norma Wong was my assistant for eight years. Seemed to be a pattern here, or perhaps fate and aligning of the stars. Or it could be that the number eight in Chinese translates to wealth and good fortune. It was my good fortune to be blessed with assistants who weren't just lucky for me, but created an atmosphere of magical efficiency.

The first thing I noticed about Ivy Leung was her mature personality and calm manner. She was only in her late thirties but projected wisdom beyond her years. Ivy had previous experience as an executive assistant, great computer skills, comprehension of budget management, a warm persona, and fluency in spoken and written English. This was the perfect combination I needed to support the complexity of running three soft goods teams and managing the department's budget. Ivy was hired and I soon realized she not only had the executive assistant skills, but she also had hidden creative talent. We instantly bonded and she gained my trust to handle all the heavily detailed documentation and budget analysis. Then the absolutely fabulous discovery that Ivy had creative computer skills to enhance my already famous presentation style was an added bonus.

A few months after Ivy started working for me, the party for the annual Chinese New Year dinner in China was being planned. In the early years at Mattel these dinners were just banquets with traditional food and lots of red wine that turned the white tablecloths into what looked like a blood-stained battleground. Vonni Yung continued to help me turn the AD&D annual dinner into fun, with games, photographs, and a dress-up costume theme. The success of major creative events was revolutionary for Mattel and became the tradition.

The 2009 Chinese New Year dinner at our China location, the plan was to have the head of Mattel Operations, Mr. Tom Debrowski in attendance, as well as all the VPs of Operations from HK and China. To make it more fun, I'd suggested to the Mattel admin team that it would be fantastic to have these executives perform for the staff and show everyone they had a human side.

Of course, my suggestion turned into a request for me to organize this event. My brilliant creative muse, Vonni, wouldn't attend the dinner because she'd decided she wanted to return to the US and work at Mattel California. I was on my own. I had to think about what I could do to get the all-male multicultural executive team to perform together. We would have absolutely no opportunity for any rehearsals since the men were located all across Asia in Jakarta, HK, and multiple cities in China and California.

This performance would be in front of over two hundred staff and needed to be a showstopper. This Directors' Show was another way to demonstrate Asia's creative energy. Nothing, not even inconvenient geography, was going to prevent me from getting this act together. It must be entertaining and dramatic, with music and visual impact, to guarantee a great experience for the audience. When things are complicated, sometimes the best way to move forward is with a simple idea. I decided we should lip sync and dance to songs of the 1970s/1980s rock group **Queen**. These songs would tell the story about how tough it was to manage and to be strong leaders, perfect for a chorus of Mattel directors!

Costumes needed to be easy and create a memorable statement. I brought multicolored bandanas that the men would wrap around their heads like tough rock stars. I instructed them by email to bring their own T-shirts and jeans, which they would change into backstage. The only props were three electric guitars made out of cardboard, with realistic guitar details painted on by the Mattel model shop. The song lyrics were emailed to the team of male executives. I instructed them to memorize the lyrics and *lip sync* to Queen's music. On stage they must look like a cross between rock stars and criminal gang members. Yes, I would be up there with them, so they could shadow my movements.

When showtime was close I signaled to the men to go to the dressing room and change into jeans. Within a couple of minutes I found myself with thirteen senior Mattel male executives in a small room, where we were going to convert them from executives to gang members. I handed out the bandanas to each one and then all the guys started taking off their dress trousers and putting on their jeans. I suddenly found myself looking all these guys in their underwear, which was, at a glance, a mix of boxers, jockeys, white, colors, and a display of hairy legs!

I yelled, "HEY! Wait a minute until I leave the room." The reply was "No need, you're one of the boys!"

I really didn't know whether I should be thrilled to have finally been accepted on the team or insulted by what could be classified as sexual harassment. The sight of a not particularly aesthetic chorus line of multicultural middle-aged men was humorous. I decided not to press charges!

Lip syncing, dancing, rocking, playing fake guitars, heads wrapped tight with bandanas! Of course, none of them had ever bothered to read the lyrics I'd emailed, so their lips weren't syncing, adding comedy to the performance. I was right up front, rocking and lip syncing with my purple bandana wrapped around my head. The clumsy guys followed my every move and then got motivated to break loose and shake down the house. It was hilarious and entertaining, which resulted in uncontrollable laughter from the audience.

For an encore, I had the audience join us on stage to sing **"We Are the Champions."** I could hardly believe this display of chaotic performance was happening in China. The ovation was deafening, the accolades from my All-Male Exec Team to me was as a good as receiving an award for Best Musical Director.

I realized that I had taken my **Personal Brand Image** of performing to another level by directing the senior engineering executives to throw off their reserved selves and **Turn It UP**. My challenge now was to top this experience in as many ways as possible for my remaining years at Mattel. Not only for laughs, but to stimulate creativity that would benefit Mattel by liberating staff from the prison of ordinary to become extraordinary and not be boring. Let the show go on!

Personal Brand Image:

To be more effective and get support from management, spread your Brand to your bosses.

Chapter 25

Still Blazing after All These Years

It was 2009, the Chinese **Year of the Ox**. According to my Chinese horoscope for my birth year of the Rat, it was predicted I would have changes, both personally and professionally. Can't go wrong with that prediction, since if you live long enough personal and professional changes are certain.

This Year of the Ox, I was focusing on two milestones that couldn't have been more opposite. March 2009 was Barbie's 50th anniversary celebration. Yes, the famous Brand was turning into a golden girl and Mattel had planned global celebrations with extravagant events. Perhaps the most significant was that **Barbie Shanghai**, a store in Shanghai, China, would have its grand opening in March, coinciding with her 50th birthday. The planning of this store was basically an experiment conceived by Mr. Richard Dickson, Mattel's General Manager and Senior Vice President of Barbie. With a Brand as old as Barbie it wasn't surprising that her popularity had fluctuated over the fifty years. Mr. Dickson was a brilliant visionary and Mattel had assigned him to the Barbie Brand to invigorate her sales. Richard had a philosophy that Barbie wasn't lost—Mattel had lost sight of Barbie's Brand Image, which was always there.

Richard was in his late thirties, a tall guy with a lean frame and quite striking looking with shoulder-length black hair. When I first met Richard I loved his passion and warm personality. He was engaging, and I thought it refreshing to meet a Mattel California executive who didn't have a hard outward demeanor. To put it simply Richard was fun to be around. When he spoke of his vision for the Barbie Brand, a casual artistic nature was mixed with sheer brilliance.

Over the years working at Mattel, I'd witnessed the deterioration of the Barbie Brand through complacency, due to the lack of competition in the fashion doll business. This was no longer the case and the slip in sales was only a symptom of the underlying problem that the previous executives had sacrificed Barbie's **Personal Brand Image** for bottom-line profits. This situation was like a mirror reflecting my own philosophy and the central topic of this book. Barbie was suffering from what I dreaded to be: she was becoming *ordinary and boring*.

Richard Dickson's vision for the Barbie Shanghai Store was on one hand an experiment in retail and on the other hand an attempt to make Barbie extraordinary. In 2009 the significance of opening an American Iconic Brand store in one of China's largest and most cosmopolitan cities was a display of courage and a huge amount of guts. A few months before the Shanghai store was to open, Richard contacted me for support on a project. The new Barbie store was actually a three-story building that would have a bookstore, play area for children, photo shop, gourmet café, chocolate shop, theater, spa, and clothing for girls of all ages.

The building was to be a Barbie experience in every detail, with a central feature of a three-story spiral staircase giving customers access to all the floors. Richard's vision was that as you walked up or down this staircase, you'd be surrounded by a clear Plexiglas spiral wall with cubicles holding hundreds of different Barbie dolls, each wearing a different fashion. A tower of breathtaking Barbies. Richard asked me to have my soft goods team in China make all the sample fashions to be displayed on the staircase, designed using various pink and purple tones. They would need nearly one thousand unique fashions.

I directed the design and colors and after about a week of sewing samples in all the pink and purple fabrics we had available, I lined up dozens of dolls in these fashions for review. What seemed like a straightforward assignment made me feel uncomfortable. Considering their end use in the display, the way the fashions were looking disturbed me. The proportion of eleven-and-a-half inch dolls on a human-size staircase in the center of a three-story building would be underwhelming with these small, pale Barbies. These sweet little dresses would have zero impact, except one might say, "Oh look at those sweet dolls!" And no one would ever think about them again.

The fashions had no **Brand Image**. They were just a bunch of dresses that would literally disappear on the giant staircase and be forgotten. The staircase Barbies were being looked at as only window dressing. I thought that the real meaning of the staircase should be a *work of art*, a *magnificent installation* specifically designed for the space in Barbie Shanghai. It wasn't just a collection of dolls—it was a statement creating an entire environment.

The design details in Barbie fashions are very small. Therefore, the fabrics and sewing aesthetics were secondary to the long distance from which they would be viewed. The real attention should be paid to the impact of a color statement. Just like Tiffany & Co. has a special blue color that is totally identifiable as "Tiffany Blue," Barbie had her pink color, her signature hue. Not just any pink, but "Barbie Pink" identified by its **Pantone** reference number, the worldwide **Pantone Matching System (PMS)**. Barbie's specific pink color is **PMS 219C**, an edgier deep pink, almost shocking pink, not like a pale pastel in a baby girl's nursery pink.

Barbie PMS 219C was what I would use to convey her Brand Image in the installation. I used the silhouettes from contemporary Barbies and some fashion designs from the iconic 1960s era and remade them all entirely in PMS 219C pink. No other colors. That meant Barbie's famous original black-and-white bathing suit and sunglasses were 219C pink, the white bridal gown, veil, and bouquet was matched to 219C pink, fur coats, shoes, jewelry, accessories, dresses, pants, shorts, hats—all from head to toe on every doll in different fabrics were all, without exception, 219C pink!

I was designing the connection between doll and art to be the Shanghai store's centerpiece. Of course, I was completely disregarding the request of the head of the Barbie division. I deeply felt this installation would make the statement needed to convey the Barbie Brand Image. I went full speed ahead to present forty different Barbies in 219C pink fashions to Richard Dickson and his staff as a sample for my idea. The Barbie executive team was thrilled and we immediately made samples of **one thousand different 219C pink fashions** to be dressed on beautiful, blonde, blue-eyed, American classic Barbies. They were each placed in individual Plexiglas cubicles constructed in the giant spiral staircase in the middle of the store. They looked like magnificent jewels in an art museum. The finished product was amazing. Nowhere else would Barbie's iconic color be displayed in a statement that was three stories tall.

This Barbie Shanghai project was a creative liberation for me. I could have taken the easy way, completing the project by fulfilling the original request for pretty pastel pink and purple dolls. I couldn't give less than 110% effort to this project and I knew Barbie's Brand Image, as well as my **Personal Brand Image** to be extraordinary, was at stake. Richard Dickson was totally supportive of my efforts, deeply appreciative, and very happy with the outcome.

Richard was in Shanghai for the store opening and had a phone conversation with my boss Mr. R in HK. When he found out I wasn't planning to attend the store's grand opening he was furious. After speaking with Mr. R, Richard immediately called me and was shocked to hear I wouldn't be in Shanghai that evening. I told him that I couldn't justify Mattel's expense of a flight and hotel to attend the event. I lived in HK and could visit the store at my own expense in future.

Richard then started to yell at me. "Of all people that should attend this event it's you! The Pink Staircase Installation is the focal point of the store. You get on a plane today and be at this grand opening. I have already told Mr. R that you must be there!"

My professor from Hunter College, Robert Huot, nearly forty years after ripping up my artwork and telling me I was boring, would have been very proud of me. I took the idea of a dull display and created an exciting piece of iconic art. I had come full circle, geographically and creatively, from New York to Shanghai!

At my own expense I asked Melvin to join me at this historic Shanghai event. I felt like Cinderella unexpectedly being transported to The Ball. In my case I already had *Prince Charming Melvin* with me, so the dream needn't end at midnight. The Shanghai press and various global newspapers photographed the Pink Barbie Staircase multiple times. And everyone wanted their photo taken by the Staircase. This was the magic of the evening. The only thing missing was leaving a pink glass slipper at bottom of the Staircase as I left to return to our hotel.

Personal Brand Image:

Repeat your Brand Image, whether it's in the office or on a staircase. Make sure your Brand is recognized at every opportunity.

My second big event in 2009 was Haris's graduation from **Rochester Institute of Technology**. I don't think Haris cared much that his graduation year was also Barbie's special birthday. If I ever forget the year he received his college degree, I can always remember it was Barbie's 50th birthday in 2009 and vice versa. The unexpected housing crisis, caused by too many folks approved for home mortgages who couldn't pay their loans, changed the job market. In 2008 the United States was at the peak of the homeowners defaulting on loans, causing a severe recession. Millions of jobs were lost and companies weren't hiring.

Usually from a prestigious school that Haris graduated from, jobs would be waiting as diplomas were handed out. Haris, with millions of others who graduated with college degrees that year, were jobless. Part of me was concerned about him not having immediately available employment, and the other part of me, after being separated from Haris for the majority of the past four years, was elated that he'd be returning home to HK for his job search.

Job opportunities, applications, and résumé submissions were all online. The interviews that would result started with phone screenings or video conferences. If those milestones were passed, there was a final in-person interview. Haris had advanced in the interview protocol with a company in Melbourne, Florida, located south of Daytona Beach on Florida's east coast. Coincidentally the name of the company was **Harris Corporation**. After a couple of phone interviews between Florida and Haris's room in Hong Kong, Harris Corporation invited him for an interview at their Melbourne headquarters.

The only time Haris had been to Florida was during one of our summer holidays to visit Disney World in Orlando when he was about ten years old. Being an international traveler, Haris accepted his interview location with a calm attitude. Within a week he'd arranged a trip to Melbourne for his meeting with multiple levels of the organization, and a few days later Harris Corporation offered him a job. Considering the recessionary reality of most American companies at this time, my advice to him was, "Take the job, stay three years for experience, and then decide your next steps in your career. It will all look good on your résumé."

Personal Brand Image:

You have to start somewhere and a good offer makes the start even better. Oh yeah, and listen to your mother.

Just as I never thought I'd be offered a job in HK, I'd never thought about Haris working in Florida. New York, LA, or San Francisco seemed more probable to me, and Haris as well.

However, when there aren't many options you have to do what is best and see where it leads. I needed to remain in Hong Kong for work and the plan was for Melvin to accompany Haris to Florida, help him buy a car, rent an apartment, and get settled in a place that was definitely more foreign than HK or China to Haris.

Chapter 26

The Fire Ignites

Melvin and Haris had only been in the US a few days, and it was my time to meet with Mr. R for our weekly update. This day didn't seem unusual when I walked into Mr. R's office. But I soon discovered his typical way of sitting at a computer and not focusing on my arrival was different. Mr. R was sitting at his small conference table, away from his electronics, and asked me to join him because we were going to have a conference call in a few minutes, with the human resource representative from Mattel California. The reason for this discussion was to review the options for my future *departure from Mattel*. The heads-up I'd received years ago about Mattel limiting expatriate assignments was being implemented.

It was Miss Q, from Mattel HR, on the conference call. I'd known Miss Q for many years. She was a soft-spoken, intelligent young woman whom I always felt was respectful toward me. She knew about my successes during the more than seventeen years of my HK assignment and that I was still the only female expatriate executive for Mattel in Asia. After the polite salutations, Miss Q explained that I had three options for my future with Mattel, to take effect in eighteen months on April 8, 2011:

1. Remain on the job in HK as a local hire, without housing allowance or benefits.

2. Repatriate and work in Mattel California. Job to be identified.

3. Take an early retirement package.

The call ended and Mr. R looked directly at me and said that I should have expected this at some point, yet he was really sorry he had to tell me when he knew Melvin had just left for the US with Haris. Mr. R hoped that with Haris working in the US, as well as my intention to retire in a few years, the options I was given would fit into my plan.

I can't say I was shocked or surprised with the corporate decision. I certainly had seen my share of major staff changes over the years and I kept calm because Mr. R wasn't my family or a friend. He was my boss, doing his job and what he felt was good for the company. Sure I would've liked his usual engineer-stiff, robot-like style to be softer and for him to tell me how wonderful I was and how amazing my contribution to Mattel had been. The part of me that is human, very passionate, and addicted to being loved was being disappointed. This was business, not a family matter. I left Mr. R's office with my feelings on hold to conduct business as usual.

I wasn't quite as calm when updating Melvin. We'd expected this discussion at some point. My "temporary" assignment was approaching nineteen years and we always knew this was a **Finite Project**. What kept me full speed ahead was my constant growing of my **Personal Brand Image** to fit the business. I was expensive to keep on staff and my organization was mature, so the inevitable business decision was made to reduce cost by eliminating my expatriate position.

Of the three options Mattel presented to me, there really was only one choice: take an early retirement package. My travel in Asia and long days kept me away from Melvin the majority of the work week. Returning to the US, at least we'd be on the same continent as Haris and we'd be together to enjoy our lives. What were we waiting for?

I would work another eighteen months, retire gracefully at the age of sixty-three, and return to the US. Of course I would've liked to determine the timeline myself, so I could be in control of my life. However, I did have control of how I would spend the next eighteen months on the job and in HK. I didn't want my staff and colleagues to have a "lame duck" leader and Mr. R agreed that I wouldn't immediately announce my pending retirement but would wait a few months, to avoid the lingering goodbyes. This would also give me time to find my replacement. For my remaining time in HK, I wanted to make sure the foundation I built was reinforced to withstand a new boss.

Perhaps I could have negotiated a better exit, but why stress over who got the winning trophy at this time? I was already a winner after this amazing assignment and the phenomenal life my family had in Asia. I was grateful and decided that Mattel had always played fair with me, which shaped my attitude regarding the current "deal." I would expect no less from myself but to exit with a professional and classy attitude for my closing Performance of this long-running engagement.

Haris needed to be told about our move back to the US. I felt really bad that I couldn't talk to him in person. It didn't matter that he was now living in the US. The fact was, HK was his home. Haris identified himself as a Hongkonger, currently living in the US only to develop his career. I called him to explain the situation and tell him that we'd move back to the US in January 2011. The only place we had in the US was our vacation home in Arizona so that's where we'd live.

I couldn't see Haris's face, but I knew he was extremely upset with this news. HK wasn't just the location for my job—it was home for our family. Our future in HK was never guaranteed. I told Haris that I understood his disappointment and that we should make the most out of the next eighteen months. He should try to come back to HK for whatever vacation time he had.

The days passed quickly and I was anxious to break the news to my staff, since the burden was heavy on my heart and I needed to concentrate on finding my replacement and prepare the group for my departure. I was like a mother preparing her children for my long vacation and what they needed to do in my absence. Only in this case I wasn't coming back.

Less than a year from my exit date I publicly announced my retirement and return to America. After my staff's shocked reaction I was asked, "Why now?" I told the truth: the expatriate benefits were changing and it seemed like a sign to spend more time with my husband and be able to see Haris more often. I had completed my job in HK and the group was strong enough to continue without me. There wasn't a dry eye in the office. I had swelling emotions as well. I was obviously sad, but in control. After that announcement the expression of unhappy emotions from my staff was a daily event. I guess I would've been totally disappointed if they were less than upset. I loved them all and separation from them was like leaving family.

The question about my replacement was asked. My answer was direct, that we would be looking from within Mattel as well as at outside talent. The search was ongoing. I was determined to make sure they were in good hands with someone who would take good care of them.

Chapter 27

This Is It

It was six months before my return to the US. I was totally engaged in completing my Mattel Asia assignment and transferring responsibilities to my soon-to-be-named successor. Mattel HR had asked me to speak to the staff about effective communication and I was actively working on my closing remarks for a year-end presentation. This assignment raised similar feelings as in my senior year at Hunter College, with Professor Mac Wells's final assignment to have a beginning and an end. Well, this was my end at Mattel and I needed to share my story to inspire staff.

My finale had to be a colorful focus on the many ways you can create a **Personal Brand Image**, so staff could be inspired to create their own Brands. My examples had to be dramatically visual, making sense to a multicultural audience. Finishing my job at Mattel and leaving the organization after a twenty-five-year affiliation wasn't the milestone I had to overcome. The real life-changing experience for me was leaving my beloved HK home of nineteen years, the organization that I created, the people that I'd mentored, and leave them with a strong message: they all had a Superhero inside them.

My main sources to create the vision for my performance were internet research and ideas from my fabulous assistant Miss Ivy Leung. Keywords that came to my mind for visual images allowed me to find dozens of great ideas from the internet. Ivy was phenomenal, taking the photos, music, and videos I found and orchestrating them into a smooth, glitch-free, e-presentation. I think Ivy was having as much fun and excitement with this assignment as I was. It became her **Performance** as well.

My first presentation was just a few months before I'd return to the US. Over 150 Mattel HK staff were invited. Everyone knew me, but they had no idea what they were about to witness. Weeks before this presentation, entitled **"This Is It,"** I sent mysteriously vague emails and videos to all who would attend the meeting, to build suspense. When the actual day arrived for **"This Is It,"** I opened with silence, staring at the audience, then dimmed the lights in the room, echoing the atmosphere in a theater when the curtain raises and the audience sees the actors on stage. With everyone a bit confused as to what was happening, I announced that I would *not* give a presentation—instead, I'd be doing Performance Art.

Explaining that by definition, Performance Art is presented to an audience and may be either scripted or unscripted, random or carefully orchestrated, spontaneous or carefully planned. I then kept silent, while my talented assistant Ivy Leung was on the sidelines like *The Wizard of Oz* behind the curtain, watching for my cues to insure perfect timing for each image projected on the huge screen behind me.

The introduction began with loud music and amazing, deep, bright, rich colors presented in a video of the **Blue Man Group**, famous in the US since 1991 but relatively unknown in Asia. They were three guys from New York, who dipped themselves in blue paint from head to toe, conveying ideas about creativity and out-of-the-box thinking through their visual **Performance Art**. They were spraying paint, catching gumballs in their mouths, rocking, rolling, playing music on utility pipes and other exotic actions to stimulate ideas. The result was magical. This was the **Blue Man Group's Personal Brand Image**, their performance that was right in your face and stayed in your mind, unforgettable. This opening aroused the staff and demonstrated that there was an alternative to just lecturing and showing slides with complex, boring words.

Following the blue guys I stepped into the physical world of HK actor **Mr. Jackie Chan**, sharing short videos of his famous acrobatic martial arts style and innovative death-defying stunts, another form of physical talent to represent a Personal Brand.

Since this Performance was for Mattel, I would've been negligent not to have Barbie represented as a famous Brand Image. Digital displays of Barbie celebrating her 50th anniversary in the flagship **Louis Vuitton** Store in HK appeared on the giant screen behind me: the #1 Luxury Brand meets the #1 Fashion Doll. Barbie is **More than a doll**—the mere mention of blonde hair, blue eyes, pink, and glitter makes you visualize Barbie, who stays true to her Brand. The same could be said for the Brand recognition of the famous **Louis Vuitton** brown luggage logo.

I'd never shared my personal story with Mattel staff, about how I got my job, moved to HK, and kept my job in Asia for nearly two decades. I did give some key personal facts in my

Performance to establish how you can develop your Brand, which became the short version of this book, including the appropriate highlights of the "whipped cream pie construction" demo, my dressing up with rhinestones, and a video of the Chinese New Year Director Show. I included these visuals to emphasize that the perception of a person is what follows him or her, and you can create a winning perception and make it your own **Personal Brand Image**. After sharing my story, the most important thing to me was to have a Grand Finale that exemplified what I'd been talking about.

Personal Brand Image:

Be your own constant example of how you want to be perceived.

The finish of my Performance had to be guaranteed awesome and make the staff think about who they were and what they could do to Brand themselves. I had to reach my goal now. After all, **This Is It**, my last Mattel event. Once again I had the same feeling as I'd had with my Mac Wells's *Finite Project*. I was thinking it would be unbelievably terrific if I'd thrown a pie in 1969 in NYC, then in 1989 in California, and now in 2010 in Asia! This would be a symbolic "Around the World Pie Tour" and the perfect conclusion for my Inspirational Showtime.

However, this wasn't America, and slapstick pie throwing in this part of the world would be interpreted as humiliating and insulting. The Asian audiences wouldn't get the meaning, even though my point would be connected to my Brand. I had to find another way to make a Pie-in-the-Face acceptable. My years in Asia taught me that the Chinese love what they call a "Lucky Draw," which is similar to a raffle prize. A Lucky Draw with a Luxury Brand as the payoff is very desirable. I decided to end my **Performance** with a Luxury Lucky Draw as my Finite End. This was my thinking, but in my heart I felt this was too ordinary. I'd been preaching **Brand Image** and not to be boring for my entire career and now I was going to settle for an easy and predictable finish. Ordinary *and* boring!

"This Is It" would definitely need a Pie-Throwing episode. What did I have to lose? I had more to gain to visually show staff that you never can give up, even at the end of your assignment! It was a no brainer: A PIE WOULD BE THROWN!

I was summarizing my main points with the staff, after nearly two hours of "Performing" before an engaged and warmed-up audience. I stood behind my demonstration table, where I had rhinestone props and a large, freshly made, whipped cream pie. I told the staff, in keeping with Asian custom, we'd end this festive **Performance Art** with a Lucky Draw. The items were announced as I placed them on the table:

- In a dark blue package, **3rd Prize**: A **Blue Man Group** CD.

- An iconic Tiffany-blue bag containing **2nd Prize**, a **Tiffany & Co.** sterling silver item.

- After the screams from the audience died down, I displayed the **Grand Prize**: A brown **Louis Vuitton** shopping bag containing a genuine **Louis Vuitton** unisex handbag.

The audience loudly moaned with joy and I explained the rules of the Lucky Draw. For anyone who wanted a chance to win one of the prizes, they needed to write their name on a piece of paper and put that paper in the Lucky Box. The person who was lucky enough to win the **Grand Prize Louis Vuitton** bag had to agree to let me throw the whipped cream pie in his or her face! This action would complete my pie-throwing New York-California-Hong Kong journey. If they didn't want to risk being *creamed* they didn't have to enter the Lucky Draw. In other words, being my pie-target was completely voluntary.

After the laughter stopped from this surprise announcement, I took a deep breath because I was worried that only a few people would enter the drawing. The audience was large and it would be an embarrassment for me if only a few folks volunteered. It would be a disaster no one volunteered, and I had no backup for another Finale. I passed the Lucky Box to the first person, then one by one the movement in the audience was a rush for a chance to win the prize. The entire audience placed their names in the box for a chance to receive a *whipped cream pie in the face* from me.

The anticipation in the room was enormous. The moans and giggles now turned to utter silence, except for the annoying crackling sounds as I mixed up the tiny folded papers with the hopeful names in the box. I took a long time to dramatically mix the papers as I put my hand into the Lucky Box and pulled out the name of the 3rd Prize winner, then the 2nd Prize winner. Tension was mounting as I slowly unfolded the paper with the name of the Grand Prize winner. I stared for a moment, then gasped as I announced that the winner of the **Louis Vuitton** item was Mr. Ted Chiu. Everyone started to scream as Ted stood up to receive the LV Bag and the Pie!

Ted Chiu had joined Mattel HK only a year earlier. Although Ted was Chinese born in HK, he was a Canadian citizen who had left his design job after many years in Canada to return to HK, where his parents and sister lived. He sought an opportunity in the dynamic HK business community. Being a toy designer, Ted made a great choice to join Mattel, where he was hired as a senior manager for the Girls Design team.

In the short time Mr. Chiu was with Mattel he'd made a great impression on me and I wasn't alone in this feeling. Ted was unique, with a Western, outgoing style and great fashion flare. He was funny, charming, extremely talented, and quite an ambitious guy. Ted was in his late forties, average height by HK standards, and very handsome. His personality and talent opened many hearts and opportunities for him at Mattel.

I'd announced my retirement almost a year earlier. The knowledge of my good reputation was enough reason for Ted to make sure I was a priority for his networking. This was very smart on Ted's part, as well as complimentary. During the last few months I'd been actively looking for my replacement. Since my star staff, senior managers Winnie Kwok and Jessica Choi, had once again declined the opportunity to take my job, I'd had no choice but to start searching for a qualified person from outside Mattel. The recruiting had resulted with a couple of candidates being considered. One day Ted Chiu had stopped by my office and asked me how I'd feel about him being my replacement.

Ted was a respected toy designer, but he had no soft goods background. Perhaps not a requirement since my staff was a very experienced and capable team. Ted's enthusiasm, great design sense, passion to manage my team, and a vision to integrate the soft goods team with the fashion designers who worked for him appealed to me. I thought his style and attitude was a good mix of East meets West. His communication skills in English, Cantonese, and Mandarin were definitely an advantage. He would make a good "foster parent" for my beloved staff and he was from inside Mattel. The position would be for a director, a promotion for him. After a few days of thinking over Ted's proposal, I recommended him as a candidate for my job.

The very week of my Performance, Mattel was in the process of considering Ted to replace me. What were the odds that of the 150 staff sitting before me, who'd entered their names for the Lucky Draw, that Ted Chiu's name would be selected for the Grand Prize, which included me slamming a cream pie in his face? Was this a *symbolic rite of passage* or just *good feng shui*?

When I read his name, Ted and I made eye contact and shared a smile. Only a few in the room knew he was being considered as my replacement. Ted was dressed in a dark brown, long-sleeve, stunning custom-made shirt, which I knew would be soon covered in fresh whipped cream. He was shaking his head and strutted with confidence as he left his seat to receive his Prize. Just as he stood before me, fidgeting to find a place to stand, I immediately picked up the pie with both my hands, aimed, and smashed it gently but firmly into Ted's face!

One thing I did remember from my two previous pie throws many years ago: never warn your "target" that a pie was coming.

Leave no time for them to avoid being hit. There was Ted, whipped cream and multicolored sprinkles dripping from his face, ears, and hair, in front of all of his staff, peers, and bosses. The cheers and screaming reaction was the effect I wanted and I certainly got it. After letting Ted wipe his face and dry his once crisply pressed shirt, I handed him his **Louis Vuitton Grand Prize**.

I was actually passing the pie like the Olympics torch to Ted. Symbolically reminding him to continue to keep the HK, China, and Jakarta soft goods teams as a trusted Mattel Brand.

A standing ovation followed.

Ted said the **Louis Vuitton** bag wasn't really the prize—the honor of me shoving a pie in his face was special!

Personal Brand Image:

Take a risk and make a statement to keep true to your Brand.

Chapter 28

The West Is Soon to Come

The next morning I sent out an email to everyone who'd attended **"This Is It"** stating, *"Never forget there is a PIE in everyone."*

The additional two performances in China were even more amazing. The audiences were larger, they'd heard rumors I was doing something different. The emotions of the Chinese were more visible than in HK and their responses were overwhelmingly appreciative. It was surreal that I had completed my Pie #4 *and* Pie #5 in China. Who would have thought that a nice girl from Brooklyn, New York, would be in China throwing whipped creams pies in the faces of the local Chinese staff as a part of a Mattel mentorship program?

A few weeks before my final **Performance** in Jakarta, I announced that my replacement would be my **Pie #3** recipient, Mr. Ted Chiu. Ted was the right choice for many reasons. Most of all, Ted wanted to succeed. A great **Brand Image** for my team. This position was a big leap for him, getting this responsibility and a promotion after less than two years at Mattel. He was ready for me to devote the next few months to handover the department to him.

These first three **Performances** literally took my breath away. A couple of days after I returned from the China events I woke up early feeling really ill, nauseous, and breathless. I asked Melvin to take me to our doctor. Without going into the painfully shocking details, I was diagnosed with pneumonia and hospitalized. Okay, you may say, that's a common problem—get some antibiotics and in a few days all is back to normal. In keeping with my Brand, my case wouldn't be ordinary.

All the time I'd worked in HK I'd never had any illnesses except for a sinus infection. Now, a few weeks before I was to perform in Jakarta, two months before I was moving back to the US, all of a sudden I developed pneumonia and was hospitalized for the first time in my life (except for when I gave birth to Haris). What was supposed to be a five-day hospital stay turned into three weeks, with an oxygen mask and two bronchoscopy procedures to clear my lungs. Melvin, my staff, and my Mattel colleagues all thought I was going to die.

Finally, between the right antibiotic cocktail, deep breathing exercises, and practicing hours of meditation to open my lungs, I was released from the hospital. Good news except for doctors' orders confining me to my home for a few more weeks of recovery. It was now almost Christmas 2010. The schedule was for me to move back to the US at the end of January 2011, leaving me less than two months to wrap up my work. I resisted being ungrateful and inconvenienced when I was joyous to have had good medical treatment in HK and recover from a disease that could have had a sad ending. I was a lucky girl.

The medical treatment included massive doses of steroids that left my immune system extremely weak. The doctors told me I had to be careful not to get an infection, which could land me back in the hospital. My human contact was limited. No visitors, no outings unless they were outside in open areas, no work, certainly no travel to China, and definitely no presentation in Jakarta. I was devastated. All these years in Asia, traveling in the poorest areas with bad/no hygiene, sitting next to coughing, spitting, sneezing passengers and dying chickens on the train, I'd never caught their germs. Now, at the end of my journey with Mattel, I'm infected with pneumonia!

I didn't consult Dr. D or any other psychologist, but I could "hear" Dr. D's voice in my head saying, "Of course you got sick. You are under extreme stress. You are completely changing your lifestyle, you're retiring after forty-one years of working and leaving your home in HK. You are returning to an unfamiliar situation. Your mind is weak and didn't defend you from a germ attack on your body."

The Dr. D voice could be right. I actually was in denial about how hugely upset I was to leave my job, stop working, and move away from HK. Rather than be emotional about the situation, I took the path of least resistance and went the physically ill route as a way for the stress to find a release.

The current circumstances of being ordered not to have any interaction with people caused me to cancel all the goodbye parties. I really didn't mind cancelling; it eliminated the opportunity for me to break down and cry in front of everyone. My staff and friends were very unhappy because they were being denied closure to my departure. The public displays of affectionate goodbyes would have to wait.

My final Christmas in HK was rapidly approaching. I usually gave all my direct reports a small gift. I had no time to shop or permission to mingle in crowds. It was important to me to personally select items and find a situation that would protect me from germ contamination. I decided to keep the Brand Image theme for the gifts as an example of practicing what I preached.

Melvin drove me to the nearest shopping mall at opening hours, when it was completely devoid of customers. I went directly to **Tiffany & Co.** As their first customer of the day I purchased sterling silver bracelets for the ladies and sterling silver key chains for the men, packed in Tiffany blue boxes. This Luxury-Brand statement of my appreciation was completed and I quickly left the store uncontaminated. My staff deserved these gifts as a reminder that they should always pursue their Personal Brands.

I returned to the HKSG office to hand out these Christmas gifts, impart well wishes, and show everyone I was alive and well after six weeks on sick leave. It was a very emotional experience. As I entered my office I was greeted with a standing ovation. I couldn't hug anyone, but I cried at every smile, loving glances, loud cheers, and the purple "Welcome Back" decorations that covered my office. This was really *My Victory Party* for so many reasons.

My last week in HK the Mattel staff planned a traditional Chinese dim sum lunch in HK for me. I was happy with this low-key exit since the separation would be extremely difficult, and this made it less emotional for everyone. I knew I'd return to HK and China for a visit the next year and we could plan my *Welcome Home Party*, complete with hugs and human contact. For now it wasn't goodbye Asia, but see you soon.

By the end of January 2011 I was back in the US, working in Mattel's California office until my final day in April. My assignment was to mentor staff in California and conduct two special Presentations. One would be a repeat of my **"This Is It"** Performance from Asia and the other would be to address the **Women of Mattel Group**. All these requests seemed like a perfect way to exit, aligning with my **Personal Brand Image** message and hopefully inspiring someone on the east side of the Pacific Ocean.

The California Performance was held in the Mattel Design Center Theater, attended by most of the Barbie and Girls Design teams. I followed the same format I used in Asia. I did consider a pie-in-the-face for Mattel's Senior VP of Global Girls Brands Design, who sponsored my California assignment and had asked me to conduct these two presentations. How perfect, I thought, to come full circle with my pie-throwing statement, NYC, CA, HK, China, then back to CA! This was the good old USA, close to Hollywood, where they're used to theatrics. The audience was mostly designers and I was a couple weeks away from retirement, soon to fade into the Arizona desert sunset. Why not just aim at another Mattel VP and let the "cream and crust" fall where they may?

As tempting as it was, I decided to use the Lucky Draw scenario instead because my message about Brand Image was more important. My desire to be famous for targeting a VP was only a secondary motivation and was put to rest. **Tiffany & Co.** and **Louis Vuitton** were examples of the importance of what a

Brand can become. If I could convey the importance of a Brand Image, then someone would risk getting a pie in the face for an opportunity to win that famous **LV** luxury bag.

The same result as in Asia, with screams, cheers, and hysteria from the Mattel California audience were outrageously gratifying after I smashed **Pie #6** in the face of the Lucky Draw Winner from the audience. Whipped cream, graham cracker crust, and multicolored sprinkles flooded the stage. I heard one woman sitting in the front row shout to another person, referring to me, "I don't know her, never worked with her, but I want to spend the holidays at her house. I really needed this today and I will remember it forever."

Personal Brand Image:

Continuously expand your scope of Brand recognition.

It was March 23, 2011, and my talk at the **Women of Mattel Group** was scheduled for that afternoon. It was open to anyone who worked at Mattel but was focused on the subject of a more equal balance of female and male executives at the company. Perfect venue for me to speak about and share my experiences as a female executive. I had no dress-up tricks or pies for this one. I spoke about what it was like to be a woman executive working in Asia for Mattel. Most of the stories I have I already shared in this book. My audience included over one hundred women and only about five men.

I decided to speak the truth and not sugarcoat anything. I shared the difficulties of being a female executive in the male-dominated Mattel atmosphere and what I did to overcome the bias in order to be accepted by the "good old boys," the opposite of the relationship and immediate respect I received from the Asian men who were my colleagues or vendors.

The audience got an earful and I felt I was only confirming feelings they had working with their male colleagues in the US.

This was the corporate mentality in America, but a **Personal Brand Image** could get them recognition.

You bet I ended with a Lucky Draw. Instead of luxury items, the gifts were artifacts from China, to hopefully leave the winners with a good feeling. That evening I was on a plane headed for Phoenix to join Melvin and start our new adventure together. My Mattel assignment was complete. Part of me was so sad to leave my professional career, the people, the passion, and my HK home.

Personal Brand Image:

Make your Image recognizable no matter the audience.

Chapter 29

Desert Life

Back from Asia, we moved into our Arizona home. We had a house to decorate, with a mix of our Chinese furniture, paintings, and porcelain vases combined with chrome-and-glass contemporary items. My choice of purple, turquoise, orange, and lime-green walls was a relief from the continuous beige, sandy desert. Almost every day the weather brought sunshine, a novel experience for us after living in HK's polluted gray atmosphere. The open space with miles of rock, cacti, and mountains was invigorating. It was like being on vacation since we had no schedule and could calmly have fresh-brewed coffee every morning.

I started to wonder what was next for me. Haris was still in Florida, 2,200 miles away, making my desire to have him over for dinner every Thursday night impossible. We had no family or close friends in Arizona. I didn't have to work and I didn't want to consult for another company. I felt I had something to give back, after all the Performances, lectures, and the hundreds of people I'd positively affected. Why did it have to stop because I was no longer working for Mattel?

I thought about being a mentor to folks who needed help with their careers. Where I came from, how I managed to achieve my career successes, how I created a Personal Brand, was a great story to share. I had no idea how to start looking for an opportunity to volunteer in the community. Having lived outside the US for almost a generation, I was unaware of available organizations where my skills might be a good fit.

On the internet I searched "mentoring in Phoenix, Arizona." After a few minutes of sipping some red wine and clicking links for interesting sites, I visited the website of an organization called **Dress for Success (DFS) Phoenix**.

Reading about **DFS**, I found their mission was to promote economic independence for disadvantaged women. They provide network and development support to help these women's careers, as well as professional clothing for interviews and a week's worth of professional clothing if they found a job. In addition, they weren't just in Phoenix. **DFS** was in over twenty cities in the United States and over 140 international affiliates in nineteen countries. I thought that this was a good place to start.

Holding out a carrot to **DFS** to see if they wanted a taste of what I had to offer, I sent an email to Ms. Lisa Doromal, founder and president of **DFS** Phoenix, with a statement reflecting my **Personal Brand Image**. The email subject line was *"Successfully Dressed One of the Most Famous Women in the World!"*

I attached a photo of me posing in front the Pink Barbie Staircase in Shanghai and a brief work biography. I offered to volunteer for DFS, where they could use my people skills to make the ordinary become extraordinary!

Life is so simple and predictable when you know the right way to get what you want. Lisa Doromal responded in less than twenty-four hours and arranged for me to connect with the DFS program manager, Miss Jessica Gonzalez. I had no idea what I could contribute to the program, but I knew if there was an emphasis on how to present yourself professionally, coaching, mentoring, and inspiring, I could do it.

I met Jessica Gonzalez at the DFS boutique store, where women could browse, look for clothing to be worn at interviews or on a job, all for free. Jessica was a very stylishly dressed, attractive young lady in her late twenties, originally from the East Coast and was studying for her master's degree in nonprofit leadership at Arizona State University. She was welcoming and happy to have someone with my work experience volunteer.

We discussed the options to be part of the organization. She scheduled me for the DFS program called **Going Places Network (GPN)**, a program sponsored by Walmart aimed at helping women who are unemployed or underemployed. DFS clients gain professional skills, accelerate their job search, and build confidence through weekly training sessions, career coaching, and networking. After an hourlong conversation and sharing, Jessica, with Lisa's support, asked me to speak at a **GPN** session.

From my experiences, I felt I could help these disadvantaged women by inspiring them to believe they could be successful, even if they think they have little going for them. In the 1970s I too could have been one of these ladies, sitting in a DFS office in New York City (if they'd had one then) looking for a job. Perhaps I could share what I'd learned during my struggling years, tell my story, and that would inspire someone.

I accepted the offer to be a volunteer keynote speaker. Although I'd never been altruistic enough to volunteer for a nonprofit, I wanted to see if I could take my performance out of the Mattel arena, broaden its scope to help anyone who was open to a commonsense idea of the importance of a **Personal Brand Image**. I was going to continue with my **Performances**.

This GPN group was twenty-four women, a manageable number for what I'd planned. To throw a pie in the face of a woman who was in a difficult life situation wasn't the right approach. Therefore, I would do a mini, modified version of **"This Is It,"** focusing on my life choices that had helped me establish my careers.

This Performance was in an intimate setting in the DFS training room. I therefore eliminated the fancy PowerPoint as well as the music. The big difference was that I wanted the ladies to understand visually how you can take something simple and make it special. The first thing I did was set up a strikingly stunning display of small gift bags to be given to each partici-pant. The colors were all Barbie's iconic look of pink, white, and black. Everything was coordinated—ribbons, bags, and tissue paper, which concealed the gifts of professional stationery to be given to the women.

Three special bags in luxurious pink, white, and black wrapping contained Lucky Draw prizes of a shoe- or handbag-themed item, to echo DFS's focus on dressing appropriately. The grand prize was a fashion-themed charm bracelet that could easily been worn to an interview.

After a ninety-minute lecture, complete with my story, Barbie connection, whipped cream pie demonstration, and rhinestone dress up, I made the final point with the display of gift bags. This giveaway idea was multipurpose:

1. The gift bags were a "thank-you note," a reminder of how a small thing can make a big impact.

2. The gift bags also were meant to be a statement that you don't need to spend a lot of money to present an image that conveys a strong message. You just have to make it special.

3. The gift bags provided an example of how to make the ordinary become extraordinary.

At this GPN Performance I asked the ladies if they'd heard of **Louis Vuitton**, and would winning a real LV be incentive enough to let me throw a pie in their face? To my amazement I got a **100% LV Brand** recognition! Without exception every woman said she would let me throw a pie in her face to get that **LV** prize! This was astonishing, that these ladies from multicultural and low- to no-income backgrounds could all recognize the Brand and desire a **LV** bag. They confirmed my message of exactly of how powerful a Brand Image can be.

Personal Brand Image:

A strong Brand Image has no social boundaries. When You're Great They Remember Your Name.

This venue gave me a perfect opportunity to share my Brand with a different type of audience in Arizona. I loved the DFS vision to help women help themselves. The gratitude from Jessica, Lisa, and the women who attended the **GPN** talks invigorated me. I looked forward to speaking with the women and sharing my experience to inspire them that they could be special and successful as long as they gave 110% of whatever is that they do best, no matter how insignificant they feel their best is!

After a year of volunteering I was unsure how to help more people. I actually wasn't sure what I wanted to do with my life. Arizona wasn't cosmopolitan New York City or international Hong Kong. I was now living in the desert, looking for a chic café to have cappuccino, or desiring to stroll into a trendy bar, to sip a glass of merlot after looking at some contemporary artwork. This was not going to happen in Arizona.

But what did happened in July 2013 changed everything for me.

I was in a car accident, hit by an oncoming vehicle as I made a left turn just one mile from my house. My car was totaled and I only suffered fractured ribs and bruises. I have to give credit to my Toyota Highlander's strong structure for saving my life. This was my first and only car accident. I was an emotional mess after the experience and I sank into depression, wondering what life was all about. All my **Personal Brand Image** philosophies seemed meaningless at this point. Now, at the time when I thought I knew what my life was about, I had a near-death experience that did more than wrecked my car—it demolished my self-esteem. All that I'd worked for, all that I lived for, could have been over in a second.

After tears and self-pity, I knew I had to do something to improve my state of mind. I couldn't believe that my journey around the world had brought me to Arizona to become mentally paralyzed and ruin everything I'd worked for. I wasn't practicing what I preached. I couldn't regress back into the 1970s. There was only one way to find a way out of this darkness. I had to use the ace card up my sleeve to win the game that was dealt to me. I called Dr. D!

I told Dr. D the situation and my emotional state. It was all there for her to hear and in her blunt style and loud voice, she told me this was very simple. There was nothing wrong with me, but it's always good to talk with a professional so you don't jeopardize the relationship with your family. I had to find a therapist in Arizona to help me.

I had a new family doctor, Dr. B and I asked him to recommend a psychologist. Dr. B smiled and said, "Yes, I do know a psychologist if you don't mind someone old." I didn't care, since I was old. He laughed and explained he meant really old, over eighty years old. His recommendation was good enough for me. I figured that if the doctor was over eighty, he'd get to the point quickly because he didn't have a lot of time to waste. That day I called Dr. K and scheduled an appointment.

Walking into Dr. K's office I didn't know what to expect. I only wanted relief from my sad feeling and low level of ambition. The first thing I noticed was that Dr. K wasn't just old, he was also very short. I'm five foot two and I was taller than him. Prior to my appointment I'd checked his website and reviewed his long list of credentials for over a forty-year career as a licensed psychologist, professor at the University of San Francisco, and a pilot who flew his own plane.

I sat in the designated leather chair for patients, which had worn-out areas on the armrests. I silently thought these shredded areas been created by previous patients, squirming in the chair from Dr. K's verbal torture. He sat at a desk opposite this abused-leather chair. His opening remarks, in a calm, low tone, made me feel I had nothing to fear from him, especially when he took the first few minutes to adjust his hearing aid. I wasn't sure if he could actually help me, but I was so depressed I had no energy to get up and leave.

After my emotional outburst stopped, I was able to tell Dr. K my current situation. He then proceeded to tell me how **he** is incredibly brilliant, multilingual, with a photographic memory, works with children, adults, and prison inmates, and is a MENSA member. To be a MENSA member you must have obtained an IQ score in the upper two percent of the general population. This was his way to let me know he was of the genius category. Without comment on my emotional display, Dr. K then pulled out a book from behind his desk. He announced that he'd just published his first book, about his life experiences as a pilot.

At the end of the session Dr. K asked me what I was doing in Arizona. The minute I'd walked in his office, he thought I was from New York and craved a cosmopolitan, not desert living, lifestyle. He sized me up quickly, telling me I had every right to feel miserable and gave me a homework assignment: write down what I really wanted to do with the rest of my life. He'd see me in two weeks with my homework. That an intelligent, impartial, experienced doctor could see my inner self immediately made me feel less upset. He told me that sometimes things happen for a reason and you need to open your mind to get the signal.

I really didn't think I could identify my life's vision as home-work. I'd always listened to Dr. D, so I thought I should give Dr. K a chance. Number one on my list would be to see Haris more often, but that wasn't a life occupation, since he had his own life. It all came down to my Performances, my lectures to inspire others. I love the show biz part and I was proud that I actually could help people. Yes, this was something I'd like to continue.

Then I pictured Dr. K showing me his book during our session. A long time ago I'd learned from Dr. D that a good psychologist doesn't do things by accident. Everything had a purpose. I believed Dr. K bragged about his genius ability to show me that even though he was old and short, he could do many things, including writing a book. Nothing was impossible.

Many years ago Dr. D had encouraged me to write a book. I didn't take her seriously. I didn't think I was capable of writing a book. Now I was thinking how I'd never thought I was capable of doing much of anything, but I'd acted appropriately all my life and did what the situation called for and was successful. Perhaps this was another situation that I didn't feel capable of accomplishing anything. Most people, when they meet me and hear that I worked for Mattel in Asia and developed Barbie dolls, want to know how I got that job. There was no simple answer and I'd joke, "You need to read the book!"

Two weeks later at Dr. K's office I pulled out my homework and read aloud, "I want to write a book based on my autobiographical performances that I have done in Asia and now in Phoenix. I want to speak to young people, perhaps high-school students or undergraduates and people starting to think about a career. I could help them get what they want." Dr. K smiled and thought it was a great idea.

I wanted another opinion and I wrote to Dr. D about my decision. She immediately responded, "What took you so long? I told you years ago to write a book."

So it seems reasonable to repeat the advice from Melvin:

If ten people tell you that you are drunk, even if you never had a drink, you should probably lay down!

Chapter 30

Brand Images Get Personal

I accomplished my goal and extended my **Personal Brand Image** to be an author. I completed this book over a 3 year period focusing on what I knew best...my personal story.

Nothing in my life was planned or even dreamt about. Events occurred when I took advantage of what I did best, and then moved on to the next situation. No matter how small it seemed, I focused on making a big statement. If I knew then what I know now, perhaps I could have done better at an earlier stage in my life and avoided lots of aggravation. Life isn't like that. You have to live the events in your life, and then look back to understand how your past choices led you to the next milestone.

The choices you make should be as impressive as the reaction you can get when you throw a pie in someone's face. I admit that most of the time I feel uncomfortable speaking in public or trying something new. Deep down I have the imagined rejection of my mother wanting to abort me, or a self-image problem that I don't have the "right style." However, when I concentrate on my strength, my Brand, I'm empowered. I feel the Superhero inside me. If I work hard I can accomplish anything. Even write a book.

My goal is to help you become great by finding something inside you, your Superhero, which has been hidden. Now you have the inspiration to look inside yourself, pull it out, and continuously strengthen what you find and create your **Personal Brand Image**.

Instead of simply being a reader of this book, you were an audience member viewing my story as a **Performance**, then you guessed it: this *Finite Project* would have ended with a whipped cream pie aimed at you, smashed in your face before you blinked.

Superhero Powers

Performance Encores

Throughout this book I have provided clear relevant **Personal Brand Image (PBI)** statements. Please note that I used all of the **PBIs** listed below over a forty-year period! You must adapt your **PBI** as needed. So here is a chapter-by-chapter list of the **PBI** statements to use for ideas, not just reference. Whatever you choose for your **PBI**, do it better than anyone.

Chapter 1: One Room

- Find something that you will instantly be recognized for, even if it is as simple as the color Purple.

- When faced with disaster, keep your attitude positive to create a better situation.

- Be creative and change your weakness into a strength. Presentation style can change perception.

Chapter 2: College

- Use the skills you have to reach another opportunity.

- After trial and error identify what you are good at to accomplish a goal.

- Look at what you're doing until you find something that's extraordinary.

- Do everything possible to never be boring. You can change ordinary to become extraordinary.

Chapter 3: Get a Job

- First impressions count. Show confidence and dress the part to help make up for lack of experience.

- Create a strong Brand Image that fits the job, which can compensate for weak qualifications.

- Use strong points to enhance and even create the skills you need.

- Be recognized as an expert in something, even if you think you'll never need the skills help create your Brand.

Chapter 4: In Fashion

- Make positive action a habit. Be enthusiastic, make every effort to be perceived as professional and competent, even if you don't feel that way. If you keep acting appropriately, after a while these actions become habit.

- Consistently present yourself as a professional.

Chapter 5: Breakthrough

- Personal hang-ups are no excuse for failure. Push past them and find a way to discover the root cause and then change your behavior.

- Project a positive attitude, and you will benefit in life and business with what you get back from those interactions.

Chapter 6: After the Letter

- The same attributes that help you in your career can work in you private life as well.

- Being bold in your career also works in your love life.

Chapter 7: The Wild West

- Whether in work or love, fix the issue before it becomes a problem.

- No need to follow the crowd—be an Entrepreneur.

- Even something as mundane as a résumé can be made to stand out with style and be part of your Brand.

- Emphasize your strengths, which will lead you to the next step.

- Be aggressive to network and be creative. The payoff will follow.

Chapter 8: Resignation

- Be flexible and see beyond the conventional.

- A horrible job isn't an excuse to fail, but an opportunity to be a hero and reinforce your trusted Brand.

Chapter 9: Change of Plans

- A trusted Brand attracts opportunity and gives you options.

Chapter 10: Repeat Performances

- Feeling comfortable will limit success, since challenges aren't comfortable.

- Find something to be great at so the negatives will go unnoticed.

- When doing the usual won't achieve your goal, break the rules.

- Make your point without being dictatorial, demanding, or angry. Be different and get the audience's attention.

Chapter 11: Proposals

- When confronted with a crisis, if you remain silent, you are part of the problem. Don't just complain—offer a solution.

- Common sense isn't always obvious. Put the problem in simple terms to find the reasonable expectation.

- Big opportunities can be scary. Don't be chicken—take them it on.

Chapter 12: Way out Far East

- To maximize what you get from a job, maximize what you give to it.

- The people you hire must be a reflection of your Brand and have the ability to implement your visions.

- Ready or not, just do it. Being wrong is better than doing nothing.

Chapter 13: Riding the Dragon

- Analyze problems rather than stay frustrated.

Chapter 14: Wonder Woman

- Lead by example and exaggerate to make your point.

- Set a high standard by your own example.

- Do whatever it takes to get the job done, without being a criminal or a monster.

Chapter 15: Change

- Adapt to the culture you're engaged with. The respect gained is above expectations and adds to your trusted Brand.

- One of the most important things to do as a manager is protect your staff because they see you will take care of them. When you go that "extra mile," this builds your team's trust in you.

- See things from the other person's viewpoint. Think before you act. Being appropriate for the situation maybe the opposite of what you feel like doing.

- Observe and decide for yourself. Preconceptions are not reality.

Chapter 16: On the Road to China ... Really?

- Doing the same gets the same results. Get out of your comfort zone and learn something new.

- Pursue what would make business better. Be a visionary and eventually you'll figure out how to achieve the goal.

Chapter 17: Barbie

- Make it personal and be an advocate for your product. To inspire, empathize with your customers to magnify the degree of passion that you share.

Chapter 18: The Fishing Village

- Even if it looks impossible, but you know it's right, support it—you will find a way.

- Keep the trusted brand, deliver what you promise.

Chapter 19: The Handovers

- It may take a while, but good ideas will not go unnoticed.

- If you want to be treated as creative, show creativity in your personal style as well as in your workplace.

Chapter 20: Tone It Down

- No matter your career status, either get used to change and adapt or become a dinosaur.

- Take advantage of all inspiration sources, whether from a teacher or a student.

- Humor is a great equalizer and can get you recognition no matter who is in your audience.

- If you continue to be true to your Brand Image you will be trusted, understood, and followed.

Chapter 21: Bittersweet

- Regardless of feelings take the opportunity for self-improvement. Feelings can change but self-improvement is lasting.

- Hold on to your Brand—you'll need it. Don't break under emotional pressure when you need your Brand Image the most.

- You have to be flexible, adjusting your Brand to attract the audience you want applause from.

- Change your Image when needed to get the result you want.

- Find a mentor to help grow your Brand.

Chapter 22: Turn It Up

- Take every opportunity to exaggerate your Brand and reinforce your image.

Chapter 23: Small Bowl, Big Bowl

- Stick to your Brand, even if you feel hopeless.

Chapter 24: Blaze of Glory

- Continue to strengthen your Image. The longer you do so, the longer you can hold on to your dream.

- Reputation can give you the edge with a new boss.

- Use the power of your Brand to strengthen your team.

- A strong Brand can overcome corporate politics.

- Help subordinates to excel. It will strengthen your own Brand and it is the right thing to do.

- To be more effective and get support from management, spread your Brand to your bosses.

Chapter 25: Still Blazing after All These Years

- Repeat your Brand Image, whether it's in the office or on a staircase. Make sure your Brand is recognized at every opportunity.

- You have to start somewhere and a good offer makes the start even better. Oh yeah, and listen to your mother.

Chapter 26: The Fire Ignites

- You did not miss it...No PBI for this Chapter

Chapter 27: This Is It

- Be your own constant example of how you want to be perceived.

- Take a risk and make a statement to keep true to your Brand.

Chapter 28: The West is Soon to Come

- Continuously expand your scope of Brand recognition.
- Make your Image recognizable no matter the audience.

Chapter 29: Desert Life

- A strong Brand Image has no social boundaries. When You're Great They Remember Your Name.

Chapter 30: Brand Images Get Personal

- Visual **PBI**... a picture is worth a thousand words!

Because You Were Great
I Remember Your Name

Personal Brand Images that influenced my careers, my life and this book.

Mom and Dad: Creativity and education will be your foundation. I am grateful for your love and life-lessons you taught me. Proud to be your daughter

Dr. D: Act appropriately for the situation no matter how you feel. Thank you for picking up the lost keys and opening the door of life, work and love for me.

Melvin Bazerman: Take a risk, be a rock star and never let your family down. Melvin you have never let me down, your courage allowed me to soar. Symbiosis at its best!

Haris Bazerman: Be fearless while being a gentleman and listen to your mother. I don't just love you... I like the man you have become. You can take the kid out of Hong Kong but you can't take Hong Kong out of the kid.

Nancy Harrington Morgan: Common sense approach to everything. Nan you hired me at **Mattel**, you saw my potential. What a *gift* you gave me!

Mattel Soft Goods Design and Development HK, China, Jakarta Staff: Loyalty and strong work ethic no matter what the challenge. The privilege of my life to work with you all.

Gene Insley: Mentoring to help others surpass their goals. You were the icing on the cake...thank you.

Special Superheroes inside this book:

New York City: It's true *"If you can make it here you can make it anywhere."*

Mattel Inc: Thanks for giving me a *temporary job* for 25 years.

Dress For Success Phoenix: Thank you for the phenomenal opportunity to help women improve their lives. It was a huge honor for me and inspired my pursuit to mentor.

The Editorial Department, Tucson, Arizona: Thank you **Ross Browne, Peter Gelfan,Amanda Bauch.** You made this book a reality with first class service and tutorials.

Dynamic Designworks, Huntington Beach, California: **Suzanne Mills-Winkler** and **Jackie Estillore**, grateful for the book cover design and art direction. Thank you for creative and dynamic advice keeping my **Personal Brand Image.**

Honorable Mention: To all the other Superheroes, as well as those Supervillains I met in my career. Thank you for making it necessary to create my **Personal Brand Image.** I learned from you what to do and what **not** to do to be successful.

CPSIA information can be obtained
at www.ICGtesting.com
Printed in the USA
LVOW06s0746280317

528698LV00041B/860/P

9 780998 653808